Praise for

The Far Away Brothers

"*The Far Away Brothers* is impeccably timed, intimately reported and beautifully expressed. Markham brings people and places to rumbling life; she has that rare ability to recreate elusive, subjective experiences—whether they're scenes she never witnessed or her characters' interior psychological states—without taking undue liberties. In many ways, her book is reminiscent of Adrian Nicole LeBlanc's *Random Family*. It's about teenagers who raise themselves."

—Jennifer Senior, *New York Times*

"You should read *The Far Away Brothers*. We all should."

—NPR

"This is the sort of news that is the opposite of fake. . . . Markham is our knowing, compassionate ally, our guide in sorting out, up close, how our new national immigration policy is playing out from a human perspective. . . . An important book."

—*Minneapolis Star Tribune*

"An indelible picture . . . of one imperfect family driven apart and astray—not by inequality or lax enforcement, but by the humanitarian crisis of gang warfare."

—*Vulture*

"Painstakingly reported . . . a compassionate look at the lives of two young men and the family they left behind when they were seventeen years old . . . [This] book could not have come at a more relevant time."

—*Mother Jones*

"Markham recreates each step of the story in rich detai~~l~~

~~rd~~

"Deserves a place alongside the strongest in the genre . . . By the book's end, it's impossible to not be rooting for [the Flores brothers]. The book's true victory, however, is in its insights into how the gang crisis in El Salvador and neighboring countries is impacting individual lives—and what lengths these individuals will go to, in chillingly descriptive detail, to persevere."

—*PopMatters*

"Markham functions as an empathetic intermediary amid ordinary and extraordinary struggles. She is implicated in the boys' search for a livable life, but her closeness to the situation does not impede her analysis. . . . [*The Far Away Brothers*] tells a story of courage and failure, tenacity and loss, loyalty and fumbling steps into an unknown future."

—*The Christian Century*

"Timely and thought-provoking . . . Markham provides a sensitive and eye-opening take on what's at stake for young immigrants with nowhere else to go."

—*Publishers Weekly*

"One of the most searing books on illegal immigration since Sonia Nazario's *Enrique's Journey*."

—*Kirkus Reviews* (starred review)

"A stark examination of youth migration and the extreme risks taken to access a better life . . . Markham questions the accessibility of the American dream while compassionately narrating Raúl and Ernesto's experiences."

—*Booklist*

"This brilliantly reported book goes so deeply into the lives of its protagonists and is so beautifully, movingly written it has some of the pleasures of a novel—but all the force of bitter truth, the truth about the lives of unaccompanied minors in the USA, about poverty, the ricocheting wars here and there, and the caprices and brutalities of immigration policy. Anyone who wants to understand more deeply how we got here and why we need to keep going until we get someplace better should dive into this book."

—Rebecca Solnit, author of *The Mother of All Questions*

THE
FAR AWAY
BROTHERS

TWO YOUNG MIGRANTS AND
THE MAKING OF AN AMERICAN LIFE

LAUREN MARKHAM

B \ D \ W \ Y
BROADWAY BOOKS
NEW YORK

Library of Congress Cataloging-in-Publication Data is available upon request.

ISBN 978-1-101-90620-0
Ebook ISBN 978-1-101-90619-4

PRINTED IN THE UNITED STATES OF AMERICA

Book design: *Anna Thompson*
Cover design: *Michael Morris*
Cover photographs: *(twins) cheapbooks/Shutterstock;*
(landscape) VallarieE/E+/Getty Images

10   9   8   7   6   5   4   3   2

First Paperback Edition

For Ben

CONTENTS

Long and white,
the road twists like a snake toward the far-off blue places,
toward the bright edges of the earth.

—ISABELLE EBERHARDT

War gathers everything under its black wings.

—RYSZARD KAPUSCINSKI

THE FAR AWAY BROTHERS

AUTHOR'S NOTE

I n the winter of 2013, I received an assignment from the *Virginia Quarterly Review* (*VQR*) to travel to South Texas and write about the recent uptick in immigration by unaccompanied minors and what happened to them once they'd made it into the United States. These were children, mostly from Central America, who had crossed the border without papers or parents. I spent that spring reporting the story, digging into the massive infrastructure of apprehending, detaining, caring for, and litigating the cases of these thousands of young migrants who, that year, more than tripled their historical annual average. The article, "First the Fence, Then the System," came out that June.

Since 2006, I'd been working with refugees and immigrants in Oakland, California, at various nonprofit agencies and then the Oakland school district. In 2011 I started working at Oakland International High School, a school for newly arrived English-language learners, where I coordinated programs for students and families, such as parent classes, after-school programs, and health and mental health services. Our school had enrolled a few unaccompanied minors over the years, but I understood little about their circumstances and even less about their experiences navigating the immigration system.

In the *VQR* story, I had focused on the children who were caught, but I soon found myself chasing another story: what happened to the children who *weren't* caught? My article on the growing number of unaccompanied minors working in the California agricultural system, "The Lost Boys of California," was published in *VICE* in March 2014.

Just as I was filing the first draft, Mr. David, a co-worker at Oakland International, came into my office to tell me that "we really need to do something about all the kids with upcoming court dates."

What?

He explained that a number of our new ninth and tenth graders had been ordered to appear in immigration court in the coming months. The students, who were undocumented and had been apprehended by the authorities after crossing the U.S. border, were almost universally unaccompanied minors, or "unaccompanied alien children." They had all been ordered deported and would have to fight in court for the right to stay. They were terrified of court; none of the students David had spoken to had a lawyer. Of the twenty-five or so students he advised, seven were unaccompanied minors.

While I had been away reporting on the issue outside Oakland, this population had been surging at my school, the place where I spent four days a week, right under my nose. By spring of 2014, more than sixty unaccompanied minors had enrolled at Oakland International High School, out of a student body of just under four hundred. By the following fall, the number surpassed ninety. Today, in 2018, when the number of minors crossing our border remains at historic highs and the issue of immigration has taken front and center on the polarized stage of American politics, unaccompanied minors make up over a quarter of Oakland International's student population.

After my conversation with David, I spent many an afternoon shepherding kids to pro bono legal agencies and court dates and setting up intake appointments and "know your rights" information sessions at the school. The students needed counseling and tutoring and doctors' appointments; some of them needed help finding homeless shelters and access to food and clothing. Supporting unaccompanied minors quickly became one of my primary responsibilities.

In February 2014, I met the Flores twins.*

They told me why they had come, but I had so many more questions. What were these children really risking—and enduring—to come here, and what was the likelihood they would gain the right to stay? Would they really be better off if they did? Were the stories I was hearing overblown, and could I take their reasons for coming to the United States at face value? Answering these questions became a personal imperative, one that would help me better understand my students, my country, and the endless churn of southern migration into the United States.

To learn more about the Flores family's story, and that of the hundreds of thousands of migrants like them, I traveled to El Salvador, Mexico, Guatemala, and Texas, reporting from various fulcrums of violence in El Salvador as well as at stations along the migrant trail north. Parts of this book I witnessed myself, and other parts have been reconstructed through extensive reporting and interviews, all in service of investigating the changing dynamics of migration.

Since reporting that first article for *VQR,* I have heard countless stories from young people traveling alone to reach the United States. Every story is different, but there are also striking similarities, often having to do with mounting violence in the children's home countries. These girls and boys are crossing into the United States in search of the fabled "better life" that has attracted migrants, authorized and unauthorized, since before the *Mayflower* landed. But in the Northern Triangle—Honduras, Guatemala, and El Salvador—a "better life," for many, means a life where they are not afraid of being killed.

I began reporting this book during the Obama administration, a time rife with anxiety for undocumented migrants. It was completed after the election of Donald Trump, marking an era of unprecedented fear among immigrants and refugees past and present in ways that, at the time of the election, we as a country could have only imagined. In a time when immigration is in the daily headlines yet is too often

---

* To protect the anonymity of the "Flores" family, I have changed their names and those of many others who appear in this book, as well as the name of their hometown.

reduced to a matter of sweeping rhetoric and binary politics—keep them out or let them in, wall or no wall—this book seeks to offer a complex understanding of why immigrants leave their country, what struggles they endure to get here, and the challenges they face setting roots in a foreign land.

The story of the Flores twins isn't the most harrowing, or the most unjust, or the most extraordinary I've come across as an educator and a journalist—far from it. But something in their story illustrates, roundly and heartbreakingly, the wounds of war, the spirit of a new generation of immigrants, and the impact of migration on the United States as well as on the tiny, time-battered country of El Salvador.

The United States is still young and is ever reiterating itself as demanded by its people, both those who have lived here for a long time and those who have just arrived. Immigrants have always shaped our country's future. Yet our country has not always done well in welcoming our newest immigrants or integrating them into society; this is particularly the case for newly arrived young men. Once it was young Irish and Italian men who, excluded from parts of the workforce and stereotyped as undeserving thugs, sought belonging, purpose, and livelihood in the tenements and organized crime rings of society's margins. The Trump administration credits the new wave of young Central American immigrants with gang activity in the United States—focusing in particular on MS-13, a gang born in Los Angeles and eventually deported back to El Salvador, and the very gang now causing many unaccompanied minors to flee home. Trump is vilifying these youths much like former generations of young immigrants and is signaling that they are not welcome here. Young Central Americans are coming here in unprecedented numbers, and how they are or are not received and supported will determine, in part, the next chapter in the American story.

"For a child to choose to make that journey," an advocate told me during my first trip to South Texas, "there's a reason."

Since 2012, hundreds of thousands of minors, paperless and parentless, have crossed into the United States. "Why are they coming, and why so many?" I wrote in my first piece on unaccompanied minors. It was an earnest question. Every answer raised another question, and the result is this book. It is about who these young men and women are, where they come from, the choices they've made, and what their stories reveal about who we are as a country, and what we will, or might, become.

PROLOGUE

It's a few minutes after nine o'clock, and the Flores twins are buckled into the backseat of Wilber's Toyota, lurching through downtown San Francisco in search of the courthouse. As their older brother brakes and curses his way through the flurry and gridlock of the morning commute, the twins' identical faces press against the windows, hunting for street names and building numbers. They are lost.

Their messy packet of immigration papers states the courthouse address (100 Montgomery Street) and the time they've been ordered to appear: February 19, 2014, at 10:00 a.m. Sharp, they remind themselves. Every appointment in the United States, they have learned, is expected to be on time, *en punto*, sharp. A counselor at the Texas detention center had explained this to them, and Wilber has, too. This morning they'd left the apartment with a two-hour window. It's important to be not just on time, but *early*, in the Estados Unidos, Wilber said.

"Shit," he spits from the front seat, as the network of one-ways forces him across Market Street and into the wrong side of downtown. The morning traffic roils and churns around the 4Runner, now stopped in the middle of the intersection.

At twenty-four, Wilber is now, for better or worse, for lack of a better option, his brothers' guardian. "Will you agree to be their legal sponsor?" the woman at the shelter had asked in her Tex-Mex Spanish. Of course he would. He'd signed a paper promising to provide for their basic needs, to feed and clothe them, to enroll them in school, and to get them to court on time.

In his seven years here, he'd become somewhat of an expert on the United States and its rules. A rule of the landscaping business, for instance: no work, no pay. He'd miss another day of wages today.

New Montgomery! That's the street they've been looking for—Montgomery! They drive past strangers in coats and scarves, carrying briefcases, earbuds plugging their ears. The boys are not allowed to use earbuds in class, but Ernesto sometimes tries to sneak them in. He likes the way they make him look: cool, indifferent. New Montgomery, New Montgomery, New Montgomery. They reach the end of the street, but the numbers don't seem right. The clock is ticking.

"Maybe New Montgomery and Montgomery aren't the same?" suggests Raúl.

THE twins have been dreading this appointment for months, ever since they were picked up out of the Texas desert, their shoes ripped to raggedy flaps, their matching bodies swaying with thirst. They thought for sure they'd be deported right away, back to El Salvador and all that awaited them there.

But they weren't sent back. They were taken to a detention center, where a woman explained to them that, as minors, they'd have a choice: they could opt to go back to El Salvador on their own—*impossible*—or they could go to court and fight for the right to stay.

Court? In front of a judge? They'd need a lawyer, for starters, and the prospect of obtaining official papers seemed absurd. Why, out of all the so-called illegals like them, like their brother, should they, kids who'd been here only a few months, get papers?

It is 9:06. They have just under an hour. Wilber has plugged the address into his phone's GPS, but the place it directs them to doesn't make sense. It seems to have stopped working altogether. Raúl snatches the phone from his twin. "Asshole," Ernesto hisses. Raúl hands it back with a shrug.

At seventeen, the twins have never been to a city before—unless you count the outskirts of San Salvador, which they'd been to only a few times to visit relatives, or Mexico City, where they were practically shackled to their coyote, hunkered down in the spectral underbelly of the pass-throughs. San Francisco looms like no other place they've ever seen. Raúl used to picture these buildings in the quiet nights back home, rising upward like ladders, like possibilities. But now that he's under them, they're just endless, indistinguishable boxes. They make him feel, as most things in the United States of America so far do, small and out of place.

The twins still have the lingering feeling of being chased, of needing to look over their shoulders. Every few nights now, Ernesto wakes up screaming and slick with sweat. He won't talk about it, but Raúl knows his brother. As surely as he knows when Ernesto feels like cutting class to go smoke a cigarette, he knows how afraid Ernesto was before he was run out of town. And during that night in the desert weeks later. The road can change a person.

The shelter staff members had explained how court works: The judge will come in, and everyone will stand up. The judge will say the name of each kid with an appointment that day, and the kid should respond *presente,* here. Last night the boys reviewed what they remembered. Look the judge in the eyes, they reminded each other. In America, their instructors told them, looking down makes you appear disrespectful.

Now the boys' faces are hardening into matching masks of dread. When they get to court, what will they even say to the judge? With no lawyer, no English, no idea what to argue on their own behalf, they worry they'll be deported this very day. And then what?

The courthouse is here among these buildings somewhere, but where? One hundred Montgomery, the twins read on the court paper again. Everything sounds the same—*Montgomery, Market, New Montgomery, Minna, Mission*—crossing and crisscrossing like the tacky, glinting strands of a web. Son of a bitch.

"Fucking," Ernesto says in English, like a noun. He had learned that word, *fucking,* in school. It sounded more raw than the other swears he'd learned.

Sacramento Street, California Street, more towering stacks of steel and stone. El Salvador didn't have buildings like this—not that they'd seen, anyway. There the streets weren't so clean, and people tended to walk with more vigilance about their surroundings. Graffiti on the walls marked gang territory you could be killed for crossing, and masked police patrolled with M-16s and AK-47s. Teenagers like them were posted on corners, texting the bosses any strange comings and goings. In parts of some towns, hardly anyone walked at all. Here in San Francisco it was just coffee cups and commerce—but the foreignness was its own quiet form of terror.

Nine-thirty, nine-thirty-five. The numbers keep shifting on the defunct phone the twins use to keep track of time. Another confused, traffic-laden circuit loops them back to Market Street. The big white clock tower stands resolute against the bay like a cruel joke.

Wilber cranks the heat high. Outside it's cold, and the twins haven't brought anything to wear over their almost-matching blue plaid shirts, their nicest items of clothing. Wilber bought them, like practically everything they have. Ernesto's is long-sleeved, a tight-fitting faux flannel, while Raúl's is a boxier short-sleeve, his collar buttoned all the way to the top. Both boys have tucked the shirts into their skinny jeans, hiked up higher than usual with the help of belts, and they've laced their sneakers tightly, instead of leaving them fashionably loose-tied like the kids at school. They've slicked their hair back, and Ernesto has even removed his earrings—the characteristic the teachers at school use to tell them apart. They look, accidentally, like twins trying to dress as twins. Ernesto scoffed when he saw Raúl in the morning. "Copying me," he said.

As ten o'clock approaches, Ernesto blinks rapidly, and Raúl breathes heavily through his nostrils, lips pressed into a tight, thin line.

"Shit," says Wilber in English. He's doing his best.

"Should we ask somebody?" Raúl finally whispers.

Ernesto shoots him a look. *Who? Who would we possibly ask?* The twins don't speak English, and though Wilber can hold his own, how could he pull over a car in the middle of the downtown rush? He can't get another ticket. In spite of his seven years here, Wilber feels just as much as his brothers do that *immigrant* and *illegal* are painted onto him like a sticky second skin.

"Fucking," says Ernesto. They now have ten minutes. They turn onto Mission and loop back toward Market. *We've been here before. No, we haven't. Yes, we have—look, that flower man—we saw him before. True.* Silence. On the map they see Montgomery station. If Montgomery station is here, where is the Montgomery Street courthouse? They'll miss their appointment, they'll be sent home, they'll wind up dead, and what would have been the point of any of it—the journey, the debt, all this wandering?

Ernesto wants to scream at his brother—*How long have you lived here? Can't you find us this fucking courthouse?* But his throat seems to have closed up. He blinks even faster, as if to incarnate something better to see.

At a certain point, you just give up. They boys know it at the exact same moment, as with many things, but Wilber feels it, too: it's that time, the giving-up time. It's an hour past their appointment. It's over.

"Okay," Wilber says. The twins say nothing, just watch out the windows as the throng of people drifts away, and they ascend the on-ramp to the bridge. The highway drags them above the slate-gray sea like a conveyer belt toward what is now, for now, home. They won't go to school today, probably not tomorrow. It would be too easy for Immigration to find them. But *la migra* has Wilber's address, too. They could go hide out somewhere, but Wilber is the only person here they really know.

They've been hunted by gangs, by packs of wild coyotes in the desert, by bad spirits, by rumors, by debt, by *la migra*—an easy, two-for-one prey. The twins look up at the sky as they emerge from the Yerba Buena Tunnel, which shoots them out and slings them back into Oakland. They've been chewed up and spit out all over this godforsaken continent, and after all this, just for missing an appointment, they're sure they'll be delivered back to El Salvador for good. But they can't go back.

For too long, the Flores twins have been dodging what now feels inevitable. In the jinxed maze of their lives, at the age of seventeen, they may have reached a dead end.

Enter the examination room in San Salvador's Instituto de Medicina Legal, where a masked doctor cuts into a new corpse and the ammonia fumes will burn your eyes. After determining the cause of death, he'll slide the body back into the freezer until someone comes to identify the remains. If no one comes, which sometimes happens—it's too far, or the family doesn't have the money, or the deceased doesn't have a family, or the circumstances of the murder are such that it's best for the next of kin to lie low—the body will be incinerated. But any corpse in San Salvador that has gone undiscovered long enough, decomposing in a cornfield, say, or cast into the dump, is taken to the Department of Forensic Anthropology.

In contrast to the fecund, overgrown courtyard outside, the anthropology room is antiseptic, all right angles and order. Metal examination tables gleam; file boxes are stacked atop the counters and tables and floor. Like puzzle masters, the forensic anthropologists turn over the contents of each and fit the pieces together to figure how a human being turned into a box of bones.

Some of the skeletons are old and weather worn, turning the color of rust; they look as though they would flake at a touch. These bones were exhumed from the site of the 1981 massacre of El Mozote during El Salvador's civil war, when government troops stormed a suspected guerrilla haven and slaughtered more than nine hundred men, women, and children. Some they killed with guns and machetes; others they corralled into the town church, then set it on fire. This skeleton here, laid out on the butcher paper, strewn with bits of the El Mozote soil mixed with the dust of his own bones, was a man "in his thirties," one anthropologist estimated. "A farmer, most likely."

The bones on the neighboring table, sturdier and whiter and in far fewer pieces, are from a newer war, a war more elusive and harder to track: the gang war.

"This one here came from a clandestine grave in San Salvador." A pit behind a San Salvador slum. She'd been a young woman—they estimated about seventeen, killed within the last year. Based on markings inside her pelvis, she'd once given birth. In the front of the skull, just above where the girl might have tweezed her brows or dusted a shimmer of shadow, was a splintered hole.

"A heavy object," the anthropologist says, running her fingers along the breach.

"Last week a man came in with thirty-seven bullets," recalled a morgue administrator. "Thirty-seven! Can you imagine?"

They cut a neat rectangle out of the young mother's femur for DNA.

It's hard to know who the particular killers in this new war are. Most homicides—especially the mass graves, like the one from which the young mother was pulled—are known to be the work of the gangs. Yet around 95 percent of crimes in the Northern Triangle go uncharged. To report a mass grave or denounce a gang member for murder carries a near-certain death sentence for the accuser and often for his or her family, too. So people keep quiet; the bodies pile up.

At the front gate of the morgue, a woman cries quietly, her shoulders quaking as she presses a tissue beneath her eyes. She leans into a young man, her son perhaps, who wears a stiff expression behind aviator sunglasses. The armed guards notice, then look away.

A different woman enters the gate. "I'm here to register a disappeared?" she says, like a question. She signs her name in the tattered logbook, and the guard points where to go with one hand, holding his gun with the other.

If your local police haven't found the person you're looking for, you go to the morgue to make another report. The Instituto de Medicina Legal staff affixes the photograph to a wall, along with dozens of others. They hang beneath a plastic cover so clean it reflects the onlooker, a flickering superimposition against the black and white faces of adults and children arranged by date last seen. THESE PHOTOGRAPHS WILL BE KEPT ON THIS BILLBOARD FOR TWO MONTHS, DEPENDING ON SPACE, the sign explains. It is late July; April's disappeared have just been taken down.

THANK YOU FOR YOUR ATTENTION, the sign concludes.

A police truck pulls into the compound, and two officers, clad in boots and balaclavas, hop out and escort a scowling young man, no more than sixteen or seventeen. He is handcuffed, his hair is gelled into spikes, and he sports low-sagging shorts, barely laced high-top sneakers, and a bright red T-shirt. The police move him roughly toward one of the doors.

"A gangster," someone says after he passes.

"They get a psychological evaluation here," the guard explains, "before going to jail."

The courts are so backed up that this young man could be in jail for weeks, months, even years before a trial. Thus he, too, becomes one of San Salvador's missing.

CHAPTER 1

You boys from eighteen?" one of the young men said, pointing his gun toward the retaining wall marked by a small graffito tag: BARRIO 18.

It was 2008. The Flores twins, twelve, were playing poker on the town soccer field with their older brother and six friends when the pickup pulled up. Ten or so guys stood in the truck bed brandishing guns and machetes, sporting hip-hop clothes and tattoos. They were MS-13, or Mara Salvatrucha, the twins knew—members of the gang that was then slinking into the small town of La Colonia. The Flores boys and their friends were high on adrenaline from having won a big soccer match that morning, a feeling that mixed nicely with the bravado of early adolescence. But the sight of the armed men scared them silent.

They shook their heads no.

"I asked you a question!" barked the guy in the truck.

Ernesto's gaze was lowered, but he could feel the men staring down at him.

"I asked if you fuckers were from eighteen!" the man shouted. At that, one of their friends took off running into the woods. Suddenly—they couldn't remember who moved first—the twins were sprinting through the forest that flanked the town soccer field, Ernesto first, Raúl close behind, panting and flying over dips and gullies, pushing past banana trees and crashing through the tall grasses while shouts and a scatter of gunshots crackled behind them.

Running away from a truck of gangsters was either an admission of guilt (in this case, allegiance to the rival Barrio 18 gang) or, at the very least, a sign of a lack of respect for MS-13 authority.

When the shouts felt far enough away, the twins hit the ground, lying on their bellies in the brush. They stayed there for what felt like several hours—until they were sure the truck was gone. They were too scared to go back to the field and look for their cards, which, for anyone *vigilando,* or keeping watch over the area, might tag the twins as the ones who ran. For a while, at least, no more poker.

THE road to La Colonia is meandering but smooth, thanks to the scant traffic. It weaves through a tangle of greenery: vines overhang concrete walls alongside tall, tight rows of banana trees, diaphanous canopies of *barillos,* pink flowering cacao, dense *cedro negro,* and flushing palms. The road begins in a valley and winds upward to where La Colonia, about thirty miles from San Salvador and home to fewer than four thousand people, spreads up and around the slopes of a gentle, low hill.

The houses along the road are simple but comfortable, built from concrete, many of them painted colors that were once bright—ice blue, cotton candy pink, white with fuchsia trim—but that now, with weather and time and dust, have faded. Less fortunate homes speckle back into the adjacent hills and farmland. Flags of the conservative ARENA party flap from electric poles and appear painted on buildings. Along the road stand La Colonia's schools—two high schools and an elementary school. One of only about a dozen Flores family photos is of the twins and their older sister, somber-faced and gangly beneath too-big dress clothes, on the proud occasion of their ninth-grade graduation.

Cows use the road as often as people do, lashed together by the horns and plodding along between farm and pasture, and dogs warm themselves in the middle of the street looking like splayed corpses. At the sound of approaching cars they rise, shake themselves, and lumber off to where the road turns to dirt. During harvesttime, families turn the two-lane road into one as they lay their bean pods and corn out to dry, the kernels spread like a blanched mosaic along the tarmac.

The road crests the hill and begins to dip downward, and that's where the Flores home sits, a stone house lined with crumbling stucco. From there it's not much farther to the center of town, a sleepy square rimmed by a block or two of houses and a few businesses—family-run restaurants, sundries shops, the mayor's office. The high-rising church is the town's main attraction, its tower wielding a hulking cross that casts a daily shadow into the central square. At noon the church bells chime.

Until the twins were teenagers, the town center was frequented day and night. Kids ran around the small playground, people took refuge on the shaded benches, and boys played soccer on the open concrete court, even in the afternoon heat. People came to use the copy shop or buy soap or soda or enter a complaint at the mayor's office. Children who'd begged spare change from their parents bought snow cones from the heavyset woman with the mobile stand, the bright, tacky syrup staining their faces. The *pupuserías* were open until eleven, midnight even, playing music and serving sodas and beers, the lady proprietors flipping the cakes of corn *masa* against the griddle until the edges were crispy yellow-brown.

"It was a beautiful town," Raúl remembers. "It was."

LIKE the rest of the farmers in La Colonia, the twins' father, Wilber, regarded the mountain and its fertile land as a divine inheritance. The land was good to him; God provided. This was Wilber's credo. "The way to survive this world is to stay close to God," he said to his children. "And keep *manos limpias*": clean hands.

Wilber carried a small Bible in his pocket at all times, the binding frayed and worn from use. Tucked inside were several prayer cards, his Salvadoran national ID, the photo taken when he was a very young man, and a picture of his bride, Esperanza, now faded and tattered. Every now and then he'd pull out the keepsakes to have a look.

"See how young you were!" he'd say. Esperanza tittered like a girl, waving her hand as if shooing a fly.

Wilber and Esperanza had always wanted a big family, but for many years they'd felt they might be cursed. They got married in the midst of the country's civil war, in 1985, and when Esperanza gave birth to her first baby, Ricardo, two years later, the war still raged. La Colonia wasn't a hot zone, but soldiers marched through it on occasion. This never meant anything good for poor farmers like the Flores family, whom the government often suspected of being guerrillas. "The soldiers came looking for people," Esperanza explained. "They could mistake you for someone else and punish you for something they did."

Once when Wilber was out of town working on another farm's harvest, news spread that the army was on its way. Esperanza snatched up Ricardo, who was barely a year old, and walked out of town up into the hills, where she stayed along with some neighbors for a couple of days, hoping Ricardo didn't cry too loudly. The army passed through without fireworks or massacres. Esperanza came down from the mountain, and they resumed their lives at home.

It was a dirty war, as Wilber put it—a war between the rightist government, beholden to the country's powerful oligarchy and operating with brute military force, and the mounting leftist guerrilla movement, fighting for the interests of the impoverished working class, especially the country's rural farmers. But the Flores family thought it best to stay out of politics.

In cities and in the countryside, mutilated bodies showed up in the streets. Political prisoners—dead and alive—were heaved off the Devil's Gate cliff in the dense hills above San Salvador. Both sides played dirty, but the government death squads were brutal: a UN-appointed truth commission report asserts, with some contestation from within El Salvador, that 85 percent of the atrocities were carried out by the government. In the early 1980s, the United States trained and backed the government forces—death squads and all—to prevent a guerrilla takeover: an effort, in the thick of the Cold War, to prevent the proximal spread of Communism.

"It was a terrible time," Wilber says. He won't say much else about the war.

In 1988, as the violence heated toward its final boil, Esperanza gave birth to another son: Wilber Jr. Then, as peace negotiations were under way in Mexico City, she gave birth to a daughter who died at just several weeks old. They buried her in La Colonia. Esperanza kept praying for more children, placing offerings upon the altar and asking God and the Mother Mary for their blessings every Sunday in church. The peace accords were signed in Mexico City in 1992, and as the government and the guerrillas agreed to lay down their weapons for good, Esperanza got pregnant again. This baby, too, died at just several weeks old, and another after that made it only a few days before she turned blue and they had to bury her as well. Was Esperanza cursed? Was she too old?

In 1994 El Salvador held its first free and fair peacetime elections. The conservative ARENA party won, but the war was over. After so many years of conflict, it was a time of rebuilding. That year Esperanza's prayers were answered: she gave birth to her sixth child, a girl, Maricela. Maricela lived.

The Flores family were still farmers who scraped by harvest to harvest, who struggled to find money to buy clothes or take a child to the doctor. But as Esperanza looked back, she regarded those as good years: three healthy babies, a country out of war.

Then the curse reared again: another baby, who died another mysterious death just a few weeks after he was born. That made seven children in all, only three of whom had made it to a year. In a place with little medical care, tragedies like this were common enough, but four tested Esperanza's faith. At the end of 1995, when her belly began to swell again a few months after the fourth baby died, she prayed she wouldn't lose this one, too.

After a bit of nausea early on, she had a good feeling—this one, she thought, would keep. The closest doctor was a thirty-minute drive away, and anyway, she couldn't afford him. Prayer was more important, she felt in the end. Within just three months she was bigger than she'd ever been at that stage. By month five she was exhausted, walking wide-legged, having to heave herself out of the bed each morning to feed the children and scatter corn for the chickens. She'd squat to tug at the cow's udders for milk, her back aching, her knees on fire.

Wilber prayed for her at church, crooned hymns and strummed the guitar in the front of the congregation. He worried that the bigness and the fatigue were due to her age, mid-thirties, so he put more offerings onto their altar—corn, beans, flowers from the blooming trees, and vines around their house, a plump orange, a twin tomato. God was good. He'd let them keep this one.

"Look how big I am!" Esperanza boasted. Must be a boy, some neighbors said. She was eating so well after the year's good harvest. Maybe she was further along than she thought?

Esperanza had her own quiet suspicions. She didn't want to jinx it, but she thought she might be carrying two. It wasn't just the taut globe of her belly; she had a warm, warbling sense of it in her heart.

They saved up some money. When it neared her time to give birth, she took the bus down to the hospital, where they listened to her stomach and brought a picture onto the screen.

"Twins," the nurse said.

She'd been right. There were two little bodies, the thump of two heartbeats. Fifteen days later she went into labor. Ernesto slipped into the world first, screeching. She felt relief and then a wild need to push again. She labored the other baby out twelve minutes later—Raúl. Two identical creatures, writhing, their brown-pink bodies slick with birth. The nurses brought them both into her arms. They'd make it, she thought.

FROM the minute they were born, the twins were inseparable. First it was a matter of circumstance—they slept side by side and lay swaddled on the floor together. Then, when they got older, they rolled around on the same blanket, learning first to babble, then to form words. Even as they evolved their own personalities, they resisted being apart. Ernesto and Raúl wanted to sit next to each other in school, to eat together on the floor or the rock ledge behind the house, to walk side by side down the road to school, to work with their father in the fields in the same shifts.

When they were infants, Esperanza liked to wrap them in matching blankets and hold them one in each arm like prizes. She dressed them identically, opting to buy new clothes in sets of two rather than use hand-me-downs, despite the extra cost. When Ernesto and Raúl began to toddle down the road holding their mother's hands, neighbors and the occasional stranger would fall into prayer upon seeing them: two identical people. A miracle. Everyone in the town knew it and that the miracle belonged to Esperanza Flores.

Their older brothers took on the responsibility of keeping them safe.

"I'll be in charge of Ernesto, and you be in charge of Raúl," Ricardo declared to younger Wilber, who took it as an order. As they watched their brothers play with trucks in the yard, or chase chickens, or snatch things out of each other's hands, both older brothers rooted for their respective twin to win.

Teachers and family friends had a hard time distinguishing them. The siblings knew which was which, most of the time—Ernesto had a tiny mole under his eye, an easy tell from close range. But since they were most often together, it was easier to refer to them as one: the *gemelos,* the twins.

WHEN the twins were ten, Esperanza developed a cough and began cooking outside in the back courtyard, letting the twins take over the sooty former kitchen as their bedroom. They were delighted: a space of their own.

A few years earlier, Wilber had put the brothers to work in the *milpa.* There was Wilber's own land, two separate plots where they grew the corn and beans and tomatoes, and then the land they leased from the twins' godfather, who allowed them to plant there on his behalf and take home half the yield. Wilber Sr. needed all the workers he could get. For one thing, he and Esperanza had more mouths to feed: since the twins, they had had Lucia, then Marina, then Pablo, then Luis. A family of eleven was large even for La Colonia. Wilber also wanted his kids to understand how to make a living off the land. Work would keep them out of trouble.

The twins got up with the sun and spent the mornings in the field, then went to school for the afternoon session. This was the norm; because of overcrowding, which really meant underfunding, Salvadoran children attend school only half a day, either morning or afternoon. After school the twins' job was to take care of the livestock.

While Raúl was all playfulness, Ernesto could be severe, quick to snap at anyone he felt had done him wrong. Ernesto was also more socially attuned: he studied the older and more popular boys at school as if learning the customs of a new land. Raúl made friends easily enough but wasn't all that worried about being included. Ernesto also loved sports, while Raúl was the artsy one, often preferring drawing to football, and later taking to painting in art class at school. As they rooted into their own personalities, the contours of their faces seemed to change ever so slightly: Raúl's now appeared softer, more wide-eyed, whereas Ernesto was furrow-browed with a cultivated toughness. If Raúl saw his brother's temper beginning to surge, he'd smack Ernesto's arm with two fingers and run away to distract him from his rage. Often, it worked.

"There's always a difference with twins," their mother explained. She had Raúl's innocent laugh, accompanied by a shoulder jiggle and the squinting of her eyes. "That's what they say. . . . It happens in the womb. One taller, the other shorter, one is funny, the other angry."

"I'm the angel, and you're the devil," Raúl joked.

Ernesto conceded—he was indeed rougher around the edges. "But I'm the older one, so I have to be more serious and in charge." They argued over who was taller, using their hairdos to claim additional centimeters.

BY fourth grade, the twins ran with a steady pack of six boys from school. They floated in and out of the others' graces as if with the seasons. The pack liked to pick on each other, play pranks, and call each other names—monster, bitch—but the twins felt the others picked on them more often and cut deeper.

"You're too poor for shoes. Look at those shoes—they're falling apart."

"Stupid asshole."

"Dark-ass peasant boys."

It was unfair, the twins felt, because many of these guys were even poorer than they were.

"Just stay away from them," their classmate Edgar warned. A nice boy, quiet and self-effacing, he was a steadier friend than the pack of six. Still, Ernesto, in particular, was drawn to the group. Probably they were just jealous, the twins reasoned—a common Flores family explanation for bad human behavior. But their friends jeered at them often enough that other boys at school caught on.

"Your father's a beggar with that guitar of his," one bully, Silvio, declared. Wilber played guitar in church and sometimes sang hymns on the street, his croaky voice thick with devotion. The other kids cackled. No one came to their defense.

The teachers did little to protect them and in fact sometimes joined in at poking fun at them or their father. When a notebook appeared in the classroom scrawled with obscenities, which Ernesto knew to be Silvio's handiwork—he'd seen him do it—the teacher pointed the finger at Ernesto.

"Why did you do this?" he demanded.

"It wasn't me!" Ernesto insisted.

"Then who was it?" But he wouldn't dare say. The teacher sent him home.

Raúl wasn't in trouble, but he followed his brother back up the hill without a second thought.

"They're always blaming us," Ernesto complained on the way home. Raúl nodded.

Another day a kid hit Ernesto in the temple with a rock. He'd thrown it on purpose. It bled and left a bruise for days; he'd have the scar there forever. When Esperanza asked what happened, Ernesto lied—he'd fallen playing soccer, he said, and Raúl corroborated.

Their own relatives fueled the bullying, too. Wilber's half-sister, Graciela, had long looked down on Wilber, and things had got even worse when she'd married Don Agustín, a man from another town. Agustín was now one of the town's big men, a guy with more land and disposable cash than most and thus holder of a healthy dose of small-town power. He and Graciela had a spacious house up the road from Wilber's, a slick, well-running truck, and a profitable coffee crop. To them, Wilber's too-big family was a laughingstock and an embarrassment. As the twins grew up, they were invited to fewer weddings and family parties, then none. Their grandfather made no effort to see them.

In 2010 their uncle's house was robbed—people knew he had money. So Uncle Agustín arranged for a private security force: he would now be protected by gangs.

THEY heard about it on the news first. Bodies found dumped in secret grave sites, police officers murdered, women raped and slaughtered and left in the streets. Gang violence had spread throughout El Salvador like an invasive bloom. The gangs were growing their armies by recruiting kids, particularly in San Salvador but in smaller surrounding cities, too. The twins heard stories of beheadings and shootings of murdered police. The whole world around them began to tremble.

The first of the infamous (and infamously Salvadoran) gangs had formed in the United States among Salvadoran exiles, mostly undocumented youth who had fled violence and forced military recruitment during the civil war. They formed allegiances in the image of other Los Angeles gangs of the 1980s and '90s. Like the Italian mafia and the Irish gangs that rose to power in the early twentieth century, their lower ranks comprised young immigrants with limited economic options in a society trying to keep them out. Thousands of young men in Los Angeles were incarcerated then deported back to El Salvador, and along with them came the gang culture.

In El Salvador, the gangs made their money off low-level drug deals and extortion, charging businesses and individuals a biweekly fee called *renta,* or rent. Most of the gangster ground troops were young, poor guys not unlike the twins. Some kids chose to join, while others fell into it unwittingly, asked to do favors here and there until they were in too deep to retreat. Joining could be a seduction—poor, parentless, or abused children were lured into a place of belonging with an opportunity to become a big person, someone with means and power whom others respected and feared. Gang life did bring power and respect, but at great cost. Many of the gang leaders ran things from prison, and though the guys working the streets acquired minor trappings of success—nicer clothes, a phone—they stayed poor. Theirs was a status born of intimidation and fear, maintained by punishing anyone who crossed them and, often, by making sure that punishment was made public.

As a *New York Times* article would put it some years later, "El Salvador has been brought to its knees by an army of flies."

When the twins had been ten, a cousin of theirs was shot. He'd been crazy, they'd always been told—a thief. He'd gotten on the wrong side of the gangs. The following year the body of an estranged uncle of theirs was found in the river a few miles away. He'd been a drunk who would show up at the house from time to time, slurring and demanding food, and rumor had it that he'd joined one of the gangs. When they found him, he was cut up in pieces.

Signs of gang activity started to show up in town, too. One day they noticed MS-13 graffiti on a signpost between the main road and their house. They walked home more quickly then, heads down.

Kids began talking about *la violencia* and *la delincuencia* in school. "You know if it's a gangster because they dress good," one of their classmates said one day.

"If you're in a gang, you get rich," another explained. It didn't matter that it wasn't true; the perception of power was tied up in the perception of wealth. The twins nodded knowingly.

Classmates started to throw gang signs. Hard to know, at first, whether they were just posing, but you didn't mess with a kid who pledged any kind of allegiance, even if you suspected it was just for show. They watched who changed their style—who had the slick clothes, the confident swagger, the phone—and who was texting more often, loitering on the side of the road or in town. Were they *vigilando,* keeping watch?

The half-day of school suited agricultural families like the Floreses, but it left many other children unoccupied, out in the streets or the marketplace, vulnerable for recruitment. As the twins grew up, more youths were recruited by sheer force. A kid was told that if he didn't join, the gangs would kill him or his mother, or rape his sister. The gangs did enough throughout the country to intimidate in La Colonia without having to do much actual damage those early years. The specter of violence was powerful enough.

The twins' parents didn't say much about the gangs, preferring, as always, to keep their distance. Their father reminded them, as they shoveled and pulled from the ground, that work would keep their hands clean.

OUT in the morning sun, Wilber Jr.—the second Flores son—plotted his escape from La Colonia. He turned the central problem over and over in his mind as he worked the *milpa*. He loved his parents, but they had been irresponsible. Really, nine children? As his siblings multiplied and grew, the household's resources were stretched thin—toward the end of the seasonal rations and before the next harvest, even food was scarce. The year before, their godfather had ended the land-sharing arrangement, and so they were growing less food. Meanwhile, the country was becoming more dangerous, it seemed, every day.

One spring day during his final year of high school, Wilber took the bus to a neighboring town to take the entrance exam for university. This was his escape plan. He concentrated, terrified of failure. But he passed. He figured he could raise enough money working some nearby coffee harvests to pay for his schooling.

Right before he enrolled in a nearby college, his dad called him into his bedroom. It was evening, and Esperanza was outside cooking dinner.

"Son," he said, "do you want to go to the North?"

Like all Salvadorans who'd grown up after the massive exodus—over 350,000 people—of the civil war years, Wilber held a reverence for El Norte. "The North" was an often starry-eyed euphemism for the United States, where work and money and opportunity, despite messages sent back home to the contrary, were abundant.

Wilber Sr. could support only so many kids. He hadn't offered this to his eldest son, Ricardo, but instead to Wilber, his namesake. Ricardo had developed a drinking problem, and Wilber Jr. figured his father worried about what would happen to him if he were to be let loose in the United States. His father must have recognized that his second son was a hard worker with big dreams outside La Colonia. Of course he wanted to go. Though he worried Ricardo might be jealous, he couldn't second-guess this opportunity on account of his brother's pride.

"It's heaven up there," Wilber Jr. told the twins. He wanted to help support his family, but more than anything, he wanted to go to school in the United States. His plan was to learn English, enroll in college, make extra money to send back home, and earn his degree. It would be hard at first, sure, but in time he knew he could work his way up that ladder of the American Dream.

His father arranged a coyote to guide Wilber Jr. north through Mexico. To pay the coyote, he borrowed $6,000 from a shady local lender. Wilber Jr. understood that he alone was responsible for the debt, and would have to pay this off as soon as possible so the interest didn't swallow the family. But within a couple weeks he'd be in the United States, he figured, and after a couple more, he'd have a job and be sending money home, probably hundreds of dollars each month. (He had heard there were jobs for nine dollars an hour in California—a fortune.) In 2007, when the twins were eleven years old and Wilber was eighteen, he left for the North. Wilber Sr. slipped a small photograph of his son—a school portrait in black and white from when he was nine or ten years old, hair combed neatly to one side—into his fraying pocket Bible.

Wilber made it across on his first try. He called with the news that he'd reached San Jose, where they had a friend with whom he could stay, who had promised to help him find a job. That Sunday at church, the family thanked God for shepherding his passage.

WILBER Jr. had become a *hermano lejano,* a faraway brother—a Salvadoran who had left the country and—most often—crossed into the United States. Along the road to the San Salvador International Airport stands a large arc of stone with a sign reading WELCOME, FARAWAY BROTHER!

But they often don't return. El Salvador is home to 6.34 million people; nearly 2 million Salvadorans resided in the United States in 2013—a third of the country's population, a higher percentage than even Mexico's. In 2015 the country's exports totaled $5.5 billion, and the total from foreign remittances, nearly all from the United States, was approximately $4 billion. As the mayor of San Salvador put it, "El Salvador's biggest export is people."

Ernesto had lost his big brother guardian, the one who always picked him to be on his team, the one who rooted for him and defended him and joked around with him. His sadness at this loss was laced with resentment: Wilber had this whole adventure ahead of him and was leaving his brothers behind to take over his share of the work. They'd probably never see him again.

It's terrible to lose your kid to the North, thought Wilber Sr. the day his son rode away in the coyote's car. Yet he felt he'd made the right decision. He blamed the growth of the cities for this hemorrhaging of Salvadorans. So much of the fertile land—good earth, land he used to work as a migrant farmhand in his youth, before he married Esperanza—had been turned into houses, factories, urban sprawl. The sugarcane fields of Nuevo Cuscatlán, the coffee terraces that swept through Santa Tecla, were all now houses and stores, a big, dead carpet of metropolis. No wonder there were no jobs for young people, no wonder food was so expensive: the earth was being used up.

NOW that Wilber Jr. was gone, the twins had to guard the farm at night, sometimes sleeping in the barn and sometimes on the naked hillside under the stars. It was scary out there, the two of them alone, listening for rustles that could be crop thieves, or the armadillos that ruined the tomato plants, or bad spirits. For the first two threats they carried *bombas,* innocuous but deafening little fireworks the size of AA batteries.

The idea of robbers didn't scare them so much—they weren't really dangerous, just other poor people looking to swipe something to eat. What really scared them were the ghosts. Once, when they had lit a candle in a little shack near the barn, a long shadow emerged from nowhere. Raúl couldn't talk or breathe, as though he'd been muted by some sinister force. Ernesto, alarmed, looked at his brother, who pointed at the wall. The shadow grew longer—until all of a sudden the candle blew out. The boys ran out of the shack screaming.

"Someone committed suicide in there," their godfather told them. "He hanged himself." They never slept in that shack again. When the sky striped yellow-blue with dawn, the boys would stretch, dust themselves off, roll up their blankets, and head back to their home for breakfast. After a few more hours of sleep, they'd pull on their uniforms and go to school.

WHEN the twins were in seventh grade, a new kid moved to town. He and Ernesto got along well, even though the boy, Miguel, was a couple of years older. People whispered that Miguel's dad was a gangster, but then again, people said Ernesto and Raúl's dad was a beggar. Ernesto started hanging out with Miguel at the soccer fields after school, and, as usual, Raúl tagged along. Miguel didn't seem like a gangster. He sometimes asked Ernesto and Raúl if he could take some of the tomatoes and corn from the fields home to his family. They always said yes. Within a few months they became friends with his crew from the high school. These older guys didn't pick on them at first, which was a relief.

The twins started working the coffee harvests in the nearby plantations, picking the beans until their fingers ached but earning extra cash to buy school supplies, clothes, and eventually a small, pay-as-you-go, Internet-capable cellphone. (This they wanted primarily as a status symbol and so they could sign up for Facebook.) One harvest they worked on Uncle Agustín's coffee plantation. Agustín's kids, their older cousins Juan and Javier, had made an offer to them to come and work, which felt akin to a social invitation. But when payday came, Agustín stiffed them, paying them only a fraction of what they should have received. He just looked at them and handed over a few dollars for many days of work, as if daring them to challenge him. They wouldn't, and he knew it.

"He thinks he can do whatever he wants because he's with the gangsters," Raúl complained in a hushed voice as they walked home, famished and exhausted.

"He can," Ernesto spat.

They had stopped asking their father why his side of the family hated them so much. They knew that from Wilber Sr.'s perspective, it was good old-fashioned envy. He was a good worker, and he suspected his family resented his leaving their plantation to work his own farm. One day up on the hill he told his children, as though recounting a fairy tale, that he'd come upon a windfall of money buried underground that allowed him to buy the land, and had inherited another small parcel from his grandmother on the other side of the family. Whatever the truth of the story, to Wilber it explained everything—jealousy, plain and simple. To Ernesto and Raúl, however, it was clear enough that their cousins were ashamed of them.

Juan and Javier passed on the notion of the twins' inferiority to other people in town, including the twins' classmates and friends. Miguel, they found out, had started hanging out with their cousins. It didn't take long for the teasing and taunting to take root within Miguel's group, too.

"Fuck off," one of them would say to one of the twins, with a voice more cutting than usual, and for a few days the twins would be excluded. But it would pass, and the twins and those who tormented them, occasionally even Juan and Javier, would play soccer again, would walk home from school together, and would scramble together down to the river for a swim and, as the years went on, for a smoke. Passing Delta menthols around for deep, icy-hot drags signified belonging and status, for a while at least. Even as more staid friends like Edgar from school stuck with them, the twins—Ernesto, in particular—clung to the prospect of being a real part of this inner circle.

Eventually, Miguel admitted to Ernesto that his father was in a gang. He told him that his dad had tattoos marking his allegiance to MS-13 and kept guns in the house. Still, they lived poor—even after all the tomatoes and beans the Floreses had given to Miguel, they once watched as Miguel's dad robbed their corn crop. They never said anything, mostly

out of fear, but also out of shame on his behalf. It was upsetting to be
stolen from but even more humiliating to have to steal in order to eat. Is
that what gang life amounted to, stealing corn?

They were also a little afraid of Miguel, when it came down to it.
They avoided going to his house, making up excuses about having to
work on the farm.

IT'S hard to know whether the men in the truck that day had been seriously out to get them, or if they were just messing with a pack of boys
playing cards, flaunting their power and stoking fear. But the threat felt
real enough to the twelve-year-old twins.

Meanwhile the boys sprouted into adolescence, growing taller and
ganglier, a dark fuzz taking root along their upper lips and chins. They
took a liking to girls, and their slim boy arms hardened into small bumps
of biceps. A year or so after the truck incident, the twins went to the
river for a swim to cool off before getting to work in the fields. When
they came through the brush onto the main road, a pack of young men—
all well-dressed bluster and darting eyes—started following them.

They recognized one of the guys as their rumored half-brother, Wilber's supposed son with a woman before Esperanza. Wilber denied the
boy was his, but who knew. Either way, this guy had always seemed to
hate the Flores family. The twins had heard rumors that he had fallen
in with Juan and Javier and had clicked into the local MS-13 ring. When
the twins saw him leading the pack, they quickened their pace.

By now, gangs were no longer confined to the communities of deportees sent back from Los Angeles in the 1990s. They were a large-
scale network of small-time criminals, decentralized but with affiliates
all across the world. The local shot-callers were people the community
knew but often only by reputation, their nicknames so cliché as to be almost comical—Shaggy, the Little Devil of Hollywood, the Boxer. They
were shadow kings, spellbinding their countrymen with reverence and
fear. By the time the twins were run-walking down the road with a pack
of young men in pursuit, La Colonia was a full-fledged MS-13 territory.

Around the region, sometimes in their own town, people were shot and left in the bushes, their corpses half-rotten by the time they were found. Heads were cut off, the corpses left out in the center of towns for all to see. Bodies turned up sprayed with so many bullets that practically none of the torso remained. When they heard the brutal reports, Wilber would sigh. Devil's work. "We're at war again," he said, shaking his head. "Only this—it's a dry war." A war between the government and the gangs, and between the gangs and each other.

The twins turned back to look, hoping their followers would be gone, but there they still were, stone-faced, gaining on them. Finally they approached a friend's house and ducked inside to call the police. The pack staked out across the street. The twins could see them from the windows, waiting. Summoning the police might only invite retribution later, but ultimately they figured they couldn't get home otherwise, so they made the call. The police never came. Eventually the guys across the street left. The twins sprinted home and stayed indoors that night, asking Ricardo to take their shift up on the hill.

That crew never bothered Ernesto and Raúl again, though they saw them around town. Afterward the twins spent less time outside and more time at home, stealing balls from their younger siblings and playing in the back courtyard. The town square grew quieter as people moved around La Colonia with more care. Practically no one was out at night anymore: one wouldn't dare.

WILBER Jr. called from time to time, though the twins rarely talked to him. He had got a landscaping job and sent monthly payments until his $6,000 coyote debt was gone. Then they heard from him less and less. He sent some money now and then—$50, $100, $200. These infusions of cash allowed them to buy rice and milk and sugar to supplement their dwindling harvest. But then the money would be finished, and they wouldn't hear from Wilber for several months.

"He only helped himself," their sister Maricela said. The twins had to agree.

Esperanza was more generous; she didn't fault her son. "The dream is always more difficult when you're awake," she said.

The dream could easily snare a person in its gravitational tug. Edgar, their quiet, steadfast friend from school, had never mentioned going north. And yet one day, as the twins scurried to his familiar door, his mother stopped them.

"Edgar's not here," she said.

"Where is he?" they asked.

"He went to the North," she said, and shut the door.

It's January 2011, and Osmin, a teenager living in Santa Ana, El Salvador, walks with a limp. "They shot him in the leg," his younger sister explains—*they* being shorthand for the gangs. Their mother sells tortillas in the market, where *they* are everywhere. Crowded markets are excellent for running goods back and forth, for collecting rent, for recruitment, for generally keeping an eye on things. Santa Ana's main market abuts the bus terminal, and Santa Ana itself, El Salvador's second-largest city, is a key point on the way north to Guatemala—a strategic transit zone through which to run drugs and people.

Osmin's leg has mostly healed, and his step will balance out. Whatever got him shot seems to be worked out for now. But he wants—he says he *needs*—to get out of El Salvador. In 2011 homicide here will reach an all-time high—4,354 people will be murdered by the end of the year, numbers rivaling those of the civil war.

He's been lucky so far, but luck lasts only so long. He's got to go. "I just have to figure out how," he says.

He means how to get the money. Once you have the cash, he knows, getting out is easy enough to arrange.

Between 1980 and 1990, the most brutal years of the civil war, approximately 371,000 Salvadorans migrated to the United States, out of a population of around 5 million—7 percent of the country's overall population. Looking for both refuge and economic opportunity, they moved north in a steady stream, some illegally and some availing themselves of Temporary Protective Status, an immigration relief offered to Salvadorans as a result of the war.

But violence and instability beget migration, and just as violence often begets more violence, migration often begets more migration. After the war, Salvadorans kept leaving—for economic opportunity, to reunite with family, and because an earthquake and several hurricanes leveled homes, destroyed livelihoods, and sent people packing. By 2008, 1.1 million foreign-born Salvadorans lived in the United States, or 18 percent of El Salvador's entire population that year.

In 2009, the year before Osmin was shot and began to think of leaving, several thousand minors like him struck out from El Salvador for the North. This, in itself, was not news; it was more or less the same number as previous years. But in the fall of 2011, the number of kids leaving El Salvador for the United States skyrocketed. Osmin has friends, neighbors, and family members who are going or have gone. The same is true all over the so-called Northern Triangle. In those other countries, Osmin has heard, gang violence is spiraling out of control, just like where he lives.

The solo, underage crossers are what the U.S. media has begun to call "unaccompanied minors," and what the U.S. government officially terms "unaccompanied alien children"—kids traveling alone, without papers or parents, and crossing the border into the United States. By the end of fiscal year 2012, the number of unaccompanied minors nabbed by *la migra* and turned over to the Office of Refugee Resettlement will nearly double to 13,625. Twenty-seven percent of 2012's unaccompanied minors will be from El Salvador—almost four thousand more *hermanitos lejanos,* faraway little brothers and sisters.

Meanwhile the number of "illegal immigrant" adults is going down in almost inverse proportion to the rise in unaccompanied alien children: from 1.1 million adult apprehensions in 2005 to 326,034 in 2012. With the tanking of the U.S. economy, why go north to beg for jobs that aren't there?

There will be 13,625 unaccompanied minors in 2012.

And 24,668 in 2013.

The next year it will climb to 57,496.

"I just have to figure out how to go," Osmin repeats. It's the children now, not so much the adults, the parents, who are moving north.

CHAPTER 2

When the twins turned thirteen, Ernesto announced that he would no longer be dressing like his brother. "We're our own people," he declared. "It's stupid to dress the same."

Raúl remembers it differently: they'd come to the decision together. "We just wanted to be our own people."

Whoever made it, the decision stemmed in large part from the bullying. Being twins already made them stand out, and dressing the same made it worse. Going to school that first day wearing his own outfit somehow made Ernesto feel more powerful.

They also decided that they needed a bicycle. A bike would give them bragging rights: their friends, they were sure, would circle around them, clamoring to use it. It would also mean freedom. They imagined huffing up the peak just beyond their house, mounting the bike together, and flying hands free into town, matching kings of the road.

They couldn't afford to buy a bike with a few dollars from working the coffee harvests, so they hatched a plan. Along with a cousin from their mother's side, they made a deal with the local repair shop: they would get a bicycle in exchange for a sack and a half of corn. One afternoon when their father was out in the fields and no one else was home, the twins loaded an entire sack from the main room of the house—about four feet long and weighing over fifty pounds—onto their shoulders, then trudged a half mile into town to the bike shop. Their cousin met them there, with half a stolen sack of his own. They dropped the booty in the corner of the shop, and the owner handed over the bike with a laugh.

It was red and sleek, shimmering with newness. The boys fought over who could ride it on his own, who would pedal standing up as the other two balanced above the wheels, one on the handlebars and the other on the seat, legs splayed away from the pedals, behind the driver—Devil Style, the arrangement was called. They had to keep the bike a secret from their parents, but they wanted to show it off, wanted the other boys to see them whizzing past and taking tight turns, nearly airborne, their wheels whirring like music.

For an entire week they hid the bike in the bushes by their house, hopping on each evening to ride it to the barn. But Wilber Sr. soon discovered it.

He took the twins into their bedroom, the walls still caked with soot from the room's many years as a kitchen. "Stealing from your own family?" he shouted. That bike cost food that they needed. He took out a rope; soon the twins were muffling their grunts and screams.

Ernesto couldn't sit down for a week. Wilber's improvised whip left cuts on his ass and red welts that seeped, over the coming days, into a purple brown. It wasn't infrequent for Wilber Sr. to punish them with force. Most of the time the whacks were quick, but sometimes, if he got angry enough, like with the bike—or with an escaped cow, or for getting in the way of an argument with Esperanza, or defending her, or defending one another for doing something wrong—he'd wallop them so hard they'd be afraid of where the beating might end.

They regretted the lying and stealing, and they still had scars as souvenirs. But they cherished the memory of the bike, the thrill of careening into the distance, the ground quickening beneath them like a slick ribbon.

———

PEOPLE left La Colonia all the time—adults, kids, sometimes whole families. More kids like Wilber and Edgar were starting to leave—for opportunity, as always, but also out of fear. After Edgar left, the twins daydreamed about it more often. They imagined the places where people they knew had ended up—Arizona, Texas, California. Ernesto idealized El Norte just as his older brother had: a place with jobs, more stuff, opportunity. In El Norte, the way he figured it, he could have a bike in a matter of weeks. Wilber wrote home every now and again about how hard it was to make money, but Ernesto never quite believed it. He imagined his brother with nice clothes, a fancy car, flashy Nikes.

Raúl dreamed of the North too, but differently. He conjured it in his mind, especially the buildings: skyscrapers with gleaming windows and shining floors as tall as his town was long. He was interested in seeing it but not in living there. He didn't want to be a farmer like his father, but he took Wilber Jr. at his word about life being harder up there than they'd been led to believe. Raúl had chosen his high school career track: banking. He was getting grades good enough to consider it; his friends sometimes even copied his homework. He imagined moving to San Salvador or maybe just a medium-size city like Santa Ana or Ilobasco, where he could count money behind a computer in an air-conditioned room. The good life he imagined for himself was in El Salvador.

Ernesto wasn't so sure.

"Want to get drunk?" one of the pack of six friends asked one day when they were fourteen. They'd never been drunk before, but Ernesto was in, and Raúl by extension was too. They pooled cash with their friends and bought a bottle at the cantina, which sold to kids like them as long as they had the money. They didn't know what kind of alcohol it was, just that it was clear and nearly made them vomit. At the banks of the river, Ernesto grabbed the bottle for a second round and slugged it back theatrically, to the cheers of the other boys.

Raúl, the quiet, timid giggler, was still the same old teasable Flores boy. But Ernesto had warrior potential.

MARICELA, the eldest girl stuck between a bunch of brothers, was shy. At school she did her work and laughed at other kids' antics, batting her eyelashes in an alloy of flirtation and self-erasure. She didn't dare publicly stand up for her younger brothers—they were boys, after all, and could stick up for themselves. It hurt when people said things about her father, but she kept quiet. She, like the twins, was aware of her status as a poorer person from La Colonia. But she also dreamed of going north, of making something unexpected of herself.

When she was eighteen and the twins were sixteen her older brother Ricardo brought a friend over: Sebastian, a handsome eighteen-year-old. He stayed for lunch, and Maricela giggled when he spoke, averting her gaze while helping her mother serve the tamales. A few days later Maricela's friends told Sebastian that she had a crush on him. She feigned fury but nearly liquefied when he came up to her in the town square one afternoon.

"What's up?" he said. She shrugged and straightened, attempting to be beautiful.

She knew he was a lady-killer, that she should be wary, but the fact that she wanted to talk to her made her feel like a star.

"THE dead and pieces of the dead turn up in El Salvador everywhere," wrote Joan Didion in her book *Salvador,* a dispatch from the heart of the civil war. "A knot of children on the street suggests the presence of a body. Bodies turn up in the brush of vacant lots, in the garbage thrown down ravines in the richest districts, in public restrooms, in bus stations. Some are dropped in Lake Ilopango, a few miles east of the city." She was describing El Salvador in 1982, but she could just as easily have been describing El Salvador nearly three decades later in 2011, the year gang violence came to a head and things started to go bad for the Flores boys.

A couple of older kids approached sixteen-year-old Ernesto in the hall one day, out of sight of the other students.

"Silvio is always picking on you," one said.

He nodded.

"Your friends, too," another said.

"They won't mess with you if you come with us." They showed him their shoes, new and nice, and flashed their touchscreen phones. "You should join," they told him, meaning MS-13.

Ernesto shook his head. "Nah," he said.

"You really should," the first guy replied.

He said he'd think about it and went back to class. He didn't tell Raúl.

We measure water in gallons or liters, distance in miles or kilometers, height in feet or meters. Murders are measured in units of 100,000. In 2011, when the twins were fifteen—prime gang recruiting age—the murder rate was 71 out of 100,000 people—compared to 64.4 the year before. That meant 4,354 murders out of a population of 6 million people, amounting to an average of twelve people murdered a day. By comparison, in 2015 there were 16,121 homicides in the United States, a country of some 320 million and home to more guns, the *Washington Post* reported, than people. The United States, a country that is fifty times the size of El Salvador, had only four times the number of homicides.

One morning in the small town down the hill where Esperanza sometimes sold tomatoes, more than forty men were arrested. The tattooed guys were linked to a local *clica* thought to be responsible for eight recent murders in the area. As they were driven off to jail, they tried to hide their faces from the newspaper cameramen. Meanwhile the boys who'd tried to recruit Ernesto claimed the sidewalks in the town center. Just a little stealing here, they had explained to Ernesto, a little rent-collecting there. No big thing.

A friend invited Ernesto to a funeral in the next town over. The deceased, someone he'd met only a couple of times, had been twenty years old. Inside the house the family members and friends wailed around the open casket. Ernesto said a prayer and felt queasy. The boy's face was bloated and unnatural looking, and he could see where the bullet had punctured his skull.

"Did you think about what we talked about?" the boys asked Ernesto at school.

"Yeah," he said. "But I can't."

"You sure?"

He couldn't tell if it was a threat or not. "I'm sure."

He told Raúl on the way home from school. "I won't join," he said. "I would never."

But Raúl wasn't convinced.

After that, Ernesto started to spend more time in town after school, more time away from the family and his twin. "Just hanging out," he told Raúl. "Just playing soccer."

UNLIKE most people in the town, who dressed in worn farming clothes, Uncle Agustín always had on a collared shirt and sunglasses. While most people suffered amid the violence, Agustín had figured out how to make the gang wars, and the new exodus, work for him.

Agustín began to lend money at high interest rates, which gave him capital for a bigger enterprise: a coyote ring, or human smuggling outfit that helped people, for a fee, navigate the tricky and dangerous routes north to the United States. Providing routes north had become a growth industry, and Agustín had some guys who would take people through Guatemala and into Mexico, and get them across to the United States. The price was steep—$7,000 or so—but the real cost, and profit, was in the interest on the loan. When would-be migrants wanted to go north but couldn't pay the full fee, Agustín was said to lend them money at 10, 15, or 20 percent interest and take their property as collateral.

It was the kids who were driving the boom in Agustín's new enterprise. Families knew they were going into debt just to line a predatory lender's pockets, but people like Wilber and Esperanza, and like Edgar's parents, didn't want their children to make the journey without a guide.

The richer Agustín grew, the higher the stakes. Hence his hiring of the gangs as a security force. Protection deals like this one were becoming commonplace. They didn't always mean direct involvement with gang business, but Agustín's proximity to the gangs meant that Juan and Javier, and by extension many of the boys in the twins' circle, were spending more time around MS-13.

IN 2012 the Salvadoran government, then led by the leftist FMLN party (a vestige of the guerrilla movement during the civil war), made a controversial decision: it would sit at the table with key gang leaders and broker a truce. Led by an ex–guerrilla member and a well-known Catholic faith leader, the leadership of MS-13 and Barrio 18, the two most powerful gangs—all of whom were imprisoned at the time—met at one of the country's highest-security penitentiaries and negotiated a deal. Allegedly in exchange for lighter prison sentences and more privileges for the top brass in the country's maximum-security prisons, the gangs agreed to a cease-fire.

And for a while, they seemed to be keeping their word. In 2012 homicides fell almost in half, from the record 4,354 in 2011 to 2,576.

On the other hand, gangs had been given a seat at the bargaining table. They were now legitimate actors with officially recognized power. Countrywide, though the body count dropped, the menace remained. In 2012 the region where the Flores family lived registered more than 200 disappeared; the next year it surpassed 300, and the following year nearly reached 600. Sometimes the disappeared would turn up dead, sometimes alive, and sometimes they wouldn't turn up at all. La Colonia started reporting people vanished. The extortion rate skyrocketed; people knew what the gangs were made of. The threat of death, it turned out, was just as powerful as death itself.

MEANWHILE, by 2012 Wilber Jr. had fallen out of contact. The Flores family hardly heard from him anymore, and although he had never sent money often, he wasn't sending any at all. When he did call, often to a neighbor's phone because the Flores family couldn't always afford to maintain an active cellphone (loading it with credit every now and then when they had the cash), Esperanza answered the phone with a hungry smile, cooing at the sound of her faraway son's voice.

"We're fine, we're fine!" she said, surrounded by her eight other children, all hungry. The harvest was bad that year; the family worried that they might run out of food; the portions got smaller every night. Ernesto and Raúl watched her lie cheerily.

"He has enough to worry about, up there all on his own," she said after hanging up.

As things got worse in their country, the older Flores siblings spent more and more time imagining what it was like in the United States—where Wilber was, and what he was up to, and what was so bad, or causing him to be so selfish, that he was no longer sending money back.

Maricela, in part to slip out of her family's dire situation for moments at a time, was hanging around with Sebastian. She dropped him coy smiles when they passed on the road and texted him via her friends. It soon became more: she lost her virginity to him gladly—she was ready and felt that he was the one.

By the time she found out she was pregnant, he'd lost interest not only in sleeping with her but even in talking to her. She told him anyway and asked him not to tell anyone, terrified of her parents finding out. They should have used protection, she knew, but she hadn't wanted to force the issue.

Maricela decided she'd have to hide for a while, to buy herself some time to figure things out. She had a friend who lived a few towns over; the friend's family said it was okay for her to stay there for a bit. So one day, four months pregnant, she left school at midday, grabbed one of her family's two suitcases, and started packing.

"Where are you going?" Her youngest brother, Luis, age seven, had peeked into the room where the girls slept.

"Nowhere," she said. "To theater practice." A play was to be performed in town in the coming weeks.

He shrugged and left her alone. Within minutes, she was a runaway.

Later that same afternoon the school health promoter, who had given Maricela the pregnancy test that confirmed her fears, showed up at the Flores family door to deliver the news. Wilber Sr. was furious. Who was the father, and didn't his daughter know this was a sin? he raged. Esperanza sat in front of the altar and prayed.

They didn't hear from Maricela for days and didn't know where to track her down. She eventually sent a message that she was safe but wasn't ready to come home yet. She was too scared. But as the weeks passed, her parents imagined her belly growing and started to think of the baby less as a sin than as their first grandchild. What could they do now anyway? They hoped they could at least persuade her to marry the guy.

But that wasn't an option. Not only did Sebastian not call her or see her or send money, he was courting several other girls—three of whom saw fit to inform Maricela that there was no way Sebastian would acknowledge this bastard baby as his own. Maricela ignored their threatening texts, though her heart billowed and heaved—just a few months ago she'd been an innocent girl, and now? She'd made a mess of her life. She did what she could to earn her keep around her friend's house, but after a month she was ready to listen to Wilber.

"You're our daughter. We want you to come back. We want to support you," he said. "Nothing will happen to you," he promised.

She went back home.

The day Maricela went into labor, Esperanza took her in a friend's car to the hospital where the twins had been born. Maricela sweated and panted and pushed, then was taken to the operating room for a cesarean. There was the baby, a little girl whom she named Guadalupe, or Lupita for short. At the hospital, when they asked for the last names, she hesitated. In the end, she gave Sebastian's name as well as her own, so that her daughter would have both a mother's name and a father's name, as was customary. No child of hers would be seen as illegitimate.

Back at home, her siblings were eager to hold the baby. Like the rest of the family, Ernesto and Raúl had been angry with her at first, but they'd softened. The only exception was Ricardo, the eldest. He didn't make eye contact with her and spoke to her only when necessary. He did everything he could, she felt, to make her feel unwelcome and ashamed.

Fifteen days after Lupita was born, Maricela still hadn't heard from Sebastian. She'd give him time—eventually he'd want to meet his daughter. When at last there was a knock at the door, instead of Sebastian it was his parents. Maricela handed Lupita to her paternal grandmother.

"Sebastian left," his mother said, as she took her granddaughter into her arms.

"Left?" asked Maricela.

"*Al Norte,*" she said. To the North. Exactly fifteen days ago he'd climbed into a car with his coyote and left for the United States—just a few hours before Lupita was born.

ERNESTO could go north, he thought in secret. He didn't want to, but he could. The family was still struggling, and now there was a new baby in the house, another person to care for. Ernesto was a hard worker, and tough—if Wilber had survived the journey, and so had that asshole who'd knocked up his sister, he could, too. If he made it there, he knew he could make something of himself and support his family back home.

"You're crazy," Raúl told Ernesto when he waxed lyrical about the North one day as they lay in the fields, guarding the tomatoes. His twin had been spending more time either inside the house or up in the mountains with Raúl, tending the animals and guarding the corn—which meant, to Raúl, that he was at least dodging the gangs' entreaties to join. Mornings and afternoons on the farm gave them time to dream, and the more Ernesto turned the notion of the mythic North Country over in his mind, the more real it became.

Juan and Javier were now fully clicked into MS-13, along with Miguel's dad, and so, perhaps, was Miguel. Meanwhile the gang boys at school kept pressuring Ernesto to do the same. He remembered the boy at the funeral with the gunshot through his head. The gang kids talked about the perks of the life with cool ease, but what about the dead kid, or the guys in the truck?

The North offered everything he wanted—success, belonging, respect, something better. He didn't want to leave, he thought in the quiet dark after Raúl nodded off, but at the same time he wanted to go.

IN the late spring of 2013, someone hacked down Uncle Agustín's tree. It had been a giant tree, a *barillo* with a strong, sturdy trunk and smooth branches that spread into a thick canopy of waxy, tear-shaped leaves. Agustín was furious. Its fall, he said, had taken out a large swath of his coffee plantation in the adjacent field, ruining a good part of the crop. The whole town gossiped, wondering who had knocked it down, and how and why.

By that time the family was awaiting the May harvest, stretching their food to their last kernels of corn.

Ernesto officially decided to leave town. One evening while his mother was outside cooking, he went into his parents' room, a separate structure from the main house, to talk to his father. "Dad," he said. "I've been thinking about it, and I think I should go north."

His father was quiet for a few moments. "Why do you want to go?" he asked. "And how would you get there?"

Ernesto took this as a no. He didn't respond, just turned around and walked back into the main house.

The next night, his father came to talk to him. "Okay," Wilber said. He'd done the caluclations in his mind, and knew they needed more money than was coming in to stay afloat. "You can go." They'd take out another loan. The family didn't want to lose another son to the northern vastness, but they knew that it was probably best.

Ernesto promised that he'd pay off the debt quickly and then continue sending money home each month. It wasn't just his future he was concerned about, he insisted, but that of the whole family. He didn't tell him that, by leaving, he was also hoping to avoid the gangs' widening net.

Raúl knew that Ernesto had been thinking about going, but he was stunned into silence when Ernesto announced his plan. He stepped outside for air. He was hurt not because Ernesto was going to the United States, specifically, but because he was embarking on this new life without Raúl. Ernesto hadn't invited him, hadn't pleaded with him to come along. Raúl wouldn't so readily be able to leave Ernesto behind.

"You sure you want to go?" he asked later that night, in their room.

"Positive," Ernesto replied. They didn't talk any more about it.

The coyote would cost $7,000. He knew of people who'd gone on their own, with no coyote, no guide, and just enough cash for food and bus fare and the occasional bribe. But Ernesto had barely ever left the quiet radius of towns around La Colonia, and now he'd have to cross through a swath of El Salvador, Guatemala, and Mexico. Horror stories riddled accounts of the road like potholes, far more than when Wilber had left seven years before: children raped in the desert, children dying of thirst, children with limbs severed beneath the cruel rims of a train.

He, like Wilber, needed a guide. So they asked the most obvious person for money and for a coyote: Uncle Agustín. Wilber Sr. trudged to his house, took off his bowler hat in deference, and asked for a loan.

"No," Agustín told his brother-in-law, who was showing his age, his arms just suntanned sinews stretching along his slight frame.

Wilber thanked him and walked back home.

He had a cousin, Erick, who also ran a coyote business, but Erick didn't loan money. So Wilber went to a loan broker in town, a woman who did business on behalf of an ex-military guy a few towns away. She'd loan them the money for the coyote, plus a few extra hundred in case of emergency. The interest, she said, as far as he remembered when he got back home, would be 20 percent.

When Wilber signed for the loan, he put one of his plots of land up as collateral. The woman handed over the cash, which Wilber then took to Erick. Ernesto's trip was arranged for two weeks' time.

In the following days, everything looked different to Ernesto. Every signpost, every view from an outcropping, every friend, was something he would miss. Raúl most, though he wouldn't let on.

When just a week remained before he was to leave—one week to say his final, real goodbyes—the family heard an ominous rumor. Something, it seemed, had led Agustín to believe that it was Ernesto who had cut down his tree.

WHY would Ernesto have done it? And where had Agustín got the idea that he had? That Ernesto could even manage such a thing strained credulity. The twins decided it must have been Miguel, or one of their friends from school, who had started the rumor. They were jealous, perhaps, that Ernesto was going north and were trying to stay on Juan and Javier's crew and curry favor with big-man Agustín.

The twins soon heard about more stories heading Agustín's way, that Ernesto and Raúl were gossiping about Agustín's livelihood and his gang connections and that they claimed to have seen stores of guns at his house. The twins had certainly heard dark things about Agustín; he was rumored to have had people killed who stole from his business. They didn't know if it was true, and they'd certainly never seen or gossiped about the guns, but the story added to Agustín's menace. That he might have a store of guns at his house seemed plausible. But Ernesto and Raúl insisted back through the grapevine that they'd never said such things and they never would have.

Agustín, the gyre of rumors reported back, wasn't satisfied.

Juan and Javier showed up at the Flores house. "Talking shit about my family?" Javier spat. He got close to Ernesto as if he might hit him.

"We didn't say anything!" Ernesto insisted.

Raúl backed him up. "We wouldn't talk about your family!"

The cousins looked at them side-eyed, then walked out the door. This kind of bad-mouthing was treated as treason in the gang world. Agustín had always looked down on the twins' family, and now he had reasons—the tree, the twins' alleged shit talking—to seek revenge.

Soon afterward Ernesto and Raúl were kicking a ball back and forth along the road outside their house. Juan and Javier, heading toward town in one of Agustín's trucks, saw the twins and picked up speed. They had to jump to the side of the road and flatten themselves against their house. As they tore by, Juan and Javier stared at Ernesto as if to say, *Next time, we'll mow you down.*

If Ernesto had had any doubts that he had to go north, they now vanished.

He went onto Facebook for some solace, posting:

Feel so sad today cuz there's only a few days with my friends.

Raúl thought he was stupid to blast out his plan like that. Neither of them understood that because his decision to go north was now posted on his public feed, it wasn't just his few dozen "friends" who now knew of it but anyone who cared to track him down.

ERNESTO was to spend his last night in La Colonia in a safe house outside town, where he'd be picked up by his *coyota,* a woman, the next morning. Raúl had decided to spend the night with his twin—the last time, it was both conceivable and completely inconceivable, that they might ever see each other.

Late that afternoon the woman who ran the safe house got a call from Uncle Erick: *Tell them to leave,* he told her. She tracked the twins down at a friend's house. "Go hide up in the hills," she said.

It turned out that Agustín had found out Ernesto was leaving and was using not just a rival loan broker but, worse, a rival coyote company. Even though he'd refused to give Wilber a loan, Agustín took it as another slight. He was looking for Ernesto.

"We're changing the trip," the safe house woman explained to Ernesto. It was too dangerous to leave while Agustín and his boys were all lit up at him—they knew Erick's routes and might have them followed.

So Raúl and Ernesto slipped out of their friend's house and spent the night up on a hill, much as they had many times amid the corn, but this time more scared than ever—not of ghosts or spirits, of wailing women or thieves, but of Agustín's boys. They startled at every rustle and movement in the forest and didn't sleep at all.

"You have to go," Raúl acknowledged. It was no longer a choice.

The trip was postponed for over a week, during which both Ernesto and Raúl stayed inside. Ernesto was a bona-fide target now—and Raúl, his identical twin, could easily be mistaken for him. Uncle Erick set a new date, with a new route, to leave town.

Ernesto once again took to Facebook:

Ummm friends the 20th of this month I'm leaving I want you to know that I'm going to miss you.

"Don't do that!" Raúl said. But Ernesto couldn't help himself.

IT was late July 2013 and seventeen-year-old Ernesto's backpack was ready to go, packed with a few changes of clothes, a sweatshirt, a bar of soap, and a small cellphone that his father had bought him that, he said, would work in Mexico. "Don't tell them you have it," Wilber said. "You can use it to let us know how you are." He handed his son a plastic rosary, which they tied around his waist under his shirt for protection.

An aunt came over to say goodbye. "It's good he's going," she told Wilber. Earlier that day she'd been over at Agustín's. "I'd like to crush that boy's face in with a rock," she reported Agustín having told her. He'd slammed his fist into his palm by way of demonstration.

That last night Ernesto was restless. Raúl was too, but he eventually nodded off, leaving Ernesto awake and alone. Finally Ernesto slipped into a doze, his vapor-like dreams peopled by his cousins and his family, but set against the backdrop of a new life in the United States.

Just after dawn his mother roused him. He grabbed his backpack and hugged his parents and Maricela, who was up with the baby, goodbye, while fighting back tears and the jitters of departure, fear knocking around against excitement like pebbles in a can. Raúl was still sleeping; Ernesto decided not to wake him. He walked out the door without even looking at his twin.

THE CHURN

I t's early morning on an unseasonably hot February day in Reynosa, Mexico, and a group of six young deportees step out of a white U.S. immigration van. The young men, all Mexicans between the ages of nineteen and twenty-five, walk toward the reception center on the Mexican side of the Hidalgo International Bridge. They're originally from places farther south in Mexico, but the U.S. immigration authorities drop them right over the border. The van turns around and heads back into Texas.

"Excuse me," one deportee asks a man on the street. "Where are we?"

It's not yet eight a.m., but the roads are already packed with cars, and the walkways of the bridge, this international no-man's-land, hum in both directions. Beggars and hawkers appeal to the passersby: a man missing a leg and an arm balances on crutches, holding out his hat in hopes of spare change, a woman with a baby and a toddler sits on the ground, her back against the railing, peddling packets of gum.

The border is punctuated by small cities like Reynosa: last stops and transit zones, places of free trade, the mutual territory of the businessman, the migrant, the coyote, and the narco. Most of the time Reynosa appears orderly enough, but beneath the surface, it roils. In the past decade, violence and crime in Reynosa's state, Tamaulipas—and throughout Mexico—have been on a swell, catching up to the reputation of its upriver neighbor, Ciudad Juárez, once infamous for having one of the highest murder and kidnapping rates in Mexico.

By now, the migrants know all about the perils of the border. You move people, you move drugs, and more often than ever, you move them in tandem. The face of the coyote is changing: no longer just a guide trying to make a buck while navigating people north but often a drug smuggler, too, or at least working for one—and almost always working with permission from the narco-traffickers to move through their territory.

A Good Samaritan with a pickup drives the deported men to a nearby migrant shelter, run by a group of Catholic nuns and international volunteers. They rest in the truck, holding their bags of provisions. The truck pulls into the migrant shelter and they unload.

Last night Reynosa had several shoot-outs. When the Zeta and Gulf cartels splintered in 2010, Reynosa became a turf war battleground, leading to a major spike in homicides and other crime. *Los malos,* everyone calls them, the bad guys, shorthand for the *narcos*—but you avoid saying *narcos* here out loud. Even journalists and police, when they talk among themselves, tend to refer to them as *los malos.* As with Salvador's *la violencia,* the violence, shorthand is safer.

Migrants aren't just wrapped up in the currents of the drug trade; they've also become its targets. In the past several years, the cartels, whose supply has reduced due to intercartel wars and international crackdowns, have realized that migrants are lucrative marks. To reach the United States, Central American migrants have to move through more than six hundred miles of Mexico. That makes them potential drug mules. They often carry large sums of cash and have family waiting for them across the border who could pay a ransom. They flee the violence of the Northern Triangle only to pass through another unconventional war zone.

In August 2010 Los Zetas pulled seventy-two migrants from one of the northbound buses, shot them, then buried the corpses in and around the city of San Fernando. Dozens of suitcases arrived at the Reynosa bus terminal with no one to claim them.

The next year, in 2011, authorities uncovered 193 more bodies, often mutilated, scattered among forty-seven clandestine graves in and around San Fernando. In 2012 the corpses of forty-nine people were uncovered in the adjacent state of Nuevo León. The majority of the dead, many of whose remains have yet to be identified, were migrants heading north.

A few miles from the adult shelter, and less than a quarter-mile from the border, is a locked facility for migrant youth. Today it's home to six Mexican boys waiting for their families to pick them up or send bus fare to bring them home, as well as sixteen Central Americans, all of whom have been nabbed by Mexican authorities and await being sent home via plane to Guatemala, El Salvador, or Honduras. The unlucky ones, they'd say. Today is music class, and an energetic older man strums the guitar with gusto, encouraging everyone to sing along—the girls on one side of the room, the boys on the other. Occasionally, a few chime in or shake a maraca.

All but one say that for sure they'll be back.

"I'm not worried," a boy with a backward cap says with the bravado of a high school football player predicting a Friday-night win. He sports long basketball shorts and soccer sandals and spreads his arms back over the rim of his chair. "I'll make it there."

They slap cards on the table. They peel tangerines and organize the rinds into piles, then rocket the seeds through their tongues so that they ricochet off the floor.

"I'll go home, see my family a little, rest up, then come back again," a boy from Santa Ana, El Salvador, announces.

"How do you get refugee status in the United States?" one of the boys asks the table.

"You need a lawyer," another replies.

"Money," another says, rubbing his fingers against his thumb. "Those lawyers cost a lot."

They discuss the merits of turning themselves in at the border versus making an all-out run for it.

"Safer to turn yourself in" and try to get status, one says, than to risk the Texas desert. But then again—you're more likely to be deported if you're caught.

The music teacher picks up the guitar and starts again. "Ay, ay, ay, ay," he croons with gusto, ducking his head in front of the boys who aren't participating. The backward-hat boy shakes a maraca and sings. Then, at the chorus, they all join in, with mocking enthusiasm: *"Canta, no llores"*—sing, don't cry. The sound of their voices echoes out the window to the too warm day.

CHAPTER 3

Raúl awoke to find Ernesto's bed empty, his brother and his packed backpack gone. He took to Facebook.

Today I feel so sad.

A few hours later, he posted more.

Today on this sad day God take care of us and protect us.

A friend commented:

What's up man?

Raúl responded:

It's that part of me, well like my best part, left since I'm a twin.

The family was relieved that Ernesto had made it out of town without incident: despite his and Raúl's public Facebook posts, Agustín didn't seem to know he was gone. But they were also uneasy: if Agustín thought Ernesto was still around and was still looking for him, was Raúl at risk? Anyone could mistake Raúl for his twin and think he'd found his mark. Or, the family reasoned fearfully, when Agustín's guys figured out Ernesto had left, they could take out Raúl to punish them all.

"I don't think you should go to school," Wilber Sr. said to Raúl, "just for a while," until things calmed down.

So Raúl stayed inside the house. He watched TV, ate, and played with Lupita, who by now was crawling around the house, knocking things over and causing trouble. His other siblings were at school, and Ricardo was out in the fields, covering the twins' former work shifts.

Raúl was relieved, at first, to stay indoors. He wouldn't be able to look his friends in the face—they, he was sure, had ratted his brother out to Agustín. Plus, he was worried about running into his cousins or his uncle in the street. Would they try to run him over again? Would they crush his skull, as they had threatened to do to Ernesto, with a rock? Their family's previous threats could turn out to be just macho bluster— but how could they risk that they weren't?

In the frenzy of his brother leaving, he hadn't had much time to think about what it would be like to miss him. "When you're a twin, you share a heart" had long been Raúl's refrain, and though Ernesto had never said it, Raúl knew his twin felt it, too. It was always funny to them, if predictable, how they thought the same thing at the same time or instinctively knew how the other was feeling. Pain, too—Raúl remembered that time the boys at school threw a rock at Ernesto, how he practically felt the shock of the blow in his own body. Without his brother, he floated through the dark house like an apparition, as if he might waft away.

He knew Ernesto could die on the road. Everything he'd heard about the journey north was about its perils: thieves and rapists and killers, the treacherous trains and buses, the Mexican *federales* and U.S. border patrol hunting migrants like beasts, the fast-moving Angry River, the Río Bravo (what those north of the border call the Rio Grande), and that long stretch of punishing desert into which so many migrants disappeared. He prayed for his brother's safety, in bed and in front of the family's altar. Before he rose each morning, he could hear his mother and father's supplications, but their prayers were just part of the backdrop: they prayed for everything and always expected the best, even in the face of the worst. The notion that bad things could happen needlessly to good people did not fit into their worldview. Raúl couldn't kick his certainty that the worst would happen.

It had been an unseasonably hot couple of weeks, and the air inside the house was stifling. He listened to music to ease the doldrums. He'd asked Maricela to load more airtime onto his phone in town so he could log on to Facebook again.

> Some of the songs I'm listening to make me feel like it's December it almost feels like it hahaha.

That same day he posted:

> A unique, beautiful God is in all of us. Today is a new day I know that sweet God will take care of my brother because God is love even if we are bad he is always on our side.

"Everything will be okay. We'll just give it some time," Esperanza insisted.

Like Raúl, Maricela wasn't so sure. She took Agustín's threats at their word.

The next day Raúl posted:

> It's so boring in this house. The moments are so short but the heart is stronger.

That afternoon it rained, an all-out downpour that shut everyone inside. The storm cooled the air, which was nice at first, but Raúl caught a chill and felt even more hemmed in as he listened to the rain clatter and bang against their tin roof. He posted a link to the Ten Most Romantic Songs. Then:

> How nice is life you just have to know it and live it.

The next day the rain stopped.

Hi friends from chat how are you doing since the night it rained I
imagine okay.

No one responded.

SOMETHING shifted. Depleted from missing his brother and the ex-
cruciating routines of life indoors, Raúl began to dissect how he had
gotten here. In the makeshift bedroom that was now his alone, he obsessed over what his friends, *ex-friends,* had done to his family. To make
up these lies about Ernesto and rat him out to Agustín? Raúl knew for
a fact that Ernesto had never talked shit about Agustín's business, the
guns, the coyotes—his brother knew better than that. And the notion
that he would cut down that tree? In his mind, the other boys had only
wanted to curry favor with the town's big man. For all Raúl knew, the
ex-friends cut down the tree themselves to frame Ernesto. As the idle
days stretched on, paranoia settled in like a hook.

There are people who just are not capable of growing up . . .

He would regret those friendships for a long time. He and Ernesto
should have known better; but human nature was dark. Everyone
wanted to get and stay close to people with power. Stuck inside the
shadowy house, listening to the doves' hollow croons from the rafters,
Raúl's thoughts cycled through endless, rattling loops.

He vowed to get back at his *enemigos.* In his best moments, when
he could think clearly and let God into his heart, he'd vow this: *If God
gets me through this, I'll become someone, and my brother, too, and we'll show
them.*

He changed his profile picture to a meme of white chalk against a
black background:

SMILE: the enemy hates that.

———

THE *coyota* noted the car, and the driver looked behind him, grunted in agreement, and sped up, weaving through the traffic to see if the car would follow them. It did.

The morning he'd left, Ernesto's uncle Erick had driven him without much talking to San Salvador. There they'd met the *coyota*, Sandra, a Mexican woman in her forties, who would accompany him across the Salvadoran border with Guatemala and up through Mexico to where he'd cross into the United States. She introduced herself. Sandra was short, with long hair, younger than Ernesto's mother but, like her, sweet and smiling and maternal. She immediately put him at ease. On a crowded street in the center of San Salvador, he said goodbye to his uncle and changed cars. He sat in the back, Sandra and their driver, a guy in his forties, in the front. But as they were pulling out, they noticed a car peeling out behind them.

Ernesto turned around and thought he recognized the car from La Colonia, as well as the guys in it. The car sped and swerved as if trying to crash into them. One of the riders brandished a machete, and the other had his hands against his waistband as though holding a gun. Were these men actually in pursuit or just harassing Ernesto and Sandra? Was it only his imagination that he recognized them? Ernesto's fear painted the whole world the color of risk. The driver sped up, bobbed and dodged through traffic, and turned onto back streets.

When it seemed they'd lost the car, they pulled over, and Ernesto and Sandra exited quickly, ducking into a small house that belonged to a friend of hers. They'd stay there "until things calmed down," Sandra said. They ate the thin Mexican tortillas that Ernesto called *lengua de gato,* cat tongues, for their floppiness, so unlike his mother's thick, soft tortillas with the thin crust. After a few hours, they climbed into the car again, headed to the border.

As they got back on the road, the *coyota* and the driver, who seemed to have taken this route together many times before, began chatting—about her daughters in Mexico, his family here in El Salvador. They didn't seem worried anymore. The view outside appeared strange; hard to believe that this was still El Salvador. Toward the border, the roads were packed with cars and people, and exhaust dimmed the sky. Even the trees looked different here, though he couldn't put his finger on why.

When it was fully dark and they were near the border, they stopped at a small bus depot alongside a gas station, bustling in the bleak, inscrutible way of truck stops at night. "We'll take a bus from here," Sandra said. Not a public bus but a private one, with which Sandra had some sort of arrangement.

But it took a while to figure out which bus was theirs, and approaching the wrong carrier would risk outing themselves. Sandra walked off to sort things out, leaving Ernesto on the roadside.

A serious-faced man in his forties ambled up to him. "You her son?" he said.

Ernesto froze, then nodded. The man walked away, and Ernesto feared he'd given the wrong answer.

"Who was that?" Sandra asked. But the man didn't come around again.

Finally she found her contact and walked with Ernesto toward a large black bus. He sat down in an aisle seat with his backpack, as the bus lurched into gear. At the Guatemalan border, Sandra paid his entry—a tourist visa, she said, for her and her son. He fell asleep to the soothing whirr of the wheels on the tarmac.

After eight or so hours, they disembarked, Ernesto woozy with sleep and squinting in the sunlight of some Guatemalan back road. This was the first step he had ever taken on land that didn't belong to El Salvador. They walked for a while, passing only the occasional house tucked into the densely forested hillside. Sandra seemed to know where she was going, and the isolation didn't worry Ernesto—he felt at home on foot in the dark among farmers like himself.

They came to a small house—the next stop, apparently, on this underground railroad. They were shown to a stuffy room that they would share. The bed looked too dirty to sleep in; Sandra took the couch, Ernesto a hammock. He barely slept. The next morning they got on a nearby bus, this one public, packed with people and chickens and sacks of corn and coffee.

All day they rode through the mountains, dense and green, where indigenous people dressed in handwoven clothing worked the fields. No one talked much, and Ernesto just stared out the window. Another country.

This bus took them to the next bus, even more packed in than the first. He wondered if he stood out as a foreigner, but no one seemed to notice him. They passed through a small town that led to a smaller town. They moved through forest and then, eventually, to a larger town again. Ernesto watched the world go by. He caught Sandra's faint murmurings here and there into the phone. He tried not to ask too many questions.

"Eat something," she said, handing him a piece of bread.

As the light dimmed, they reached a gas station, where they waited for a car. No one showed up; the *coyota* was getting antsy, texting and calling again and again. "Stay here," she told him. "Don't move, and don't worry—I'll be right back." She hopped into a taxi.

But she didn't come right back—in fact, she didn't come back at all. After about two hours of waiting on this dusty corner, Ernesto assumed he was abandoned. The phone his father had given him was still tucked in the bottom of his backpack—but who, besides his parents, could he call? And what would he say? *The lady left me here. All the money has been a waste.* He tugged at the rosary wrapped around his torso and waited.

Finally a van pulled up with a grumpy driver who shouted at him to get in, then grumbled something about the traffic. Ernesto hesitated, but the man knew his name and seemed to know where he was supposed to go. "Get in!" he barked again, and Ernesto did.

Inside the van, a young man ordered Ernesto to take off his clothes. *I should never have gotten in here alone,* he thought, frozen to his seat. But then the young man pulled out a pile of clothes and dropped them on the seat next to Ernesto.

"Put these on," he said in a voice that didn't sound like a killer's or someone who was shaking him down—just a tired guy doing his job.

So Ernesto obliged, stuffing his old clothes into the bottom of his backpack. The new set was baggier, dirty and tattered, "so you look Mexican."

The guy handed him a hat, too. "You're going to pretend to be the bus driver's assistant," he explained, "when you cross the border."

Blending into the crowd was one thing, but a game of pretend was entirely different. How did he know what a bus assistant in Mexico did, or what a Mexican kid would move or talk like? But this was the plan.

The van pulled over, and he got out and boarded a small, empty commuter bus. He pulled the hat low onto his forehead to shade his face and sat quietly, as the bus driver instructed him.

They pulled into the immigration station on the Guatemalan side of Ciudad Hidalgo. Ernesto held his breath as he handed over a stack of documents. He feigned calm while the immigration officer scanned some papers. He looked him in the eyes and then waved them on.

Ernesto slept again as they wove up through Mexico, awakening as they slowed into the lurch and heave of morning traffic on the outskirts of an unknown city. When the bus pulled over, he felt pangs of hunger—he hadn't eaten in almost a day—and worried once again that he'd been abandoned. But there was Sandra, cleaned up and smiling, waiting for him. He got into the taxi with her, and they rode through the massive metropolis (Mexico City, he later learned), meandering through crooked streets until they reached a middle-class neighborhood where all the roads were named after birds.

They stopped at a two-story house (in Las Aguilas, he also later learned) with plastered walls and a staircase inside, much nicer than Ernesto's home, with its bare bulbs and ragged curtains in place of doors. "Welcome to my house," Sandra said cheerily. He was about a thousand miles from home.

She lived there with her two daughters and a son, all a few years older than Ernesto. She showed him to the room where he'd be staying, then pointed him to the shower. It had been three days since he'd left home, but already, he saw in his reflection, he looked skinnier, older. The water was hot—a luxury. He scrubbed the grime and unease from his skin.

Then he took out his hidden cellphone and called home.

THE call from Ernesto was short, as he needed to preserve his airtime, so Raúl didn't get a turn to talk to him. He was happy to hear his brother was safe in Mexico, though he had figured as much. He'd know for sure if something had gone wrong. But Ernesto still had a long road ahead.

"He didn't sound so good," Maricela told him. "He's fine, but he didn't sound good."

Meanwhile rumors in La Colonia circulated that Agustín remained furious—about the gun rumors, the tree, and now, as he had finally learned, that Ernesto was on his way north. The fact that he'd split seemed to affirm, in Agustín's mind, the boy's guilt. Raúl still hadn't left the house, except, occasionally, at night, and then he'd always remained on the farm.

"Maybe," Wilber said to his son, "we should think about you going north, too."

Raúl still didn't want to leave home for the uncertain, unfamiliar, and to his mind, spiritually empty terrain up north. Couldn't he just go somewhere else in El Salvador for a while? But he worried that Agustín could use his connections to track him down. And anyway, he had nowhere else to go. Who would he live with, and what would he do? You couldn't live always looking over your shoulder.

The second time Ernesto called from Mexico, Raúl got to talk to him. "I'm nervous," he said. "I haven't gone outside. What if they think I'm you?"

Ernesto was silent on the other end of the line.

"I'm wondering . . . should I go, too?"

"No," Ernesto said.

Wilber took the phone. "We're thinking it might be better if he goes," he told Ernesto.

"It's too dangerous," Ernesto replied.

"We'll see." They said goodbye and hung up.

After Raúl heard his brother's voice, "it's like he changed his mind in a second," Maricela later recalled. "I think I should go," he told his dad.

Things were not calming down, and Raúl was still stuck inside the house, so the family decided there was no other option. "It's better," Wilber said, "for you to be with your brother." He didn't mention the tacit threats.

Wilber Sr. would later remember Raúl leaving because Ernesto had begged him to join him. "He missed his brother," he would say. But everyone else in the family insists that Raúl made the decision along with the rest of the family, without Ernesto knowing. Though Wilber worries often about the future, the rest of the family contends, he doesn't like to dwell in the hard, sad stuff of the past. Better for him to remember the story of Raúl's departure, his third child to be wrested from him by the North, as a story not of violence or family dissolution but of brotherly love.

Raúl logged on to Facebook, announcing to his imagined audience of real friends, good people:

Facebook friends, I really love you. Facebook friends, I'm going to miss you.

Like his brother, he published his plans onto his public profile.

You could have a thousand adventures, a thousand loves.

They arranged for a *coyota* from the same company that took Ernesto—Uncle Agustín's rival business. In fact, it would be the same woman who took Ernesto, which gave the family some comfort. For safety reasons, they'd take a slightly different route to Mexico City—if a coyote always travels the same network, he or she has a higher risk of being caught. Raúl would meet up with Ernesto in Mexico City, and then, back together again, they'd travel through the rest of Mexico and into the United States.

They'd have to borrow more money from the lender for Raúl's trip, another $7,000 for Uncle Erick for the *coyota* fee, plus some additional spending cash. That brought their total debt up to $14,000, with interest

compounding each week. As collateral, they put up their second parcel
of land. The debt amounted to more money than they had ever possessed, but certainly, the family reasoned, they'd be able to pay it off
quickly once the twins got to the United States. They would have their
older brother Wilber Jr.'s help, once they got in touch with him. No one
told Wilber Jr. that his twin brothers were coming north until they were
already gone. It had been a long time since he'd called. Raúl posted:

Something tells me, that I'm not coming back.

A friend of his, a girl, replied:

Noooo don't be like that!

Another girl chimed in:

Xq amigo?

She asked. What is it, friend?

Ernesto's going to be waiting for me in Mexico and from there we'll go,
the two of us.

You could have a thousand adventures, a thousand loves.

The night before he left, Raúl lay restless, listening to a pack of dogs
howling into the dark. The same thing had happened the previous two
nights. The town dogs always barked now and then, but this seemed
different—a prolonged chorus of howls and saw-toothed yips. He felt
sure the sounds weren't made by dogs at all but by prescient spirits,
warning of things to come. It had been nine days since Ernesto left.

The next afternoon Raúl got in a car with his uncle Erick, his mother,
Maricela, and her little daughter. In his backpack was a gift from his
father that, he promised, would keep him safe: *Prayers for El Niño Divino,* the Divine Child. They met up with the *coyota,* and he hugged his

mother goodbye and looked at her in the eyes one final time. She was crying. Maricela bounced Lupita on her hip and told her brother to take care of himself.

"I'll bring them there," Sandra said, mother to mother. "Don't worry, I will."

They got in the car, shut the doors, and the driver shifted into gear.

ERNESTO woke up in Sandra's house, and she was gone.

"She left," explained the elder daughter. "Another trip from El Salvador." But she'd be back, the girl explained, in a few days, and then she'd take Ernesto to the northern border. She motioned for him to help himself to breakfast.

When Ernesto called home, Maricela picked up. She handed the phone to Wilber, who said a prayer for him by way of greeting. Ernesto asked to talk to Raúl.

"He's already gone," Wilber explained.

"Gone where?"

Wilber gave him the news. He'd left that very morning for San Salvador with Uncle Erick. "He's on his way."

Ernesto hadn't expected them to actually send Raúl north—not yet, anyway. His heart had skipped a beat when Raúl told him it might be best if he came, too. The guilt of the situation agitated him: *What if Agustín thinks I'm you?*

And if something happened to Raúl on the road? He'd been lucky making it this far; sending his double here too seemed to be testing fate.

At the same time, he couldn't wait to see his brother. They hadn't even said goodbye.

Sandra was gone, Raúl was gone, but Ernesto didn't put two and two together until Sandra called his phone. "I'm with your brother," she said. He let out a sigh of relief.

He didn't mind being stuck in Sandra's house for a few more days—there was food, a clean bed, a shower, a TV, and the two sisters. He was especially drawn to the elder, Fernanda, with her long, thick hair, dark eyes, and brash confidence. Unfortunately, she had a boyfriend—not that Ernesto thought he stood a chance with her, as a ragamuffin kid from El Salvador. Still, a few more days here wasn't so bad.

Mexico was hotter than El Salvador, and the heat swelled the house, making everything hazy and slow. Ernesto spent the days wiping sweat from his brow, eating food the daughters made him, and avoiding the son, who in any case stayed in his room most of the time, not seeming to do much of anything. On Sunday the kids' father came over and made breakfast for everyone, making sure to prepare a plate for Ernesto. They didn't ask him much about himself—they knew better, it seemed, than to pry.

A few days later the phone rang. Fernanda picked it up; it was Sandra. Ernesto, from his spot on the couch, heard the elder sister's voice go tense.

"What happened? What's wrong?" he asked. On the other line he could hear the frantic voice of the *coyota*.

Fernanda didn't answer him. She hung up the phone and turned around to walk upstairs. He could tell something had gone wrong.

"What happened?" he asked again. She didn't answer him.

FROM San Salvador, Sandra directed the driver along the back roads to the Guatemalan border. Like Ernesto, they crossed through an official if remote checkpoint, where an officer waved them through after Sandra showed some papers. ("Just visiting.") They continued on into the thicket of Guatemala.

Sandra and the driver chatted like old friends, twisting the radio dial every now and again in search of a good song. Raúl felt embarrassed about his status as cargo; he just stared out the window. It was so quiet, and so little moved on these isolated roads, the darkness outside shrouding the whole world from view. It made him nervous and, despite how tired he was, he couldn't sleep. "Don't worry, just relax," Sandra said from the front seat. "Nothing's gonna happen. We're fine." They drove on for a while through the blank stillness of the night, and he tried to settle in. Suddenly, Sandra gasped.

"*¡Dios!*" the driver whispered.

They had come to a roadblock where a large black truck pulled out in front of them, and an officer in uniform motioned for their car to come to a stop. In the back of the truck were about ten men, all in uniforms, each clasping a machine gun between both hands.

An officer approached the car and bent over to talk into the window. "We're antinarcotic officers," he said. "We need you to come with us."

Raúl stiffened. He didn't think they had drugs in the car, but he had no passport, and he assumed they would know from his accent that he was from El Salvador.

The driver pushed their car into gear, and they followed the truck off the main road into a dim thicket with few lights, no houses, and no traffic.

The same officer approached again, a photograph in hand. He held it up to Raúl's face. "Yep," he said, nodding, and flipped it around. "This is you, right?"

It was the photo of him, Maricela, and Ernesto wearing their best campesino-fancy clothing and grave expressions, at their ninth-grade graduation.

"Get out," the man ordered.

Raúl stepped out of the backseat, trembling. One of the officers grabbed him and threw him down, pressing his face into the ground with his boot. Raúl could hardly breathe. "Your uncle hired us," the man said, then bore down his boot even harder.

They weren't police at all but Agustín's henchmen. Or maybe they were both? The paranoia in Central America and Mexico is vast, but so are the criminal networks that inspire it—the truth and the fear caught up in a tangled dance.

They ordered Raúl to pull off his shoes and strip his pants and shirt. They yanked out his shoelaces and tied his wrists behind his back, face-down in the dirt, and did the same to the driver. Two men took Sandra away into the darkness; Raúl could hear her scream. Next to him, the driver was praying aloud to God as Sandra's screams crescendoed into the night, along with shouting and grunting, the driver's frenzied prayers, and the wicked pounding of Raúl's heart against the ground.

"Please," the driver pleaded. They took a metal pipe to his head and cracked him so hard that Raúl thought for sure he would end up dead.

Then they shook their guns toward Raúl and laughed.

This is where I die, he thought.

"Where's the money?" the guy asked. He'd brought an additional $2,000 or so—something they either knew for sure, or assumed, because migrants always traveled with cash. Sandra was holding on to it. They rummaged through her stuff and found the cash.

"Please?" Sandra said. "Leave us just a little, to get out of here?" Raúl was shocked she'd dare to ask, but they threw a few bills her way.

Then, as quickly and mysteriously as they had appeared, the men retreated into their cars, and the cars retreated toward the main road and into the night. It was now just the three voyagers again, tied up on a patch of dirt and far from anything, their money gone and, they noticed, the wheels of their car now missing. Sandra managed to get her clothes back on. She wiped her face, then untied Raúl and the driver.

"Are you okay?" Raúl asked her.

She just handed him his clothes. *Oh my God, oh my god, oh my god,* the driver kept saying. Sandra and Raúl said nothing. Raúl pulled his clothes back on. With their shoelaces now broken, their shoes flopped open, almost obscenely, as they trudged into the forest. They spent the night there, none of them sleeping much. Raúl knew it was sheer luck that he wasn't dead.

He guessed Agustín had been been tipped off about Raúl leaving and intercepted them along Erick's route. Or perhaps Uncle Erick was trying to rip their family off of a bit more cash? Maybe it was the usual migrant profiteering, people taking advantage of those out on the road, knowing that they were almost certain not to report these episodes to the police. But then why the mention of his uncle? And the photo? He was certain that the attack was Agustín's handiwork, to teach the family a lesson: *I'm boss, I'm in charge—run as far as you will, and I'll find you.*

The next morning, when the sun had risen enough to light the wooded area where they'd hidden, they took stock. All three looked as if they'd already spent months outside: dirty clothes, faces streaked with mud, a wily look in the eye. The car was ruined, unusable, but the cellphone worked. The driver, they decided, would stay behind with the car, but Raúl and Sandra would press on. They walked to the road, Raúl's shoes barely staying on. Sandra called her daughter, pulling herself together. "A bunch of gangsters caught us," she said, her voice tight. "Don't worry, we're okay. We'll take the bus. We'll be there soon."

It took two days for the three of them to work their way north on buses, with not enough cash for anything but the tickets, not even food. Sandra soothed Raúl. "Don't worry," she said, "we're on our way, we're okay, we'll be there soon." She had fully collected herself, pushing onward as if nothing had happened. Raúl wondered if maybe this wasn't the first time she'd been attacked. He was jumpy, every loud noise triggering a jolt through his brain. He tried to fall asleep. As they moved from the outskirts into the thicker traffic of the big city, he sat up at attention. Ernesto was somewhere in this massive maze, waiting.

WHEN Raúl showed up at the door of the house in Las Aguilas, he was dirty and shaking, his clothes practically falling off in scraps. Ernesto grabbed Raúl and began, uncharacteristically, to cry. As if they'd swapped identities, Raúl just stood there, emoting not at all.

Sandra went straight to the kitchen and prepared some food, like it was any regular day. When the meal was ready, she called the boys in and went to clean herself up. Ernesto set a plate down in front of his brother: scrambled eggs, spicy sausage, and those thin cat-tongue tortillas.

Raúl ate slowly and hardly at all. Between labored bites, he told his twin what had happened. "It was Agustín," he said.

"How do you know?"

"They had a photo. The one from graduation."

Ernesto was silent for a while. It was his fault: he was the one Agustín wanted. He teared up again. He'd always taken care of his brother—he was the elder, after all, if even by twelve minutes—and now he'd failed.

"Here," he offered softly. He gave his one change of clothes to Raúl.

They spent another few days in Las Aguilas while Raúl and the *coyota* got their energy back.

"You guys look *exactly* the same!" Fernanda said. Now that her mom was back safely, she didn't seem worried about what had happened: occupational hazard, for one, and her mom herself had brushed it off, as though they'd simply hit bad weather or had an unhappy accident.

"No we don't!" they said in unison.

Seeing that it annoyed them, Fernanda teased them about how alike they looked for the rest of their stay. Raúl could see that Ernesto had a crush on Fernanda, for which he didn't blame him. But he was too tired to think about love.

After a few days, they hopped a northbound bus with Sandra to Reynosa: the final border.

THEY traveled fifteen hours due north out of the city and through northern Mexico, where the scenery moved from fecund green to desert. Raúl silently prayed for no more bad encounters, while Ernesto looked steely-eyed out the window, braced for disaster—the one he felt he deserved, after what had happened to his twin.

As they entered Reynosa, they both noticed how poor it looked: not rural poor, like La Colonia, and not city poor, like San Salvador, but somewhere in between. The air was riddled with fine dust, and children ran along the crumbling roadside without shoes. Houses and businesses jostled for space. This was the border zone: the last stop, the final crossing point before America.

Tamaulipas state is shaped a bit like the silhouette of a seated rabbit: its cotton tail is puffed against the state of San Luis Potosí; Matamoros—another key cross-over city opposite Brownsville, Texas—is the bunny nose, quivering into the gulf. The city of Reynosa is at the base of the rabbit's long ear, which stands erect, as if listening, stretching northwest along the Rio Grande toward Nuevo Laredo.

The bus wove its way through the outskirts and into the city center, the roads thickening with the sludge of traffic. Raúl could see Texas from here, right there across the bridge. Its proximity seemed ridiculous.

Luckily, the twins didn't know about any of Reynosa's particular dangers. To them, all of Mexico was a threat.

Sandra walked with them to a small garage with some mattresses on the floor and a card table. A few migrants, mostly young men and a few teenagers like them, were already inside.

Sandra wouldn't be crossing with them into the United States, but she'd wait in Reynosa until she heard they were safely on the other side. She gave them a hug. "Don't worry"—she motioned to the safe house floor—"you'll be just fine."

But she made sure they still had her number "just in case." She gave them a pen and instructed them both to write it in the lining of their pants. Then she said goodbye.

Ernesto and Raúl claimed an empty mattress and lay there all day, close but not touching, limiting their movements due to the heat and their unease at their circumstances. Their fellow travelers intimidated them—who knew what they were running from? Every so often more migrants were let into the safe house; then the door was promptly shut and latched. By nightfall, more than twenty people were packed into the little garage. They had food, at least; one lady cooked in a small outdoor kitchen, and periodically someone called on one or two of the migrants to carry in plates: eggs, tortillas, beans. For two more days, the twins lay on their mattress, languishing in the heat, waiting to be told it was time to move.

The single bathroom was upstairs. A faucet jutted out from a tiled area where you could bathe, using a few flimsy bits of remainder soap. The second day Raúl went upstairs to take a shower, leaving Ernesto in the packed room.

"Help me out back?" one of the coyotes asked him, the guy who, by his firm temperament and imposing stature, appeared to be the boss.

Ernesto obliged, jumping to his feet and following the man outside toward the kitchen.

Twenty minutes later Raúl returned downstairs, cleaned up, but Ernesto was gone. After a while he walked back in through the door, ash-white. Ernesto settled down onto the mattress in the fetal position and, despite the heat, pulled a sheet up over his head.

Raúl tried to get his attention. "What? What happened?" But Ernesto wouldn't look at him, and Raúl shrugged it off. Ernesto stayed silent for the rest of the night and through the morning, only the slight up-and-down motions of his chest beneath the sheet signaling to Raúl that he was alive.

"Tonight," one of the coyotes announced the third afternoon. They'd cross tonight. The atmosphere in the room shifted instantly: people re-shuffled the items in their small bags and sat alert, mentally preparing for the next gust north.

Around midnight, the coyotes marched the group of about twenty migrants down to the river. The men pulled the first of two inflatable rafts from the bushes and pumped it up with quick huffs. The twins watched the raft's silhouette rise. On the other side, just as they'd been told, was the United States of America. The coyote ordered the first group to board the raft. "Get in," he said. Raúl and Ernesto stepped aboard, their weight sinking the soft bottom into the water. They could make out their own dark shapes against the river. The coyote pushed off, and they were afloat, adrift, on their way.

The slow, muscular tug of that fabled river, the Rio Grande. The liquid border slinks alongside the southern edge of the Santa Ana National Wildlife Refuge, not three car-lengths across. To a person tiptoeing from the river through the scrub of South Texas, everything sounds like a threat: wind rustling the palm fronds, a lizard skittering through the understory, one's own arm against a pant leg, the heavy flap of a low-flying hawk. This park preserves desert wetlands and other natural habitat home to birds and armadillo and the endangered ocelot, with the occasional crossing of border patrol trucks and those they are hunting. Thanks in part to environmentalist uproar, the infamous border wall—a twelve-foot-high red metal fence—stops, for now, at the Santa Ana's perimeter and starts up again on the other side. A laminated sign beside the river justifies the park's existence and the break in the wall: THIS CORRIDOR WILL ALLOW ANIMALS TO SAFELY PASS ALONG AND ACROSS THE RIO GRANDE. Just east of the placard is a narrow scramble path to the river. On opposite sides of the river, Mexico and Texas look just the same.

A person crosses where he can. He moves around or over or beneath the wall. She strips down on the south side and swims across, or hops into a cached-away raft. Ask anyone who's crossed: the languid look of the river is a sham. Beneath the surface, the water rips fast and cruel.

"They cross here every day!" says the woman behind the counter at the gift shop. "You can find stashes of water and clothes and all sorts of stuff back there." She motioned with a wave to the park.

"Just last week they caught twenty of them," she continues. "There was one full family, but the rest of them were all kids."

The history of the Rio Grande Valley is one of shifting borders, of hidings and crossings—this used to be Mexico, and before that indigenous land. The whole of South Texas used to look like Santa Ana does now—the Sabal palms, Spanish moss, shallow swamps, hundreds of species of birds—before nearly all the Rio Grande Valley was carved up as farmland, before the Rio Grande was both river and border, before the long chain of strip malls stretched along Highway 83, before the border wars and beheadings raged on the Mexican side, before the border patrol trucks scraping against the Texas dirt.

Now the rust-red slatted fence, like an inverted train track, follows the river on either side of the refuge as it twists along the state's edge. The call to "build the wall" along the entire southern U.S. border is a bit of a misdirection: the desert border wall already stretches for roughly 650 miles of the two-thousand-mile southern border. It's not really one wall but rather dozens that, if one traces the border by car, appear and disappear abruptly against the segmented agricultural fields and the sky. To connect all of them would mean building through massive swaths of harsh deserts and high mountains—at a cost *The Washington Post* estimates at tens of billions of dollars.

There are other, less tangible walls as well: U.S. Customs and Border Protection has organized its border security apparatus as a series of them. After the Rio Grande and the physical border wall, the next blockade is the border patrol agents themselves, cruising the valley in their green and white vehicles. And then, within a hundred miles of the border, on the few north-south roads that carve up the state, are the checkpoints.

To reach the Falfurrias, Texas, checkpoint by car, you head seventy miles north on U.S. 281, a four-lane highway that cuts through a vast desert rangeland, ever cast in the thin, dusty light of an old western or faded photograph. A sign along the road: SMUGGLING ILLEGAL ALIENS IS A FEDERAL CRIME. Border patrol agents man the checkpoint clad in fatigues, black boots, and reflective sunglasses, holding tight to the leashes of German shepherds who sniff beneath trunks and carriages in search of drugs or hidden bodies. When there's a breeze, a large U.S. flag flaps overhead. According to Customs and Border Protection, the Falfurrias checkpoint "is nationally known as a primary leader in seizures, both alien and narcotic apprehensions."

The migrants leave the road well before the checkpoint and head out into the desert's tangle of scrub and tumbleweed, the only shade provided by a rare mesquite or oak. It is hostile territory but a weak spot in the Customs and Border Protection surveillance system. A person can walk for miles without seeing much but the occasional team of cattle, a low-set ranch house, or an east-west county road, probably unpaved. Most migrants travel under cover of night, though this means stepping carefully to avoid snakes, thorns, and ankle-twisting pits.

Ranchers come upon bodies, both fresh and decomposed, often enough. Each year the remains of hundreds of migrants are found along the southwestern border—in 2012, more than 120 were found in Brooks County, near Falfurrias. Normally the bodies are desert-wrangled, burned and decomposed and picked over by scavengers, and they often carry no identification. ("There's a reason they're called undocumented," a Department of Homeland Security officer quipped.)

The county pays a local Falfurrias funeral home to inter the bodies in the Sacred Heart Burial Park. A man found dead in a field with a rotted face and nothing in his pocket will be dropped into an unnamed grave.

It's a pretty graveyard, well tended and colorful, its gravestones adorned with flags and flowers both fake and fresh, suggesting frequent visits by the living. The migrants are buried off to the side of the graveyard, a nice enough resting place, though the plots, upon closer look, are too close together. In 2014 researchers from Baylor University discovered several bodies in many of the graves—they'd been tossed into a common pit.

JOHN DOE. UNKNOWN FEMALE. CHILD. UNKNOWN MALE. SKELETAL REMAINS. UNKNOWN. The graves are marked by these small tin signs. Some signs bear only serial numbers.

One April day, amid the hulking headstones of the known, three grave diggers shoveled a new hole for a local death—the passing of a documented person, who would be given a stone with a name.

CHAPTER 4

The current yanked the small raft into the center of the river, sucking the Flores twins toward the Gulf of Mexico as the coyote fought it to the opposite shore. They couldn't see much in the blackness apart from the stars and the outline of trees against the darkness. It wasn't so bad out here, thought Raúl, compared to what he had imagined during the days in the safe house, though the raft did wobble as it cut across the current, and he could feel the cool water lapping uncomfortably close. Before they left, the coyotes had told them that migrants like them had died making this crossing; Raúl couldn't help picturing corpses submerged in the water beneath him. Once the raft bumped the Texas shore, the coyote commanded them, in a voice between a whisper and a hiss, to get off.

Ernesto, as usual, stepped off first, into water up to his knees. Once he got his footing, he reached for Raúl's hand and pulled him up the bank. One by one the migrants scrambled up into the United States, flecking the heavy droplets of the Río Bravo from their skins.

Once the second raft came ashore, the coyotes yelled at the group to run. They took off into the chaparral, struggling through dense brush as thorns ripped through the fabric of their pants. The whole group ran for about an hour; they were in the United States, but all that amounted to so far was a frenzied scramble through a thicket. They stopped to rest for a while at a roadside spot with good cover. No one seemed to sleep. At about six in the morning, just as the sky was lightening, a couple of trucks arrived and picked the migrants up. They packed in and were taken to a safe house in one of the *colonias,* the small, poverty-stricken unincorporated zones, outside McAllen, Texas. The twins were so hungry, their stomachs cramped and groaned for food. The safe house operators handed out peanut butter and jelly sandwiches and water. The boys ate fast, like animals.

They spent the night and the following day there, resting, occasionally eating, waiting. On the night of the second day, they packed into trucks again to be driven up to the desert. There they'd walk overland, circumnavigate the Falfurrias immigration checkpoint, and meet up with a truck on the other side for the drive to Houston. The twins' plan was to call Wilber once they made it there; though they were already in Texas, Houston still seemed like a long way away.

That night twelve rode in the front cab and even more in the truck bed, huddled in silence. About an hour north, away from McAllen and well into the flat, quiet expanse, the driver pulled over. But as they cut the headlights and the migrants began to get out, a border patrol car sped up, flashing.

The world went silent inside the twins' heads, as everyone scattered in different directions. Ernesto lurched into action, Raúl following close behind. They ran and ran until the lights were far behind them, then crouched in the night and caught their breath.

They looked around and spotted Edy, a nineteen-year-old from Honduras, with whom they'd exchanged only a few words. Besides Edy, they were alone—everyone else had vanished into the desert.

The trio set out walking, with no idea where they were heading but knowing they needed to move.

"Don't worry, guys," Edy said.

"We'll get there. We're close. Don't worry."

"We got this, guys. We're getting there." Edy's composure and worldliness, along with his insistent optimism, soothed the twins.

In spite of his pep talks, however, Edy groaned every few steps—he had fallen and twisted his ankle on something, a log, a piece of cattle fence, he wasn't sure. He soldiered through the night, not wanting to slow the group down. They squabbled every now and then about which route to take—this way, no that way, no this. Usually they deferred to Edy.

"Think about it—we're so close," he said. "Close to our dreams, man, close to reaching our destiny." Edy rattled on like this as they walked, his comforting voice spinning dreams in the darkness.

When the sun came up, they rested beneath a mesquite tree, desperate for shade and to keep from being spotted. They scanned the horizon, trying to figure out where, exactly, they were. Had they been going in circles? Which way now?

Beneath the tree, Ernesto rummaged through his backpack for the phone. He turned it on: two bars of signal. "I think it works!" he told Raúl.

He tried texting Sandra: "We're lost."

Within moments, his phone pinged with a message from her. The three boys laughed in relief. "Don't worry, you'll be okay. Where are you?" read the text.

"In the desert."

Pick a direction and keep walking, she told them. Once they got past the Customs and Border Protection station in Falfurrias, she instructed, there'd be a car there waiting for them.

They'd make it to a road as long as the boys could mark a straight line in one direction, ideally north. They picked a direction and tried to keep straight.

"You're at the last step," she wrote. "You're so close."

These messages lifted the boys' spirits for a while, and they walked with renewed confidence in spite of their thirst and the unbroken horizon of empty, blistering terrain.

"I can't wait to get a job," Edy said. He was planning to stay in Houston, where his dad lived. "Construction, restaurant, whatever—I'll get any kind of job. Think about it—how great will that be? We're close. We're so close."

The three spent another aimless day and night eking out a pathway through the parched rangeland. During the day they hid out and rested, and at night they walked, tangling their feet in the scrub and tumble-weed, rolling their ankles in an occasional divot or one of the cattle muck pits strewn through the flat expanse like mines.

Raúl's shoes were coming apart, the stitching unraveling. Finally the soles came undone and flapped audibly with each step, exposing his feet to the spiny brush. How would he go on like this, half barefoot?

"Here." Ernesto yanked off his shoes and demanded Raúl do the same. "Take mine."

Raúl obliged. Ernesto pulled Raul's shoes onto his own feet and undid the laces, winding them around the bottom of the soles to hold the halves together, then tied them as tightly as he could.

"Thanks," Raúl said.

Ernesto made a face to make sure Raúl knew he was annoyed at him for letting this happen. Even with the adjustment, the soles of Raúl's shoes, now on Ernesto, still dragged against the ground.

The second night Ernesto insisted on walking ahead, though he had no more idea where he was than the other two did.

"We got this, boys," Edy said periodically. "The last step. We're al-most there." The twins nodded and kept moving.

Around three in the morning, the stars bright in the sky, Raúl heard a sharp yipping sound behind him. *Evil spirits,* he thought, *on the hunt again.*

The noise repeated, louder. "What's that?" he whispered.

They all stopped. Ernesto and Edy had heard it, too.

"Fuck," Edy said. "Coyotes."

They picked up their pace, but the yipping followed them, seeming to get closer and more varied. They walked faster. Every bark felt like a prophecy: the animals caging them in on all sides, their three bodies nothing but future meat.

Edy picked up some stones and hurled them into the blackness, and Ernesto and Raúl followed suit. But the yips didn't stop.

"Shit," Ernesto said.

They found a low mesquite tree and scurried up into the slim branches, a handful of rocks in each of their pockets. Raúl knew that coyotes, those scavengers, ate corpses. Were they such obvious prey?

"What do we do?" Raúl asked. Ernesto and Edy didn't answer.

They spent an hour up in the tree, pitching rocks toward the sounds, until eventually the animals lumbered away.

The next day their thirst became unbearable. It scratched their throats as though they were swallowing bits of chaparral. But they trudged on. Occasionally they came across a cattle trough and drank, first skimming the slimy green muck off the water's surface. The water tasted terrible, but it soothed their throats.

Maybe this was where they'd die, Raúl thought. At least they'd die together. He didn't say it out loud because it would affront Edy's optimism and because Ernesto would scold him. But he was sure his brother was having the same thoughts. Sometimes he prayed for the border patrol to come and find them—though then they'd be sent back to El Salvador and would likely die all the same. Those guys in the trucks in Guatemala—there were more of them waiting for him, he felt sure. They had to make it to Houston, and then on to California.

"I wonder what the others are doing," Raúl said. The guys from their migrant group, he meant. Had they been caught, or were they also lost in the desert? Or worse? Ernesto and Edy didn't reply.

Edy's limp had grown more pronounced, but he kept up the positive talk. Maybe he'd broken the ankle, or maybe it just needed some rest, but he didn't complain. "Just a little more, brothers, we're so close, just imagine how close we are. Reaching our dreams!"

By the third day, though, Edy was sick. His stomach hurt, and as they walked, he had less and less to say. They figured he might be dehydrated, or maybe it was something in the water they drank. Normally he took a medication every day, he said—he'd been off it for a week now.

They needed help. Sandra in Mexico wasn't of much use. So Ernesto texted Wilber Jr.—they were in his territory now, after all: "We're in the desert in Texas," he wrote. "Me and Raúl." "We're lost. We have no food or water." Their parents had told him they were coming, they knew, but they didn't get a reply.

He texted the same thing to his sister Maricela. "We're lost. We have no water. We're drinking dirty water, water from the cows."

Finally, in the distance, they spotted a house. It appeared empty; no car outside. They moved toward it with caution.

The door was unlocked, so they stepped inside and into the kitchen. They turned on the faucet and took turns sucking water straight into their mouths. They'd seen a hose outside, and Ernesto went out to fill their long-empty water bottles. They were trespassers, intruders, low-down burglars, but they were desperate. Raúl apologized to God, then began rummaging through the cabinets. They were stocked with bread, rice, and cans of food. He began pulling them from the shelves.

Just then a man walked into the kitchen.

Raúl saw him first and immediately put his hands up. Edy startled and did the same. Eyes wide and hands in the air, the boys backed away from the counter, nodding, trying to show they meant no harm. The man's wife walked in, seeming not all that surprised at their presence.

"Who are you guys?" the man asked in Spanish.

"We're coming from Mexico," Edy said. "We're sorry. We're so sorry. But we're lost."

"Don't be scared," he said. He told them to call in "the other guy." Raúl yelled for his brother to come inside. Ernesto hadn't seen the car drive up, so he panicked when he saw it parked out front, and then the man and woman in the kitchen. He, too, put his hands in the air.

The man sat them down at the table and poured them glasses of water, then, once the boys emptied them, filled the same glasses up with juice. He put a stack of white Bimbo bread in front of them. They ate the entire stack, slice by slice.

"Don't worry," he said. "You just gotta walk that way." He indicated a direction. "If you go that way"—he pointed in another direction—"you'll hit a big road with an immigration station, and you want to avoid that."

The boys nodded, as the man pointed in the right direction again. "Thank you," Ernesto said. He retied his shoelaces around the broken soles, and the boys took off walking.

"Yep, that way, that's the way," the man said, waving goodbye to his trio of intruders.

They trudged on, feeling better. As the third night fell, they could hear only the sound of their feet crunching through the scrub. Lost in thought, Ernesto tripped on something and fell. Another log, or a water trough? He reached his hands out to catch himself, but as he hit the ground, his hands pressed into a soft mass that collapsed in a wet, sickly mess under his weight.

As he got his bearings and pushed himself up, he realized he'd fallen onto a human body. He screamed.

Raúl ran up behind him. They could see in the dim moonlight that the corpse was headless.

Ernesto fell back onto the ground away from it and began to shake and hyperventilate. A migrant, alone and decapitated, in their very path. "I touched it," he said. "I touched it with my own hands."

Raúl and Edy soothed him, but Ernesto couldn't speak for a long time.

They kept walking, then rested at dawn and through the heat of the next day. While the two others slept, Ernesto forced his eyes to stay open. He couldn't shake the feeling of death on him. When he finally nodded off, he dreamed that two men were chasing him to cut off his head.

He awoke with a start.

A text popped up on the screen. "Okay, *está bien.*" It was their brother Wilber.

FINALLY they came to a road—a blessedly paved, even surface, presumably leading somewhere. It was dark, but the road was busy, cars flying in both directions. Could they get anywhere on this road without being seen? They hid in the scrub for a few minutes, assessing their options, staying still. But all of a sudden a light flashed over them and a truck sped their way.

Edy, despite his weak stomach and his bum ankle, took off running again. But not the twins. They wanted to follow Edy, but their feet wouldn't move. Ernesto's shoes were torn to bits, and they were hungry and thirsty and rendered inert by the cumulative effect of the coyotes, the corpse, and all the curses that had brought them here.

"Stop," they heard in Spanish. It was the border patrol, *la migra.* "Don't move!" an agent shouted.

They stood there, hands in the air, eyes heavy and resigned. Raúl braced himself to be punched and kicked into submission, as cops sometimes did in El Salvador.

Instead the agent just patted them down. "What are your names?" he asked in twangy Spanish. He turned the boys around, patted them down, and cuffed them. Another couple of trucks had pulled up.

"Where are you from?" the agent asked as he walked them toward the truck. "Where are you going?"

The twins answered in unison. "California."

The agent passed Raúl to another agent and helped Ernesto up into his truck. They were separated.

"Don't worry," Ernesto called to Raúl. "I'll see you when we get there." He wasn't sure where "there" was, but he didn't want Raúl to be too scared.

Inside the truck, Ernesto's agent filled out some paperwork and handed him two bottles of water and a packet of crackers. Ernesto sucked down the water like a drunk. They were caught, but they weren't dead.

"How old are you?" he asked.

"Seventeen."

So they counted as "juvies," as the border patrol likes to call them—unaccompanied alien children, paperless and parentless. The agent likely knew all about these kids from the uptick in their numbers over the years. This time last year there had been no place to put them all—they'd had to lodge them in former military bases along the border, scrambling even to have enough mattresses for them to sleep on. Since then, the numbers had kept rising. By the end of September 2013, just over two months from now, 24,668 minors (87 percent teenagers like the twins) would have been taken into federal custody with the Office of Refugee Resettlement. For all of 2013, fully 93 percent of these juvies came from the Northern Triangle. El Salvador, the twins' home country, would account for 26 percent of them. The twins were just two among thousands.

In another truck, separated from his brother, Raúl figured the agents would drive them to the border and drop them off in Mexico. Perhaps after that they could try to swim across on their own. But then what?

"You boys are lucky I found you when I did," the agent told Raúl. "We just found five dead bodies not too far from here." He said something into his radio, put the truck in gear, and drove.

FOR three days, Maricela kept the phone by her side, waiting for news from the twins. Each text was a slug in the chest: "We're lost." "We have nothing to eat." "We're drinking dirty cattle water." "It's hot." "Our friend is hurt." Every time she tried to text them back—with something comforting, like "Keep walking" or "You're going to be okay"—her message was rejected. The limitations of her phone plan made for a cruel echo chamber: she could receive their messages but could do absolutely nothing to help, not even offer advice.

At first she didn't show their messages to her parents. But as things appeared more desperate in the desert, she told them what was going on.

"They'll be okay," Esperanza said knowingly. "God will protect them."

Finally, a phone call: they were in detention in Texas. "We're okay," they said. "We're okay. We're alive." But they'd been caught. After all that, Maricela thought, the twins would just be sent right back home.

IN fact, they weren't. The agents took them to the immigration station to be fingerprinted and questioned to be sure they were really minors. There the twins, thankfully, were reunited. Being under eighteen, that line in the sand of life, mattered: if they'd been adults, they would have been put into an adult detention center and ordered deported, likely without seeing a lawyer. But because the twins really were juvies, they'd be put in a special detention center, a "youth friendly" shelter overseen by the U.S. Office of Refugee Resettlement.

First they were sent to the *hielera,* or icebox, the immigration holding tank, the official limbo zone of the U.S. immigration system.

The icebox was a cold, windowless room, packed with about thirty other young men and boys. They shared one toilet with only a low barrier; going to the bathroom meant doing so in front of everyone. They held it in as long as they could. There were no beds or mattresses, and it was too difficult for everyone to lie down on the concrete floor all at once, so they took turns. The others seemed to be minors, like the twins. Immigration gave them all apple juice boxes and cookies every now and then.

Every detainee received an aluminum blanket, but it hardly kept them warm—the air conditioner remained cranked up seemingly as high as it could go, in spite of the inmates' quiet complaints. Some immigration advocates claim that the cold temperature is intentional, a tactic used to break the spirits of immigrants who, they hope, will opt for voluntary departure—that is, agree to be sent home.

Immigration authorities contend that they need the *hielera* as a temporary place to house people while they figure out where to send them. Because they have no beds or showers and are not designed for overnight accommodation, a 2008 internal Border Patrol memorandum asserted that immigration detainees should not be held in *hieleras* for more than twelve hours, pending release to an official detention center. But the reality, according to a report by the American Immigration Council, is that they are often held longer; in the fall of 2014, they were held for an average of four days. In 2015 a U.S. District Court Judge ruled that DHS must release children from their custody to that of the Office of Refugee Resettlement within seventy-two hours. In June 2014 a consortium of human rights and immigrant advocacy agencies, including the ACLU, filed an administrative complaint against U.S. Customs and Border Protection, outlining complaints of physical, verbal, and sexual abuse, as well as withholding food, water, and medical care, of 116 unaccompanied minors while they were in temporary custody in the *hieleras.*

A few months after the twins were first detained, the U.S. government and media officially christened the "unaccompanied minor crisis," and photos of children in these *hieleras* were leaked to the press. The images of dozens of children locked in windowless rooms revealed the institutional overwhelming and deplorable conditions to which these children were subjected: they were crammed into cells and slept en masse, like prisoners, on the floor. The photos spurned outrage on all sides for the poor treatment of minors within our borders, as well as frustration at the undue burden these migrants were placing on U.S. infrastructure.

First separately, then together, Raúl and Ernesto were taken from the *hielera* and interviewed by an immigration officer. She asked their age, where they were from, and if they were using a false identity. Then she asked if they had anyone in the United States they could call.

"Our brother," Ernesto said.

"Wilber."

She dialed for them.

Wilber picked up after a few rings. "Who is this?" he asked suspiciously. Despite their texts from the desert, he didn't totally believe it was them.

"Ernesto and Raúl. Immigration has us," said Ernesto.

Silence.

"Hello?" Ernesto said.

"You're here? Seriously?"

They were serious.

"How are you?"

"Hungry," he said. "But we're okay."

"Make sure you answer our calls," Ernesto added.

Wilber said he would, and then the officer took the receiver, asked Wilber a series of questions, and jotted down his information. The twins knew Wilber didn't have papers. Had they just got him in trouble with the authorities?

They waited in the *hielera* for three days or so; it was hard to mark the passage of time since the lights were always on. Then they were put into a car with four other boys, sure once again that they were being taken to the other side of the border. But soon they were pulling into the gated front lot of a two-story white clapboard house. A small sign with an orange sunburst hung along the gate: SOUTHWEST KEY PROGRAMS.

At the front desk, they handed over their belongings: a backpack each, the cellphone, Ernesto's rosary belt, and Raúl's *Niño Divino* book. They took showers and were given a change of clothes—jeans, shorts, some colored T-shirts, and sneakers. They were given several medical tests and vaccinations. They stayed in quarantine for three days, just the two of them in a room, lying around in the morning, pissing into cups, getting their blood drawn. In the afternoons they were let upstairs to watch TV, though they had to wear medical facemasks and weren't let around any other kids. When they were finally released into the shelter, they found themselves, to their surprise, among about two hundred minors, mostly teens from Central America like them.

They were put in a room with two sets of bunk beds—Ernesto took the top—that they shared with two boys from Guatemala. It didn't seem so bad in here. Much better, in any case, than in the *hielera*.

They were awakened early by the shelter staff—five-thirty a.m., time to take showers and do chores. They made their beds, straightened their room, scrubbed the bathroom sinks, and mopped the floors. They had to keep their rooms neat and orderly for daily checks. During the day they attended English classes, played soccer—always supervised—and met occasionally with their counselor, Gerardo.

Ernesto looked forward to his meetings with Gerardo. He told him things he'd never told anyone before, not even Raúl. His dreams had been getting worse and worse—like the recurring dream with a headless man chasing him down, trying to strangle him—and he'd awaken in a sweat, screaming and trembling. Gerardo was often on duty in the middle of the night, and Ernesto could ask permission to walk down and see him. In the daytime, Ernesto began to suffer from panic attacks, and Gerardo helped him calm down. "Breathe," he'd say. "Deep breaths." With each inhale, Ernesto was to focus on calming, and with each exhale, he'd repeat out loud something bad that had happened, as if he were releasing it into the air around him.

"My uncle wanted to kill me."

"My brother was kidnapped, and it was my fault."

"I fell onto a body—I can still feel it on my hands."

"What happened that day in Reynosa."

After sessions like that, he could sleep a little. But the following day the cycle would start over again, and he'd be back in Gerardo's office, breathing deep and asking for a caramel.

Raúl noticed that Ernesto wasn't doing so well. He was glad he had his counselor. But why wouldn't he talk to him?

THE Southwest Key Facility in San Benito, Texas, just outside Harlingen and about ten miles as the crow flies from the border, is part of a lucrative federal contracting industry in which contracts are awarded to nonprofit agencies for the short-term housing and care of unaccompanied minors.

Prior to 1997, unaccompanied minors like the Flores twins had been detained along with adults in prison-like detention facilities. That put them at obvious risk and violated the United Nations Convention on the Rights of the Child. In 1997 an agreement known as the Flores Settlement (no relation to the twins) laid out new requirements for child-appropriate facilities for unaccompanied minors. It also provided for an alternative detention model in which children would be released, when possible, to trusted adults in the United States pending their immigration proceedings in court. In 2003 the Department of Homeland Security transferred the responsibility for the housing and care of unaccompanied minors to the Department of Health and Human Services (DHHS)—specifically, the Office of Refugee Resettlement (ORR)—which meant the government agency that was attempting to deport children was no longer also in charge of their day-to-day care.

As was formerly common in the U.S. penal system and as remains a norm in adult immigration detention, these youth detention facilities were run by outside contractors, all nonprofit agencies like Southwest Key. But in spite of their 501(c)3 status, youth shelters are often a big business. The year the Flores twins crossed the border, DHHS budgeted $175 million for the Unaccompanied Minor Program, over 80 percent of which went to the shelter costs through federal contracts. In response to the surging numbers, in fiscal year 2014, Obama's budget plan allocated $494 million to the ORR in support of unaccompanied minors, nearly double the program's 2012 budget. Southwest Key received $164 million in government grants that year. In fiscal year 2017 the ORR's Unaccompanied Alien Children budget is approximately $1.32 billion, up more than $373 million from 2016.

Southwest Key is one of the largest UAC contractors, priding itself on its mission of "opening doors to opportunity so individuals can achieve their dreams." Though it is a nonprofit, it looks a lot like a private prison company in its reliance on high-priced federal contracts. In some cases, former prison guards have been hired to work in ORR-funded shelters.

Though the vast majority of children report that the shelters are well run and safe (even if they don't like being stuck there), abuse seems to be not uncommon. In 2007 the nonprofit Texas Shelter Care outside San Antonio was shut down over allegations of sexual abuse. There were other reports over the years, though they were kept in relative secrecy until a 2014 *Houston Chronicle* exposé. The *Chronicle* investigated 101 reports of sexual misconduct between 2011 and 2013, with unaccompanied minors in custody in New York, Illinois, Texas, and Florida; the alleged sexual abuse was often accompanied by threats if these incidents were reported. In cases of allegations, the shelters contact local law enforcement. But "in the hands of local police and prosecutors," reported the *Chronicle,* "criminal cases have crumbled because of sloppy detective work, communication gaps with federal officials and jurisdictional confusion." As a result, very few perpetrators have served jail time, and none of them were prosecuted under a 2008 federal law designed specifically to protect children in custody from child abuse. (To make matters worse, because seventeen is the age of consent in Texas, abuse of a seventeen-year-old in custody was on at least several occasions not deemed abuse by the local authorities.)

Prior to 2012 the average stay for children in ORR custody was seventy-five days before they opted for voluntary departure, were ordered deported, or most commonly, were reunited with family in other states pending their day in immigration court. In 2016, the average stay was thirty-four days. When the budget is broken down, the total cost of detaining each child has, since the initial 2012 surge, totaled between $200 and $500 per night. Profits have been healthy: in 2014 the Southwest Key CEO made $659,000, including bonuses and incentives.

THE Flores twins stayed at the Southwest Key facility for over two months. It was here that a social worker finally explained what was happening to them. They had entered the country illegally, she said, so they were being placed in deportation proceedings, but they would not be sent home before first going to court and talking to a judge. They could try to find a lawyer to fight their case, though that might cost money. If the judge did not accept their plea to stay, they would be deported. Meanwhile they'd stay at Southwest Key. If they had a family member or other close friend in the United States who was willing to take them in, they could be transferred out of the facility to live with them.

"But," the woman warned, "this does not mean you have permission to stay in the United States for good. You still have to go to court." While they were cared for under the auspices of the Office of Refugee Resettlement, the Flores twins and their peers were not considered refugees; they were illegal aliens under the letter of the law, with a pending order for deportation.

The social worker explained the release process to Wilber Jr.: he would be background-checked, and if they found him fit to be a sponsor, he would have to pay the plane fare for the boys to travel to his city, as well as for a social worker to accompany them on the journey. He would be responsible for making sure they were fed, clothed, housed, that they were safe, that they enrolled in school, and most important, that they made it to their court date.

She added, "And if you don't have papers, don't worry—this will not impact your immigration status."

This fact put the boys somewhat at ease. But still—could they trust her?

The shelters wanted to release children to sponsors to keep their time in detention to a minimum, or at the very least to free up bed space. In practice, neither the shelters nor the ORR turned over information about sponsors or their immigration status to the Department of Homeland Security. (That practice could change, however, under pressure from the executive branch.) Wilber took the social worker at her word. Within a few days, he started the process to become the twins' guardian.

Once a week they got to make a fifteen-minute phone call home. They alternated between calling Wilber and calling their parents. Fifteen minutes went quickly, and each time the staff member motioned for them that their time was up, they rambled a quick goodbye and handed the receiver back over. Gerardo sometimes let Ernesto make special phone calls home during their sessions. Talking to Esperanza was the most soothing for him and also the hardest of all. "I'm okay, don't worry," Ernesto would say. "We're okay!" But she was always crying into the phone. She didn't believe him, he could tell. Likewise, the twins didn't believe her when she insisted the family was safe back home. They worried that Agustín might go after their family to punish them.

Meanwhile they made a few friends at the shelter, who, like their old classmates, referred to them as a unit. "The twins," *los gemelos,* the boys called them as they passed in the cafeteria or the game room, all in their standard-issue clothes. They didn't share much about their past, preferring to focus on the now of the shelter: video games, gossip, and what was—*gross, what is this?*—for dinner today.

They ate their meals in the big cafeteria downstairs. The food was terrible—slop on a tray, nothing like what they were used to eating at home. On special days they'd get pizza, which wasn't bad.

There were girls there, too, but they were housed in a separate part of the campus and had meals separately.

Raúl noticed one Guatemalan boy, ten or twelve years old, who spent a lot of time staring fixedly out the windows. He carried a little blue rock with him everywhere, until one day it disappeared. "Black magic," one of their new friends whispered over dinner. Another morning the Guatemalan boy woke up to find his clothes were gone, and then, the morning cafeteria chatter went, he found a noose hanging from the ceiling—the Guatemalan's roommate had seen it, too, or so the kid reporting it said. Then his clothes turned different colors. Someone, it was clear, was doing *brujería,* witchcraft, against this kid. The more strange things happened to him, the more the other kids steered clear of him, and the more time the boy spent at the window, staring. Eventually he was taken to the hospital "because he was driven crazy," said Raúl, "by the sorcery." It confirmed what Raúl had assumed: the boy had been seeing the same bad spirits he had.

Occasionally the kids with good behavior were taken out on field trips. One night it was to the movies; the Flores twins had never been to a movie theater before. They loved the cool, dark room and the chairs like individual couches, comfortable and soft so you could sink back and stare up at the big screen. They had no idea what the film was called, or what exactly was happening, since it was in English. Something about a boy and girl falling in love. The popcorn was delicious and left tracks of butter on their hands.

They went to the park in town from time to time to kick the ball around. Once they heard a commotion and turned: one of the shelter staff was demanding that a man please put down his camera. The man had it trained on the shelter kids and was saying something about how, as Ernesto and Raúl took it, he didn't want his own kids playing with a bunch of immigrants. Eventually the guy collected his own child and drove away. The staff wouldn't tell them what, exactly, the guy had said.

The twins wanted out of Southwest Key as fast as possible. As competently cared for as they were, their life was on hold, which was maddening. Their debt was climbing, for one thing—every day in here meant another line of compounding interest in the ledger, another day they weren't earning money to pay it back. Their world was precarious. They called Wilber every other week, and more if Gerardo gave them extra calls, asking for an update, hoping he hadn't changed his mind about letting them come live with him.

In the middle of each night, a train clattered by their window, slicing east-west through Texas.

Early on a Tuesday morning in March, the Harlingen, Texas, immigration courthouse is packed. It's an unimpressive building, a small, stucco block set back from the road just down from a Motel 6 and the I-2 overpass. In the parking lot, an American flag flaps alongside the bold Texas Lone Star. Just before eight, van after van pulls up beside the flagpoles to unload their cargo: children.

A handful of adults sit quietly in the lobby, hands folded in laps, gazes cast toward the floor. More than three dozen children from the shelter vans fill the room, radiating heat and nervous chatter. One by one they step through the metal detector and snatch seats along the rows of orange plastic chairs. Each detention center has its own standard-issue dress—one group is in starched light-blue shirts and dark-blue jeans, another in primary-color cotton Henleys. The kids whisper and fidget with their packets of papers: manila envelopes stuffed with everything that matters to the court, each scrawled on the outside with a name and an alien number. The girls wear tight ponytails, and the boys—most of them are boys—have slicked their hair back and tucked their shirts neatly into their pants. They'll need to look smart today, clean and serious and well behaved. A boy around thirteen years old stands repeatedly to smooth his red collared shirt into his jeans.

Before they transfer out of the Rio Grande Valley to their families or other trusted adults, Unaccompanied Alien Children are ordered to appear in court here in Harlingen. A paralegal for a local pro bono agency, ProBAR, enters the room, legal pad in hand, cowboy boots clicking against the floor. He introduces himself to the children as Jose Chapa. "*Buenos días, jovenes,*" he says to the room. He's met some of them before. The kids fall silent and listen. Chapa, a Rio Grande Valley native in his late twenties, has a gentle, assuring demeanor as he checks in with each kid about his or her case—*Are you trying to go home today? Are you about to turn eighteen?*—marking up his spreadsheet of names. "When I call your name, come stand over here." One by one they line up in a studious single file then follow him into the courtroom. The four youngest children—ages seven, eight, nine, and twelve—sit in the back, three boys and one girl, their feet dangling off the edge of the bench. The pews are filled, hip to hip.

These kids have never seen a room like this before, and they stare wide-eyed up toward the judge's stand. Before coming here, a good number of them had never heard of a judge, or a lawyer, or a court. Most of them are from towns in Honduras and Guatemala and El Salvador that might have a police officer or two, sometimes a town office or a one-room precinct. This small-time Texas courthouse is bigger and more imposing than any building many of them have ever visited.

When robed Judge Howard Achtsam walks in, all the children stand. The shelter staff have trained them to do this. Judge Achtsam addresses about a dozen first-timers at once, explaining that their cases will be reset for a later date. "You were not given permission to enter legally in the United States," he reads from a script. "Therefore your Notice to Appear says you can be removed—that means the same as deportation—because you are not citizens or nationals." He explains to the boys and girls their rights, which they digest, via Spanish translation, while staring straight ahead. (The handful who speak indigenous languages, and not much Spanish, follow as best they can and work to look alert.) As their names are called, they stand one by one.

The clerk passes around some papers: a Notice to Appear, sometime in late May, copied on blue paper and affixed to a list of attorneys several pages long. They'll shove these into their folders.

"You have the privilege of being represented by an attorney but at no cost to the United States. If you cannot afford to pay for an attorney, there are a number of legal-aid organizations in this area that can represent you at no cost. You have to find an attorney as quickly as possible," Judge Achtsam advises them. But they might as well not bother calling anyone on this list. No one aside from ProBAR will take on these children's cases, and even then only in an emergency scenario, such as a child who is about to turn eighteen and age out of the juvenile process, or a child, fed up with detention, opting for voluntary departure—to go home. Today ProBAR is just here to help out with the logistics of court—none of the kids in this first group has an official attorney.

"Any questions?" Achtsam asks.

No one raises a hand. The cases are officially reset for the next month—by then, they may still be here in the Rio Grande Valley, or they may have been sent to live with a friend or relative where they'll stand, eventually, in front of a different judge.

"Thank you," Judge Achtsam says, and stands. The juvies file out.

Slowly, like birds coming back to life at dawn, the children begin to chatter again. They're glad it's over.

"It was scary," one says.

"It wasn't so bad," another interjects.

"I thought it was going to be worse," says a third. They'd heard what it would be like from the other kids.

As groups head out toward the vans, a huddle of kids wait for their ride back to one of the shelters. A boy named Miguel sits off to the side alone, shoulders slumped. He is seventeen and from Honduras, pale and pimply-faced with dark curly hair. Because of his family's relative wealth back in Honduras—by the standards of poverty—a local gang kidnapped his aunt for ransom. "When my father told them they had my aunt, the police just asked for a bribe." In the end, his family failed to come up with enough money to do any good. "They killed her. They killed her, and no one did anything." His cousins were killed, his uncle too. He wants to go home, to get out of the U.S. immigration system's loveless grip—but he knows the danger.

Chapa gathers a group of small children living in foster care to explain what happened in the courtroom. "Okay," he says in the honeyed voice of a grade school teacher. He explains that they will have another court date, which is listed on the blue paper. The paper is very important, he says, and they need to keep it and bring it with them next time. A little boy, seven years old, holds his manila packet and blue paper in one hand and a ziplock snack—a packet of Oreos, some chips, and an applesauce—in another. He looks up at Chapa as he speaks, nodding along. "Call your family back home and tell them about your court date," says Chapa. The boy clutches the papers and the snack bag. He continues to nod until Chapa stops talking.

"Understood?" Chapa asks. Understood.

CHAPTER 5

They'd never been on a plane before. As the wheels lifted off the tarmac, the Flores twins gripped their armrests and held their breath. The shelter staff member accompanying them took these trips often, it seemed, and wasn't impressed by the airplane, the free snacks and drinks, the rush of taking off. But for the twins, the flight was miraculous. The woman from the shelter hardly spoke a word to them or to the other California-bound boy the entire trip. The brothers whispered to one another, drank soda, and stared out the window.

Wilber was waiting for them when they landed at San Francisco International Airport. At first the twins didn't recognize him. They exchanged stiff hugs and laughed uneasily. After Wilber signed some papers, the shelter staff released them officially into his care.

Wilber had a girl with him. "This is Gabby," he said. She was shorter than he was, sturdy and baby-faced with a red rinse in her hair and thick black glasses.

"Hi," said Ernesto.

"Nice to meet you," said Raúl.

Wilber was like an entirely new person: new clothes, newfound swagger. Even his face looked different. A lot changes in seven years. They said little to one another as they walked out of the airport.

Wilber didn't look much like his twin brothers. His face was more drawn, less wide-eyed—the product, perhaps, of years on his own up North. He resembled them most in stature: at five foot six, he was only slightly taller, simultaneously brawny and trim. He walked with an adapted, tidy confidence, and his front teeth were ringed by gold caps that gave his smile, offered timidly and with a nod of his head, an actual glint.

Wilber had taken the day off work to fetch the twins in San Francisco, about an hour north from where he lived in San Jose. The past two months he'd taken on all the Sunday shifts he could at the landscaping company where he worked in order to pay for their tickets—this was his first break in weeks. He noted how skinny his brothers looked—this upset him and was now his responsibility.

They rode the train to San Jose; then at the station they hopped into his car and, at his request, buckled their seat belts. The car, a Toyota 4Runner, rode high off the ground and had leather seats that were slick to the touch. The Flores family had never owned a car. Wilber pulled into a parking lot and left the twins inside. He and Gabby came back a few minutes later, paper bags in hand. "Burgers," Wilber said. Delicious.

Wilber's working-class San Jose apartment—their new home—was nicer and more modern than any house they'd ever been in. He showed them around: it had two bedrooms, one for him and one for his roommate and his roommate's girlfriend. The twins would sleep on the couch.

They all spent that first afternoon watching TV, a convenient mask for the lack of things they had to say to one another. Wilber could see in their faces that they'd been through the wringer. He knew how bad the journey could be, but he didn't ask any questions—they'd survived, and to keep pushing forward, these things were best left undiscussed.

Maricela had recounted what had gone down with Uncle Agustín. And Wilber had followed the El Salvador news since he left, seeing the pictures of dead bodies, the statistics, the way the police covered their faces now, so the gangs wouldn't know who they were. Little by little, ragtag groups of kids with guns had taken over his country. He read stories on Facebook by Salvadoran friends and co-workers. Gabby was

Salvadoran, too, though she'd been born in the United States and had only visited once, when she was little. He had two friends who had gone back to El Salvador from the United States and been killed. Two. If you returned to El Salvador, you were an unknown, a *desconocido*. The gangs knew who belonged and who didn't, and a new guy rolling into town with nice clothes was assumed either to have money, or to be a part of a rival gang, or both. Another friend had to start paying *renta* every two weeks, extortion money, to keep his family safe. Wilber wasn't surprised that this plague of violence had made its way to his family. His country, as far as he could tell from this distance, was falling apart.

Still, seeing his little brothers grown up, no longer scrawny little boys, made him miss home: the wet smell of the hillsides, the sweet burn of brushfires, his mother at the stove. When he left home seven years ago, he had been so preoccupied with the dream of what awaited him in the United States that he hadn't really considered that he would very possibly never return. Forever is an obscure prospect, especially for a kid, even more for a kid hell-bent on the horizon.

Things don't always work out as planned. Right when he got to California, aged seventeen, he had enrolled in high school, which he'd assumed would just be a stepping-stone to college. (According to the 1982 Supreme Court decision *Plyler v. Doe,* anyone under eighteen, with proof of address, can enroll in a U.S. public school regardless of immigration status.) But without English, he found a second-rate U.S. high school harder than he'd thought it would be. Plus, though he had a place to stay—on the couch of friends of the family—financial pressures kicked in quickly. He wanted to pull his weight in the household, and he had his $6,000 debt to pay off. Feeling sure that he'd re-enroll once things stabilized, he quit school and got a job in landscaping, working on the yards and gardens of Silicon Valley's wealthy homes and businesses. They paid him in cash every other week, more cash than he'd ever had. But life in the United States was a nonstop ticker tape of bills and charges, an endless invoice. He moved out and rented a room in a house—that was a monthly bill. He needed a car. A new pair of shoes, work gloves, gas for the car, insurance—he was always behind, never ahead. But he was diligent about sending money home to work off his debt: he paid it off a few hundred dollars at a time, finishing within two years, never letting the interest overtake him.

The twins would have to go to work as he had—he understood this before they even arrived. But shelter rules said otherwise. "They'll have to go to school," the woman from the shelter had explained in her Tex-Mex Spanish. "They can't work."

So who was going to pay their debt?

"How much do you owe?" he asked them over burgers.

"Fourteen thousand dollars," Raúl said.

"When we left," said Ernesto, shaking his head. The sum, they knew, had compounded in the three months since they'd left. They weren't sure by how much.

Wilber took a bite, nodding silently. He loved them, and had missed them. Now their debt, it seemed, was his. "I'll help you guys," he'd told them over the phone. But now, hearing the impossible sum they owed, he didn't repeat his offer. They'd figure out their own path forward, in time.

THE notion that unauthorized immigration into the United States is spiraling ever higher is a myth. In fact, the number of undocumented people rose steadily from around 3.5 million in 1990 to 12.12 million in 2007, but it dropped (owing largely to the economy) to approximately 11.3 million in 2009 and has stayed relatively steady ever since. Of these immigrants, 2.3 million lived in California as of 2014, more than in any other state. But immigrant demographics have changed. In 1990 approximately 525,000 undocumented people living in the United States had come from Central America. By 2011, that number spiked to 1.7 million.

Another myth is that immigrants like Wilber do not pay taxes. Taxes are taken out of their paychecks; they pay sales tax on milk and soda and tortillas and cars, like the one Wilber purchased with post-tax cash. When undocumented immigrants use fake or borrowed Social Security cards, they are paying into the real Social Security benefit pool—benefits that they will never receive. Even those without a Social Security number often file tax returns using an individual tax identification number.

Had Wilber owned a house, he'd pay property tax. In 2012, according to the left-leaning American Immigration Council, the undocumented paid $11.8 billion in state taxes alone.

Of course, undocumented immigrants also avail themselves of public services: schools, roads, and public hospitals. They do not, however, qualify for benefits like welfare (contrary to what is so often charged), or food stamps, or subsidized housing, or health insurance—even under the Affordable Care Act.

Wilber had learned to navigate the province of the paperless. He went to work, came home, paid his rent on time, paid his car payments on time, and stayed out of trouble. Except, that is, when it came to driving. Until 2013, the year the twins arrived, undocumented immigrants weren't able to get a driver's license in California. In 2010 he'd been ticketed for driving without a license, then two years later, charged with driving drunk—four beers at the club, his friend's car with a dead battery stuck in a fifteen-minute zone, and Wilbur steering it in neutral across the parking lot. When the sirens flashed, he'd braked and tried to remain calm and deferential as the officer questioned him, though he thought the circumstances absurd. He was arrested, nonetheless.

He was slapped with a DUI, had to pay several thousand dollars in fines for both the DUI and driving without a license, and do over one hundred community service hours, picking up trash at city parks and freeways.

But it was better than what he'd feared. For a while, he waited for immigration to show up at his door. They never did, and eventually he stopped worrying. He also kept driving. He had to get to work. He stopped fully at every stop sign, never ran a yellow light, and stayed just under the speed limit at all times.

By the time the twins arrived, Wilber was just starting to feel settled, to build a life he could be proud of. He had Gabby, who spoke perfect English and came from a big family who lived, mostly, in Oakland. Gabby's Chihuahua, Nicky, lived with them inside the house, unlike most dogs in La Colonia, who roamed the streets snapping up scraps and snarling at competitors. Nicky relaxed Wilber. Anytime he was having a bad day, the dog's antics lifted his spirits. Gabby was finishing up her high school credits at the local community college, after which she'd enroll as a full-time college student. Wilber wanted to enroll in college, too, though he couldn't, just yet, because of work demands. He also wanted to marry Gabby if things kept going well; he was saving up cash to buy a home and maybe even a ring. Gabby was a citizen, and if they got married, he thought he might get papers. But, Wilber reasoned, "you have to get married for love."

Ernesto and Raúl bought new clothes with Wilber's cash. At the local mall, Ernesto picked out a black T-shirt bearing an image of Bob Marley in profile, dragging on a joint and ringed with its smoke. Back home they dressed more conservatively, with straight-legged pants and collared shirts tucked in at the waist. Here the styles were different— skinny jeans and fitted, hoodless sweatshirts, with oversize high-tops only barely laced. It was like what Wilber wore—and not unlike gangster garb back home. When Wilber saw the Bob Marley shirt, he just laughed. The shopping trip drained him of all that month's extra cash.

He was happy to see the twins, but it was also a game changer. Just when things had started to stabilize and he was thinking about going back to school, his brothers appeared, needing food, a place to sleep, and Bob Marley T-shirts. They were his blood and they needed him, so of course he'd help them, but damn.

WILBER secured another day off to enroll the twins in the local school, Westmont High. He gathered all the twins' papers—birth certificates, release paperwork from Southwest Key, vaccination documents—and walked into the main office. The twins stayed home.

"I'm here to register my brothers for school?" Wilber said to the woman at the front desk.

She took the paperwork. "They're seventeen?"

"Yeah," Wilber said.

"Do they speak any English?"

"No."

"Unfortunately," she said, "they're really too old to enroll here." Since they didn't speak English, they wouldn't be able to graduate on time. She suggested another school that had a program for English learners.

Wilber didn't argue. The U.S. immigration system required them to register in school, but that was proving complicated; the school she mentioned was in another part of town. (Though anyone under the age of eighteen is required to attend school in California, and thus eligible to enroll in school, not all schools are equipped to support newcomers.)

It would be a while before he could get another day off to try the other high school. If they couldn't go to school yet, Wilber reasoned, they should at least help pay the rent and start sending money home. His boss said he might need a few extra hands. So in their second week in California, the twins began accompanying Wilber to his job sites a few days a week, where they mowed lawns, trimmed hedges, and pulled weeds from the gardens of the big houses that draped the hills like strands of pearls.

They made nine dollars an hour and, for two months, worked whenever the boss texted that he could use them. The money they earned went to food and rent, and whatever was left over they sent home: $100, $150, every couple of weeks when they had some extra to spare.

"Can you send more?" Maricela wrote over Facebook.

THEY didn't know what the interest was—was it 5 percent or 50? All they knew was that the sum had started at $14,000, and, as Maricela reported once they'd settled in at Wilber's, by the time they set foot in the United States, it was $16,000. Of the money the boys did send home, hardly any of it even went to the debt because the family needed it to eat. The larger swath of land that Wilber Sr. had first put up as collateral had been valued, loosely, at around $60,000.

To lose the land would mean losing the family's livelihood, their food source. For Wilber Sr., the land also signified his very purpose in the world, entwined with his own origin story.

The twins' father been born out of wedlock to a mother who was just fifteen; his father had run away. Ashamed and heartbroken, Wilber's mother gave birth to him in a cornfield. She cut the cord, left him there squirming on the dirt, and then, like his father, ran away. Her sisters found the baby, miraculously alive. Their own mother had just given birth a few months before, so Wilber's grandmother nursed both babies, one after the other.

After the second grade, he quit school to become a full-time farmer. At twelve, his father, whom he'd never met, showed up. He had another family by now, and he wanted Wilber to come and live with them. He did, but it quickly became clear that he'd been brought there to work. While the other siblings went to school, Wilber was in the fields. One of these siblings was Graciela, Agustín's wife.

Wilber had wanted to get married, to have a family of his own, but his siblings dissuaded him. They preferred, he thought, to keep him working for them. Every time he brought it up, they berated him, until he nearly went mad from the pressure. He ran away to the forest for a couple of weeks, to be alone. But there, his story went, the spirit of an old woman appeared and told him she'd buried a treasure on the mountain. She told him he could find it beneath a pine next to a huge rock. He went there and dug up a stash of money—enough, he said, to purchase the land and start his own family.

Who knows what was true? Wilber Sr. told the story of his life in this sort of parable, always with a clear moral, blurring the line between fiction and fact. The moral of this tale: his land was something he'd come to through both patient suffering and divine intervention.

Now his sons' debt was putting it all in jeopardy, and Wilber Sr. felt an uncharacteristic tremor of doubt. Not Esperanza. "God will find a way," she insisted. She lit a candle on the altar.

To Maricela, this wasn't about God—it was about numbers and math, a sum of money that needed to be paid off quickly. "Can't you get more work?" she asked Ernesto via Facebook.

"If they find out we're working, they'll know we aren't going to school, and we could get deported."

To this, Maricela didn't respond.

Ernesto and Raúl received a letter from immigration court. Their case had been transferred from Texas to California. They were due at the San Francisco Immigration Court in February 2014: in less than two months' time.

BY December 2013 the boys had been living with Wilber in San Jose for two months—long enough to feel comfortable again, thus long enough for the bickering to begin. When they weren't at the landscaping job with Wilber, they were at home, confined to Wilber's dark apartment, worrying over their debt and their court cases, and what might next go wrong.

Nights were the hardest. Once Raúl awoke to a feeling of someone standing over him. He saw a thick figure against the wall, but there was no light. He thought of the Guatemalan boy at the shelter, the barking dogs the night before he left La Colonia, the guys with the photo on the side of the road. Now the dark spirits were here with him in California. He frequently spotted a flash across his wall, or felt a cold chill come over his body. He waited and prayed until these went away. Ernesto didn't see spirits, but when Raúl told him, he believed him.

Ernesto's sleep was still afflicted—worse now, even, than in Harlingen—and in San Jose, he had no counselor to help him. Almost nightly he fell into suffocating dreams. He'd be in a bus, or out in the desert, or in the forest back in El Salvador, and a dead man would rise and chase him. The first night he had that dream in San Jose, he woke up screaming. He opened his eyes and saw Wilber above him, shaking him.

"What's wrong? What's wrong?" he asked.

Ernesto brushed him away. "I'm fine, sorry, I'm fine." He rolled back over.

"You sure you okay?" asked Raúl, after their brother left.

"I'm fine!" he said, and yanked the covers over his head.

Once the dreams became a pattern, Wilber stopped coming in. Raúl would just roll over, groan, and ignore Ernesto's screams. Raúl didn't ask about what he was dreaming about. Clearly, that dead body he had fallen on had really affected him, or maybe it was the stress of the upcoming court date, or the lingering taste of fear from those last weeks back home. It used to be that Raúl could just look at Ernesto and know his thoughts, but not anymore. The twins were losing their special powers up north.

AROUND the holidays, Wilber began to talk about moving. Gabby was starting school again in Oakland. If they all moved to Oakland, about an hour north, they could rent a larger house along with her mom, Rosalinda. Wilber would have to commute to work an hour and a half every day, each way, but the rent would be cheaper, he figured. Then the landlord found out how many people were living in the apartment. He issued an eviction. They had no choice but to move.

Christmas was one of their last days in San Jose, spent at a barbecue in a parking lot across town, grilling meat and eating *pupusas* with a dozen or so other Salvadorans. They missed the nativity scene their mother always set up on the home altar, missed the songs in church and the fireworks at night. But they had something to look forward to: they were moving to Oakland. Maybe there they'd be able to go to school.

They moved into an eight-unit apartment complex in East Oakland, on a small street just off the Bancroft Avenue thoroughfare. It stood at the nape of the gradual hill that rises from crime-riddled flats to towering hills speckled with new housing developments. Oakland was busier and, to the twins, felt poorer than even La Colonia. Urban poverty was different; it was split open, glaring, and on display for everyone to see. Homeless people walked the streets, people did drugs out in public, there was litter everywhere, and sometimes even they heard gunfire. But living with Gabby, Rosalinda, and Rosalinda's two other kids—José, age eleven, and Silvia, three—provided, at first, the semblance of an actual home. The freezer was full of icy cuts of chicken and off-brand bags of cauliflower and peas. Sometimes Rosalinda would make food from scratch for her kids, and sometimes for the twins, too. Wilber bought a television and hooked it up to the building's cable.

The twins had their own bedroom again. It was small and dark; their windows leaked in heavy rains, and the carpet was laced with mold from years of too much moisture. To prevent their neighbors from seeing in, the boys tacked up large fleece blankets in the window wells—one beige and the other printed with SpongeBob SquarePants, hung upside-down and slightly askew. It was still nicer than their soot-stained room back home. It had a door.

They'd come to adore Nicky, Gabby's Chihuahua, and now they got to see her every day. Each evening they'd coax her into their room. Raúl chuckled as he flipped her over and rubbed her belly and held up chips for her to jump after. When they finally rolled over to go to sleep, usually after midnight, Ernesto would swipe Nicky from Raúl's side of the bed to his own and tuck her beneath his chin. When Nicky slept with him, he had fewer nightmares.

Gabby's younger brother, eleven-year-old José, became the twins' frequent tagalong. He bounced between his grandmother's house, his dad's house, and the apartment where the twins lived, where he often ended up sleeping in the twins' room, playing video games and watching movies late into the night. The twins could have done without a third bunkmate most nights, but José was harmless, and once they got over ceding part of their space to a strange kid, he was even nice to have around. He was younger, which took the pressure off the twins to be mature and tough, and his presence made their small world on Hillside feel more like family.

José had a computer that the boys used to check their Facebook accounts. Though they didn't post much of anything except the occasional photo of themselves and a "What's up, everybody," they still liked to scroll through their old friends' walls. But this always left them feeling adrift and far away.

Plus, they started to get private messages from their school friends in La Colonia. "You guys look good," one said. "Living the dream in North America, man!" "Hey, can you send a little money? I need to buy some shoes." The requests for money came almost anytime they posted a photo. Even their enemies, the guys who they were sure had ratted them out to Agustín, asked for favors—the audacity, fucking assholes.

They had no money, but felt a twinge of pride that those maggots thought they might. Raúl finally unfriended all his old friends, even the ones who likely hadn't done anything to him. Because who knew, exactly, where people's allegiances were anymore? They tried not to think about it but harbored a needling fear that someone might come here looking for them. On their new profiles, they said they lived in San Jose and attended high school—to throw anyone from their old life off their trail.

"Fuck them," said Ernesto. He followed Raúl's uncharacteristic lead, unfriending their ex-friends too. He wasn't in charge of much in his life, but he could block a person with a click.

THEY pulled into the Oakland Unified School District's enrollment office, in a set of trailers behind an old elementary school on Grand Avenue, abutting Lake Merritt. Wilber had taken yet another day off work.

"How old are you?" the woman behind the counter asked.

"Seventeen," they all replied at once.

"Yes, you can enroll, as long as you're under eighteen." This is what they'd been hoping for, naturally, but that it came so easily was a surprise. She handed them two long sheets, in triplicate, on two matching clipboards.

Given their limited language, they were placed at Oakland International High School (OIHS), where I worked. It was about an hour bus ride from where they lived, and it catered specifically to newly arrived immigrant English-language learners. The school's 370 students came from more than thirty countries, but at the time over 50 percent were Spanish-speaking, from Mexico and Central America.

The next Tuesday they walked a little under a mile to the corner of International Boulevard, as Wilber had instructed, where they caught the 1R bus. They rode in an unsteady silence. The route ran along most of International, one of the city's main arteries, carrying them from the littered political neglect of the outer avenues, through the throng of commerce in the Fruitvale district, and past the limp chain of street walkers alongside rows of seedy motels. They continued past the outdoor fruit stalls of the Vietnamese shops and Chinese markets, glided by the shimmering Lake Merritt and through Chinatown, and headed into the morning bustle of downtown Oakland. There the bus route hooked north, and they rode up Telegraph Avenue to OIHS.

The first day they were all nerves and jitters. In spite of their age, seventeen—normally an eleventh or twelfth grader—they were placed in the tenth grade, which according to the school's programming would give them enough time to learn English, earn all their credits, and if they worked hard, graduate in three years at age twenty-one. When Wilber filled out the registration paperwork the week before, he had agreed to this plan. He knew he wouldn't be supporting them for three years of leisurely finishing their studies. No way. But he simultaneously wanted the best for them, and for now they would be in school.

The twins were assigned to separate classes and were too nervous to argue. Settling into their respective seats, they felt as though they'd touched down on an alien planet. Back home, all their classmates had been somewhat familiar. They knew where they lived, at least, and who they hung out with, and who their grandfather was. Here they didn't know a single face, and they couldn't communicate with half the students. There were cues and customs—using a binder, for example, rather than a textbook, and working on a "do now" at the beginning of every class—that eluded them.

Instead of individual desks, students at this school sat at shared tables in groups of four to six. Ernesto made his first friend quickly enough: a kid named Diego, from Mexico. He'd been in the United States a few years and spoke English already, which he often commingled with his Mexican-slang-riddled Spanish. He was smart, and class was easy for him, so he spent his time cracking jokes and playing on his phone.

Ernesto was seated at his table. "Here, man, lemme show you." Diego leaned over to help him fill out his first handout.

The twins learned quickly: where to stand in line for lunch, how to log into their school emails, how to use Rosetta Stone to practice English, the order and location of their classes. Every morning they took great care to shower, slick their hair with gel, and don their cool new American clothes—which, because they had so few, they had to wash at least weekly at the Laundromat down the street. The finishing touch was a generous helping of cologne splashed onto their necks and hair.

They felt dumb in school for not understanding English, but not the dumbest—it helped that everyone was learning alongside them. If they came to school and tried hard, the teachers promised, they could pass their classes—they'd learn English eventually, and the more they practiced, the better they'd do. In 2014, the year the twins enrolled in school, an estimated 4.5 million students enrolled in U.S. public schools were English-language learners—nearly 10 percent of the entire U.S. public school population. (Over 75 percent of those students spoke Spanish.) Around 1.4 million U.S. English-language learners lived in California, or, as of 2012, 25 percent of the state's public school population. In Oakland, nearly a third of all students were English-language learners.

Oakland International High School had opened in August 2007 as part of a network of public schools, based in New York City, designed for newly arrived immigrant students. These schools taught language alongside content—that is, each subject was simultaneously a language class, so that students could study standard high school subjects while also acquiring the language needed to understand what they were learning. Grades at OIHS were based on a combination of skill, effort, and growth in English, and students were allowed to continue enrollment until the age of twenty-one.

Many students had gone to school for only a couple of years before starting with us; a few had never attended school in their lives. A small minority arrived at OIHS with strong educational backgrounds, or with a few years of U.S. middle school under their belts. Teachers, then, were charged with instructing an astoundingly diverse student body—in terms of language background, cultural mores, life experience—with a wide spectrum of abilities.

Like other high-density immigrant schools, Oakland International was a delayed mirror of world events. In the first ever class, of sixty students, most were from Mexico, China, and Karen state in Burma (by way of refugee camps in Thailand). Within a few years, as environmental and political crises swelled in Yemen, the school became home to dozens of Yemeni students, and as the United States began resettling tens of thousands of Nepali refugees who had been ethnically cleansed from Bhutan, dozens of them, too, enrolled. A decade after the U.S. invasions, students from Iraq and Afghanistan joined our student body. And starting in 2013, unaccompanied minors began to fill our seats.

We had been home to undocumented students since we opened— students from Mexico, Mongolia, El Salvador, China who lacked immigration papers, because they had either unlawfully crossed a border or overstayed a temporary visa. We didn't ask for students' immigration status as per U.S. law, but they and their families often confided in us as they sought support.

Most undocumented kids were unknown to immigration authorities. Unaccompanied minors, however, had been caught—meaning that they were in more immediate danger of deportation, even though their day-to-day lives, and the circumstances of their departure, were often similar to those who merely lived under the line. Eventually this created a strange hierarchy among students: those who had immigration cases were more quickly supported, due to their imminent court date; those who had not been caught, or who arrived with parents, received less support. It was difficult and unfair.

The twins were expected to talk to their classmates, in whatever mishmash of languages they could, to finish their assignments. The more students worked together on projects, the more they had to talk to one another in their common language, English. (The best way for students to learn English, we saw over the years, was for them to date someone from another country. No better incentive than love.)

They met other kids from El Salvador as well as from countries they'd never heard of: Burma, Vietnam, Yemen. Everyone had a story, but even with the Salvadorans—especially with the Salvadorans—they didn't discuss the particulars. They didn't want to out themselves as kids without papers, or kids who had problems with gangsters back home, although unknown to them they were far from the only ones. They kept their mouths shut about the fact that, within a few weeks, they might very well be ordered deported, and they left for home as soon as they could after the bell rang. Walking from the bus stop in the dark made them nervous, and sometimes, as the twins fell asleep, they thought they heard gunshots—or maybe just a backfiring car.

THE night before their court date, Ernesto and Raúl sat up worried. What would they say to the judge? What if he deported them right then and there? What if he accused them of being gangsters? They planned what they would wear—the dark jeans and light-blue-plaid shirts Wilber had bought them, buttoned up all the way. They checked and rechecked the papers in their manila envelope: their exit paperwork from the shelter, their birth certificates, their Notice to Appear. The judge might ask about their grades, how they liked school, and why they'd left home; they practiced their answers. They would do their best to look like reliable young men, diligent students, civic participants worthy of sanctioned entry into the United States of America.

So focused were they on how they'd fare and what would happen afterward, it never occurred to them to worry about how to find the courthouse.

THE DETAINED

The Mesa Verde Detention Center is a four-hundred-bed immigration detention facility in the industrial outskirts of Bakersfield, California, on a strip alongside auto repair shops, boarded-up buildings, and the El Morocco motel, whose parking lot is cluttered with rusted bicycles and shopping carts. The sky is big in this part of California, and though it's the day after Christmas, it's warm outside, palm trees fanning against the dry expanse to the east. A dusting of snow is visible on the peaks at the edge of the horizon.

Three flags flap above the sleepy entrance: the flag of California, the flag of Geo Group, the company that runs this facility, and the flag of the United States. The parking lot is about a quarter full, mostly with staff cars. Every day is a visitors' day, but today not many people have come. Bakersfield is far away from pretty much every place but Bakersfield. If the detainees have family in the United States, the odds of them living near enough to make the visit, even during the holidays, are scarce.

"They have a lot of freedom," says the guard, motioning toward the locked door that leads back into the detention facility. "Not in the sense of being free to get up and walk to the store or whatnot, but you know, they got a lot of freedom back there." On Christmas the inmates received little gift bags of chips and candy, and they were served an extra-big meal. "They were pretty happy about that."

This is a border overflow facility, meaning that they receive adults who have just been apprehended after crossing the border.

Mesa Verde's contract with the government guarantees it a minimum of 320 immigrants at any one time (out of its 400-person capacity), for a payment of $119.95 per immigrant per day. The government pays a cut rate of $94.95 per immigrant per day for any inmates above the minimum. The more detainees, the more money Mesa Verde makes.

Each year detaining immigrants in the United States costs about two billion taxpayer dollars. Over 60 percent of immigrant detainees are held in facilities managed by private contractors like Geo. Contractors often cost less per inmate than government facilities, but the quality of care often suffers, too, and there's little federal oversight. Geo is the largest contractor by far, housing between eight and nine thousand immigrants at any one time and raking in $140 million per year since 2012.

In August 2016, after decades of public pressure and several press exposés of negligence and mismanagement in private prisons, the U.S. Department of Justice announced that it would no longer outsource incarceration to private contractors, but private contracting of immigration detention remains widespread.

After that August announcement, stocks in companies like the Corrections Corporation of America and Geo—companies that also run immigration facilities—plummeted. They rebounded once Donald Trump was elected president. In one of his early executive orders, President Trump instructed ICE to begin immediately constructing new facilities and initiating new contracts. A January 2017 memo suggested the administration might double the number of immigration detainees at any given time.

Though Mesa Verde is less than two hours from Los Angeles, the facility's inmates are looped into the jurisdiction of the San Francisco immigration court—at least four and a half hours away, without traffic. Inmates patch in via teleconference to their court hearings and for weekly Know Your Rights legal training sessions. "I want to be deported," a tired Mexican detainee told a Know Your Rights presenter via teleconference. But, according to the attorney, she'd have to wait for her court date before officially requesting to be sent home. Meanwhile, she was stuck in detention on the government's dime, to the profit of Geo Group.

In 2016 U.S. Immigration and Customs Enforcement (ICE) processed 352,882 new immigrant detainees and, along with Customs and Border Protection, deported over 450,000 people. In 2015 a total of 21,920 were deported to El Salvador—9 percent of total removals. The Obama administration deported more than 2.5 million people from the United States—more than any administration to date. Toward the end of his tenure, the number of deportations declined. President Trump campaigned on an immigration hardline, and in his first one hundred days alone, his team issued executive orders and guidelines to ramp up immigration enforcement, increase expedited removals at the border (where newly arrived immigrants would be deported without first seeing a judge), and expand the priorities for deportation—including not just those with serious crimes, anymore, but those with minor offenses like driving without a license, and even those merely charged with a crime. Less than a month after the inauguration, an internal DHS memo also issued new guidelines that parents who paid a coyote to bring their children north could be subject to prosecution for facilitating smuggling. Attorney General Jeff Sessions also signaled that immigration enforcement would be a top priority in the judicial system. "For those that continue to seek improper and illegal entry into this country, be forewarned," he said in April of 2017. "This is a new era. This is the Trump era." Just before the one hundred day mark, ICE officers arrested an unaccompanied minor with a pending asylum case in an ORR-funded youth shelter in Los Angeles on his eighteenth birthday, transferring him to adult detention. Rarely had unaccompanied minors turning eighteen been prioritized for adult detention—particularly one with a pending asylum claim and family members willing and able to serve as his sponsor.

The exact nature of future immigration enforcement remains unknown.

CHAPTER 6

On a cold, clear day in February 2014, Mr. David, a math teacher, poked his head into my office.

"We have a problem," he said, motioning to two students who stood behind him. Their heads were hung in matching silhouette, their fists gripped around their backpack straps. Despite the brisk weather, the boys sported only black T-shirts and slim fit blue jeans, stylishly worn at the knees, and red and black Nikes.

"Come on in, gentlemen," David said, urging them into the stuffy shoebox of an office that I shared with the dean of discipline. The boys reluctantly obliged, stepping in from the rush of students passing between classes. A group of girls were chatting emphatically in Arabic at a library table outside my door. David pulled it shut.

"These two missed their court date," he said. He repeated it in Spanish. The two boys nodded, and I noticed they were identical.

"Twins," I said in Spanish, dumbly. They nodded again, still looking at the floor as if studying their sneakers. Given that these young men had had a scheduled court date, I suspected they were unaccompanied minors.

The twins introduced themselves: Ernesto and Raúl Flores from La Colonia, El Salvador, they proclaimed somberly, as if I, seated behind my cramped and cluttered desk, were the judge to whom they hadn't reported that day in San Francisco.

"Don't worry," I said in Spanish, though they had every reason to.

The bell rang, and David, who had a class to teach, reopened the door. "I'll let you take it from here," he said.

The twins stood in my office like living statues of fear: fixed eyes, sharp cheekbones, lips strained beneath identical flat noses. While Raúl laughed nervously from time to time as we spoke about their situation, Ernesto's jaw remained clenched, his gaze severe. In all probability, after failing to show up in court that day, they had been ordered deported in absentia. Given limited staffing and the fact that kids like the Flores brothers would be low on the priority list, no immigration authorities were likely to come looking for them, but it wasn't uncommon for people to be swept up in immigration raids or to be taken into custody by agents looking for someone else. Though Oakland was, as of 2007, a "sanctuary city"—a loose, legally undefined term meaning that, in practice, their police force generally as a matter of public safety did not hand over people they arrested or information about those people to the immigration authorities—this was not an explicit law, and there were numerous cases in Oakland and elsewhere in which contact with law enforcement had led to deportation. If the twins were picked up for anything—smoking cigarettes in the park during school hours, jaywalking, trying to buy booze—it was not out of the realm of possibility that they would end up in the hands of the immigration authorities.

"Why did you leave El Salvador?" I asked.

They shook their heads. "*Problemas,*" said Ernesto. He paused, then: "We can't go back."

Raúl shook his head again. "No," he said. "We can't go back."

They needed a lawyer, and fast.

AS the legal team who visited Southwest Key had explained to the twins, the U.S. government provided no free lawyers in immigration court. They'd have to either find a pro bono option or pay. The latter seemed a nonstarter; they had no money—far less than none, considering the debt. And they were already asking so much of Wilber. Plus, they'd been cautioned about fake attorneys, often called *notarios,* who promise help with immigration cases, then abscond with their clients' money.

Though immigrants could apply for protective status, the process was exceedingly complicated and success rare. In a 2014 study of more than a hundred thousand unaccompanied minor cases, Syracuse University found that 90 percent of children without an attorney were deported, compared to only 47 percent of those who secured legal representation. In 2015, 69 percent of the 31,158 unaccompanied minors studied had lawyers. Less than 4 percent of those minors had been ordered deported, compared to 64 percent of those who did not have lawyers. According to Kids in Need of Defense, a child without a lawyer was five times more likely to be deported. If a child went before a judge without a lawyer, the judge had no responsibility to treat the case differently: either the child won immigration relief through the paperwork-intensive official process, or he or she did not.

An American Bar Association report showed that children were over three times more likely to even show up in court if they had representation. If the Flores twins had had an attorney, after all, he or she would have helped them find the court that day.

Very few nonprofits in the Bay Area were taking on these cases, as I knew from experience. Those who might were so bogged down with pro bono work that squeezing on their caseload was unlikely. Though the majority of the unaccompanied minor students at OIHS were living with a parent who had come to the United States and had later sent for his or her children, an increasing number were being released from the shelters to live with uncles, cousins, older brothers (like Wilber Jr.), and even family friends—sometimes people they'd never met. All of the dozens of sponsors I spoke with needed help finding attorneys. That winter I had called legal agency after legal agency, navigating phone trees and leaving messages that were never returned, listening to crackly recordings that listed drop-in hours, and poring over websites in hopes of getting a rare audience with a pro bono lawyer.

The Flores twins, with their duplicate faces of fear, were now at the top of my growing list of students in need. I was worried about them. I wrote friends who were attorneys and immigration experts, friends of friends, even an old love interest who had once, I remembered, tried a pro bono asylum case.

At the time, only one local organization, San Francisco–based Legal Services for Children (LSC), specialized in supporting unaccompanied minors, providing not only legal representation but also social work support, counseling, and case management. Getting LSC's support would be like winning the unaccompanied minor lottery, but due to capacity, its caseload was limited. In the past, LSC had taken a few students from our school but not many.

A few weeks before I met the twins, I'd begun bringing students weekly to LSC's drop-in hours. The students would anxiously wait in line, and then a paralegal would mine the details of their case to see if they'd be able to represent them. Bringing the twins seemed worth a try—really, the only immediate option we had.

There was no guarantee LSC would take their case—I made sure the twins knew that. I checked my messages again and again in hopes of having a plan B if LSC turned us away, but no one had called me back.

My old love interest, however, did reply. "Sounds like they need an actual, good attorney," he wrote. What they needed was any attorney at all.

A week after we met, the Flores twins and I boarded a BART train for San Francisco, hoping for a miracle. I could see they were nervous as we settled into facing vinyl seats. Ernesto pulled the cords of his close-fit green sweatshirt, tightening then loosening the hood around his neck. The only other time they'd been to San Francisco was their failed journey to court.

We lurched west beneath downtown Oakland and then rolled out of the tunnel to the final East Bay stop, the sun-spangled San Francisco skyline coming into view ahead. The twins whispered unintelligibly. I often couldn't understand them when they talked to each other—they spoke fast, in a rural accent to which I wasn't accustomed—but this time it felt as though they were using another language entirely.

When I asked what a word they'd used meant, Raúl laughed. "That's our language," he explained. I looked to Ernesto for confirmation and he nodded, smiling for the first time all day.

"Well, some of our brothers and sisters can understand it," Raúl confessed. ("They just say things backward," Wilber later explained.)

We sloped down into another tunnel, and the train screamed against the rails. The twins clutched their backpacks until we slid to a stop on the other side of the bay.

The Legal Services for Children office was packed with immigrants, old and young—there was no place for the twins to sit but on the floor. It's a high-stakes venue, the pro bono waiting room, and the twins could feel a familiar energy of hope and anxiety in the air. They waited for their names to be called, then disappeared into a small room where a paralegal took down the details of their situation.

AFTER World War II, when millions of refugees fled Nazi Europe, the international community came together to determine, essentially, what to do next time. They drafted the 1951 Refugee Convention, defining a refugee as someone who has fled his or her country owing to past persecution or a well-founded fear of persecution based on race, religion, nationality, political opinion, or membership in a particular social group. In 1980 the United States incorporated the international definition of a refugee into domestic law. Asylum status is nearly identical to refugee status, but to win asylum in the United States one must apply from within U.S. borders.

Now El Salvador, Guatemala, and Honduras were all, due to the curse of pervasive gang activity, among the murder centers of the world. The trouble was it was difficult for someone from the Northern Triangle to prove that he feared persecution based on one of the five grounds for protection—that is, that he was, due to a socially recognized (or visible, as the law put it) aspect of his identity, at a heightened risk from the violence besieging them all. Uncle Agustín was after them, as Raúl's experience in Guatemala had proved well enough. But could they demonstrate that this qualified them for asylum?

In 2008 the U.S. Department of Justice's Board of Immigration Appeals (BIA) ruled that a young man from Honduras, whose two brothers had been murdered by a gang and whose family had received subsequent threats, was not eligible for asylum because "young persons who are perceived to be affiliated with gangs (as perceived by the government and/or the general public)" and "persons resistant to gang membership (refusing to join when recruited)" did not, in fact, constitute an eligible social group under asylum law. In February 2014 the BIA ruled against two other gang-related asylum cases, further shoring up precedent.

It didn't help that many migrants from these same countries were still coming to the United States in search of economic opportunity, a motive for which there is no legal protection. It also wouldn't help Ernesto's case that he had been planning to come to the United States even before he began fearing for his life. The complex stew of motivations that propelled kids like them to emigrate—poverty, a quest for opportunity, a desire to reunite with family, and a well-founded fear of violence—was difficult to distill. It was easy enough for a court to deem that what brought a kid north was more pull than push, even when that was not, in fact, the case.

So even if the twins did find an asylum lawyer (LSC didn't take on asylum cases), they didn't necessarily have a good case.

There were other protective statuses they might apply for. As the LSC paralegals explained, unaccompanied minors could qualify for U visas, for people who'd been victims of a violent crime in the United States and were willing to cooperate with the police, or T visas, for people who had been trafficked for labor or sexual exploitation. Neither applied to the twins. A more common option was Special Immigrant Juvenile Status (SIJS), which provides protection to immigrant minors who have been abused, abandoned, or neglected by parents. But that wasn't why the twins had decided to leave home.

As they spoke to the paralegal, these details overwhelmed the twins; it was so hard to keep track of their options. But they grasped one thing clearly, which was perhaps worst of all: if they did apply for asylum, they would have to do so separately.

"You probably have a better asylum case than a Special Immigrant Juvenile case," the paralegal told Ernesto. The catch was that Raúl didn't have much of a case at all.

Ernesto balked. He shook his head. "But . . ." he said, trailing off.

They had the same problem and the same face—shouldn't they have the same fate? But Ernesto had been targeted for violence directly, whereas Raúl was at risk only because he looked like the kid with the already shaky asylum claim. He might win, but Raúl likely wouldn't.

The twins had learned about Castor and Pollux, the Gemini twins who occupied a constellation that they had unknowingly stared up at so many nights back home. In ancient Greek myth, Castor and Pollux got into a feud with their cousins—over girls and a stolen herd of cattle. Their cousins, seeking vengeance, drove a spear into Castor's heart. Pollux tried to fight them off, but he could do little on his own. Once Castor was dead, Pollux prepared to die, too, to follow his brother to the underworld. But at the last moment, Zeus stepped in and offered Pollux a choice: he could either spend the rest of his days on Mount Olympus among the gods, or give half of his immortality to his twin. Pollux chose the option that would be entirely obvious to Raúl and Ernesto: split the immortality, just as they split everything else. Castor and Pollux were reunited, spending half of each year on Mount Olympus and the other half in the underworld.

Of course Ernesto wouldn't let Raúl get left behind. It was his fault that he'd had to leave in the first place

Regardless, as the paralegal explained, the only cases her agency took on were SIJS visas. She told them that they'd review their case and be in touch.

RAÚL and Ernesto walked out of the office and through the piss-smelling streets of Civic Center toward the BART station. They didn't talk about what they'd just learned about their chances—what was there to say? At the station, they boarded the escalator, a foreign contraption with wobbly steps, and took the train home by themselves. It would have been fastest to get off in East Oakland, but instead they retraced their earlier route exactly, traveling to the station in North Oakland near OIHS and then taking their usual forty-five-minute start-stop bus ride home. The boys lost their bearings easily, and the prospect of being adrift in this city, still so new to them, was terrifying.

At home, they got on the old, chugging computer they'd got for free from a local nonprofit and opened their new Facebook accounts. They'd decided to give up their old accounts entirely. Raúl had convinced his brother that they needed to make their new profiles private so they could monitor who followed them, and pick and choose their friends from here on out. They added only a few people from their old accounts, then set to work friending their new classmates.

Ernesto posted a mirror selfie of the two of them shirtless, flexing their pecs, then another of them in their new clothes back in San Jose, still skinny from the desert and the terrible shelter food. Raúl reposted them on his own profile. One day he'd post photos of himself in a suit, or driving a car, to show off what he'd become once he became it.

New life, new profiles. Like Castor and Pollux, they would stick together. And they, too, needed a miracle—a lawyer.

NOW that they'd been in the Hillside apartment for a few months, the living arrangement was no longer bolstered by politeness or novelty, and tensions stewed. Seven people—the twins, Wilber, Gabby, Rosalinda, and Rosalinda's two younger kids—were sharing too small a space. Rosalinda resented any mess the boys left behind, while they fought with Gabby over shower time. Increasingly the boys holed up in their own room, coming out only to fix food, which they mostly ate sitting on their beds, leaving stacked, soiled dishes on the carpet for days on end. They subsisted on pasta, the occasional eggs, and cornflakes, and they ate Takis, spicy chips that they bought at the corner store, until their lips and mouths turned red with the spicy powder flavoring. No more family meals.

The twins hardly saw Wilber, whose two-and-a-half-hour commute wore on him, as did the long hours under the sun shoveling dirt and trimming hedges. When he got home, he would lock himself in his room with Gabby, and on the nights when Gabby had class, he would drive her there and pick her up afterward. He almost never drove the twins anywhere, they noted.

When Ernesto did see Wilber, they felt he snapped at him for something small or rolled his eyes. Ernesto blamed Wilber for missing their court date, and as tensions grew in the house, the accusation deepened and bloomed. Ernesto felt Wilber didn't understand how bad it had got back home, focused as he was on Gabby and on his new life here in California. When Wilber made a joke at his expense, or even asked him to take out the trash or help with Silvia, he stormed out. "Ernesto!" Raúl pleaded each time Ernesto picked a fight. Wilber was doing his best, if you asked Raúl. "Calm down." Getting mad at the one person they had would just make matters worse.

Sometimes Wilber would go into their room to look for something—his phone, José's computer, a missing sweatshirt, Nicky the Chihuahua. Ernesto had a sixth sense for when his stuff had been rifled through.

"Don't touch my stuff!" he yelled one night.

"I bought all your fucking stuff!" Wilber yelled back.

A fight with Wilber always ended with a fight between the twins, who then slept as far away from each other as possible. Nicky cuddled under Ernesto's arm like a pillow.

When Raúl was angry about something other than what Ernesto had done, you wouldn't know it. He'd retreat into himself, quiet for the rest of the evening.

As the days of waiting to hear from the lawyers wore on, their new Facebook pages took a turn toward the dark side.

Shit me.

Raúl posted this in English next to three wailing emojis.

Alongside an emoji of a gun and a knife, Ernesto wrote:

Fuck this life.

He exchanged the giddy photo of Raúl and him in in the mirror with a stock photo of a white rose, dripping crimson with blood.

THE week after they went to Legal Services for Children, Ernesto was sent to my office with a note.

"Ernesto keeps motioning to his head with his fingers like a gun saying he wants to kill himself," it read.

He sat before me, scowling and jittery one moment, blank-faced the next. He wouldn't talk. "I'm not going to tell you what's wrong," he said. "So don't try."

"Is it the court case?" I asked. Things at home? Something with his family back in El Salvador?

"Everything," he said. "But something else, too. But I'm not going to talk about it." He told me only that it was eating at him, infecting his sleep and now his waking hours, too. He said he'd been having flashbacks more and more often, sometimes in the middle of class. "It's like a dream, but I'm not sleeping."

"I haven't told anyone about it," he said. Except his old counselor from the shelter, he qualified. He lifted his head to look me in the eyes. "Not even Raúl knows." He said it like a threat.

Of the impulse to hurt himself, he admitted, "I don't really want to." Not wanting to speak anymore, he picked up a legal pad, wrote something, and handed it to me: "Sometimes it just seems like it might happen, like I'm scared that I might do something to myself even if I don't want to."

Then he told me he wanted to go back to class.

He promised he wouldn't do anything to harm himself that night and, as is standard practice in many schools, signed a "safety contract." He swore he felt a little better. But under no uncertain terms, he said, would he be interested in talking to another counselor about any of this.

"Are you sure?" I said. "I think it would be really good for you to have someone to talk to."

But he wasn't interested in opening up again. "Can I go back to class?" he repeated.

"It's court," Raúl said later that day, when the principal and I told him we were concerned about his brother. "He's just stressed about court. I'm sure that's it."

BACK in La Colonia, things seemed to have calmed down with Uncle Agustín, but Maricela went out of her way to avoid him and her cousins in town. The vacuum left by Raúl and Ernesto left more responsibility in the fields, now, to Ricardo and the younger boys, and they were reaching the end of their stores from the fall's harvest. Spring's had not yet come, and Maricela worried that even when it did, the yield would be low.

Maricela and Ricardo had not been on speaking terms since her pregnancy, as he still blamed her for bringing another problem into their house. Their mutual silence was no small feat in the three-room residence. It was a stupid feud, anyway; Lupita was now almost two, and it was Ricardo, after all, who'd brought Sebastian around.

These days Ricardo spent ever more time out of the house, and he would come home reeking of booze, which caused her parents to fret more than was good for their health. Maricela worried he was flirting with joining a gang—or maybe he'd joined one already? She heard he was hanging out in the town where they'd busted the gang ring the year before, that he was running with shady guys. Maybe he was just protecting himself by staying on good terms with the gangsters, but it seemed foolish to mess around with any of it, given what had happened to their little brothers. *Go ahead,* she thought, *throw your life away.*

Maricela's little sisters, Marina, twelve, and Lucia, fourteen, were good kids and took loving care of Lupita, but Maricela couldn't talk to them about real stuff—they were still just girls. The siblings she'd been the closest to in age and in temperament, Wilber, Raúl, and Ernesto, were gone.

Not to mention Lupita's father and, in the past couple of years, most of her girlfriends. They had all left for the United States. *Everyone leaves,* she thought. *Everyone.* She knew the United States wasn't the land of milk and honey—she wasn't dumb, and she'd heard as much from

Sebastian, who had settled into his life in Houston and sent a nominal monthly sum for Lupita. But here she was, freighted with the debt, with the baby, and with her aging parents. Only twenty years old and already trapped.

Maricela often wondered what American streets looked like. Was it true that Converse in the United States had different, softer soles? How much did jeans cost there? How much did a *pupusa* cost in California? Was it true there were no street vendors in the United States, and that prostitution was illegal but in many places people sold their bodies anyway? She asked over and over for Sebastian to send her a pair of Converse; he promised but never did.

She missed going to school, when her days had had some outward purpose and direction. Her whole world was now in the house: all she did was help her mom with chores and take care of her daughter, who was attached to her—clutching her legs, latching onto her breasts—like a snail on stone.

One afternoon during the weeks while the twins were searching for a lawyer, Maricela turned on a popular TV program. During one segment people sent messages along with their phone numbers to be displayed on a ticker tape at the bottom of the screen, like a live OkCupid or Tinder. The show was popular especially among lower-income Salvadorans. Maricela, changing her name "just for safety," composed a message.

> Hello, my name is Daniella, I'm a single mother, twenty years old, looking for friendship from someone my age. Call me if you're interested in getting to know me.

She texted it to the program. For the next few days she watched the show religiously, holding her breath every time they read a new message. Finally, there it was, her message on the screen. Her chest felt like it might break open. Within minutes a text message popped up on her phone. All afternoon more texts pinged in, ten of them, then fifteen, then twenty. She read them all, too bashful to respond. Some of them were vulgar and explicit, propositioning her for sex. Even so, just getting so many messages was a comfort.

The next day another message came in: "Hi. I'd like to be your friend." Sweet and straightforward, no innuendo. Some internal instinct told her to respond to this one. She wrote back: "Okay. What's your name?" Cesar. They exchanged Facebook messages. Cesar was twenty-five and lived in a town on the outskirts of San Salvador, where he worked in a factory. After a few days, they began to talk on the phone. The first time she heard his voice, her heart hopscotched into her throat. He sounded like a really, truly good man.

By the second week, they were talking almost every day. They got to know each other—what they liked and disliked, what they wanted for their futures, their longings and disappointments and betrayals. She told him how her baby's father had run off to the United States the very day his daughter, whom he'd probably never meet, was born. He confided in her how sad he was that he'd never have a kid of his own, due to a childhood accident that had sterilized him. That didn't bother her. He began to say he wanted to be with her and to meet her daughter. He felt like he could be in love with her and would take her daughter as his own.

The messages thrilled her. For two months, she woke up each morning and looked at her phone, planning her day around when she could talk to Cesar. She used up money on airtime, but it was worth it. The mystery and yet the certainty of him was alluring—someone right here in El Salvador who wanted to be with her, someone not so far away.

"My real name is not Daniella," she texted him one night. "It's Maricela."

"Beautiful name," Cesar said. He wasn't even mad that she'd lied.

"You're a good mother," he told her once. Not that he could really know, but she had rarely been acknowledged for doing anything right.

TWO weeks after our trip to San Francisco, the twins and I still hadn't heard from Legal Services for Children, so I inquired about their case. The reply came almost immediately. "Unfortunately," their paralegal wrote, "due to capacity issues, we won't be able to take the Flores brothers' case at this time."

She suggested we call Amy Allen, a private attorney whom LSC highly recommended. I did and left a message. When my phone rang later that day, Ernesto was sitting in my office. He had got in trouble for throwing pens across the room in history class. He was calmer now than he had been last week, and though he was still stressed, he said he wasn't thinking of harming himself anymore. When he felt upset, he said, it helped to throw things.

I answered my phone, then covered the receiver. "It's the lawyer!" I whispered. Ernesto tapped his foot anxiously, unable to understand anything I was saying.

Amy Allen spoke in a cheerful voice suffused with professionalism. Like LSC, she took only SIJS cases, not asylum cases, but said she'd be happy to talk to the twins. "I'd love to help however I can," she said. Unfortunately, she didn't work pro bono.

My neck stiffened. Ernesto looked at me worriedly, so I managed a smile as Amy explained that she worked entirely on her own, and so, though she would prefer to donate her services, she had to charge. I let out a tired sigh. The price she quoted was likely impossible, though it was a fraction of what many other attorneys charged for the same service. It was somehow more demoralizing than if the amount had been exorbitant. I told her I'd talk it over with the boys, and we hung up.

I called Raúl into my office, and the twins settled into the small, stiff-backed chairs, shoulders touching.

"She can probably take your case," I said, "but it would cost twelve hundred dollars—each." They looked at each other, then away. Raúl dropped his head between his legs and began rocking from side to side.

Ernesto, stiff-jawed, stared fixedly into the middle distance. "Twenty-four hundred dollars is a lot," he said, laughing caustically, "but nothing like what we owe at home." What was another shovelful of money heaped onto the pile of debt?

But they had no money. They'd have to talk it over with Wilber.

After school they lingered by the bus stop and smoked cigarettes. Newport was their brand of choice—they still liked the minty feeling down their throats, a reminder of the old, untarnished days by the river in La Colonia. Ernesto carried the pack. They saved up for them from the pocket money Wilber gave them, and the Arab guy from the corner store sold to them without asking for ID. It had surprised the boys to learn that there was a minimum age for purchasing cigarettes here.

Back at Hillside, they mustered up the guts to talk to Wilber. When they told him how much the lawyer would cost, he was silent, as if doing the math in his mind.

"I don't have that kind of money," he said.

"I know," the twins both said. A long pause.

"Do they accept payment plans?" Wilber asked.

The next day the boys marched into my office. Ernesto was scarcely across the threshold when the words came out of his mouth: "Does the lawyer accept payment plans?" Yes, she did. She'd accept two hundred dollars a month from them, so they could pay off the debt over the course of a year. Emboldened, they said they'd talk it over with Wilber again.

But now they were afraid to ask him. They knew he was struggling to support just their most basic needs—even his phone bill had gone unpaid for two weeks. And they'd already asked him for so much.

As Rosalinda prepared dinner that night, she saw that they were discussing something serious and asked what was wrong. Whether out of a lack of people to confide in, or because of the maternal concern she exuded, they told her. They could get a job to pay for the lawyer, they said, but then they'd have to quit school—and that would look bad to the judge. Plus, how would they make a good life for themselves without English, without an education? And they were starting to like school, where, for the first time in their lives, they weren't dogged by bullies or false friends.

As Rosalinda prepared dinner, she looked at the boys: so young, with a mom so far away. "How much does it cost?" she asked.

They told her. She was silent for a bit, then said, "I can help you for a couple of months."

Raúl shook his head but said nothing, caught in a vortex of glee and shame.

"We'll pay you back," Ernesto said. "We'll pay everything back."

"Okay," Rosalinda said. "Don't worry about that now." The boys came in the next day and told me: *la suegra,* the mother-in-law, was going to help out.

A few nights later Gabby told Wilber about the agreement. "Isn't that sweet?" she said.

Wilber's face flushed. The twins had asked Rosalinda? He didn't want to look like a deadbeat to Gabby's family, whom he was still only getting to know. As it was, he had enough of a complex about not having papers and speaking so little English.

He stormed into the twins' room. "Rosalinda is not helping you with your lawyer," he said.

"What the fuck?" said Ernesto.

"I am your brother, I am in charge—you ask me."

"We have to get help from wherever we can," Ernesto spat back. Wilber was treating them like beggars, like the worst of their "friends" back home.

"Seriously? Look at all this!" said Wilber, pointing around the disheveled boy den, with soda cans and crumpled clothes everywhere. The beds, the TV, the clothes, the entire bedroom—he paid for all of it.

Raúl sat on the edge of the bed, silent.

Wilber slammed the door, and they heard the car pull out of the driveway. Ernesto punched the mattress hard, and Raúl closed his eyes and dropped his head into his hands. Ernesto breathed heavily. Raúl opened the door and called for Nicky, who jumped onto the bed and into Ernesto's lap.

The next day Wilber agreed to help them with the lawyer fees, at least for now. He told them they'd have to get jobs, which was fine with them. They'd have to put off sending money to El Salvador a little longer. They didn't tell their parents or Maricela about the new debt they were about to incur.

CESAR lived an hour and a half by bus from La Colonia. Maricela searched Google for images of his town and imagined what he looked like in person. She thought over the things he'd said to her that day as she cooked dinner and bathed Lupita. She lay in bed dreaming with her daughter at her side, the breathing of her little sisters an arrhythmic choir.

But one day soon thereafter she woke up feeling anxious. "I'm tired of this," she wrote to Cesar. The luster of their situation had worn to suspicion. "Why can't we just meet?"

He suggested a plan for that very day. She told her parents she was going to meet a friend and left Lupita at home.

He told her to meet him outside the cathedral in his hometown, a city of about 150,000 just beyond San Salvador, where he lived. He'd be wearing a brown shirt, he texted. "You'll recognize me from my photos." As if he knew how many hundreds of times she'd swiped through his collection of selfies.

It took three buses to get from her house to his town. She stepped off the final bus into the boiling scrum of the town's main drag and walked toward the town square, asking directions for the cathedral. Far from home, without Lupita, and about to meet the person she wanted so dearly to be the man of her dreams, she felt as if she'd swallowed a swarm of bees.

She found the cathedral, a sturdy, white edifice with two towering spires, a building so clean and white it practically gleamed. And there he was, brown shirted, waiting for her. He looked just like his pictures—broad chested, a smooth complexion, kind eyes—and even better, because here he was in real life. They hugged politely, which sent electricity down her spine, and he took her hand.

"Want to get some coffee?" he asked.

"Whatever you want to do," she said.

"Do you want some?"

"Okay."

They were practically silent at the café. She twirled a spoon into her cup, keeping her eyes on the plastic floral tablecloth. She wanted simultaneously to glow and to vanish. She adjusted her shirt and smoothed the flyaways from her ponytail.

"It's really good to see you in person," he said. She smiled.

After coffee, he said, "Come to my house. I want you to meet my parents."

The hopscotch of her heart. *Meet his family?* "Okay," she said.

As they walked to his house, she relaxed a bit. She could count the number of times she'd sat down at a restaurant on one hand, but visiting a home was something she knew how to do.

"Mom, Dad," Cesar said, "this is my friend, Maricela."

When she got home that evening, after a long and blissful afternoon on the couch sitting as near as she could to Cesar without touching him, she gave her parents the news: she had a boyfriend.

"You should have him come here to meet us," Esperanza replied.

When he'd walked her to the bus, he pulled her into a side street and kissed her, running his hands along her shoulders and arms. She fell asleep that night imagining their life together. She'd move out of La Colonia and have a family of her own.

ATTORNEY Amy Allen rented a space in the Women's Building of San Francisco, a hulking Victorian covered top to bottom in kinetic murals depicting powerful women from around the world. It commands the corner of Eighteenth and Lapidge streets in the Mission district, a rapidly gentrifying area of the city that was once primarily Latino.

The twins and I left school early on a Friday afternoon to be on time for their first appointment. Walking into the lobby, we spotted Amy, who was in her early thirties, dressed in a crisp black suit dress. She offered up an affectionate smile that instantly put the boys at ease.

"You must be Ernesto and Raúl!" she said. "*¡Buenas tardes!*" She shook their hands and led them upstairs to her office, a space with a desk and some children's toys, as it was also sometimes used as a day care center. Separately and then together, she asked Raúl and Ernesto about everything they'd been through. They talked about their home in El Salvador, about the time they stole corn for the bike and got beaten for it, about their siblings, their school, what happened to Raúl on the way north from Guatemala. Ernesto was quiet about his own trip north.

"I felt sick when I heard what had happened to him," Ernesto said. He started to tear up. "It was my fault." She offered a box of tissues.

"How do you like the United States?" she asked them.

"It's safe here," Ernesto said, "but I miss my family."

"It's better here," Raúl said. Sometimes, they admitted, they still worried that someone from El Salvador could come and track them down. It was unlikely, but it kept them up some nights.

After over an hour and a half of interviews, Amy shared her thoughts. They could qualify for Special Immigrant Juvenile Status, but didn't have the strongest case. What their uncle and cousins had done to them was terrible, and they could still be in danger, she agreed, but SIJS was for minors who had been abused, abandoned, or neglected by their parents. Wilber had beaten them growing up—a fact that was hard for them to admit to this stranger in a dim-lit room—and the family had been unable to protect them from the danger from their uncle, both of which could be deemed qualifying factors for an SIJS visa. She didn't think their case was impossible, "but there would be no guarantees." They could try to find an asylum attorney, but it was hard to get one for free; very few attorneys were taking these cases at the time, and private attorneys generally cost many thousands of dollars.

"Talk to your brother, and take some time to think it over," she said.

They retreated to the lobby. The intake appointment cost fifty dollars, for which Raúl had shyly asked Wilber. Raúl drew three crumpled bills from his jeans pocket. As he fumbled with the cash and Amy drew up a receipt, Ernesto leaned against the spiraling iron banister, hands stuffed down into his pockets, staring at the empty floor.

Amy promised to call them next week. As they walked out of the Women's Building, they were quiet.

The twins had one more thing to do that day, which was to buy a phone—not like the clock and music phone that they already had, but one that could actually make a phone call. They'd wanted a phone since they first got here, but now it felt like a true priority, not least to use to follow up with Amy. Wilber had agreed. At a Walgreens they found a plastic-encased faux BlackBerry with an orange sticker reading "29.99," including minutes. They paid and tore open the plastic to test it out; it worked.

They exited back into San Francisco. The fog had rolled in, and they crossed their arms to keep from shivering. They would once again take the BART home, a prospect that no longer frightened them. "If we can't win the case . . ." Ernesto said, fiddling with the new phone.

Raúl shook his head as the long mechanical staircase sucked them back underground.

FOR a judge to order that it is in a child's best interest to stay in the United States, there needs to be a guardian to take the child on. If the twins decided to hire Amy, they'd need Wilber to sign on as their court-appointed guardian. They'd also have to get paperwork, signed by their parents in El Salvador and sent back to Oakland, in which they agreed to relinquish their guardianship—a strange technicality, given that in the case of SIJS, parents were also being accused of being subpar care-givers. Also, Amy had explained, if they won SIJ status, they could never apply for their parents to join them in the United States. This attempt to win immigration status would mean committing to separation from their family (though if they won and got their green cards, they could apply for passports to visit—if, that is, it was ever safe). And all this would have to be decided against the ticking clock of their eighteenth birthday, less than two months away.

Wilber was the decider, and he asked for my advice.

I had late meetings the day we planned to talk, so the twins stayed after school to hitch a ride home with me. When the three of us pulled up to their apartment complex, an off-white block building hoisted up on posts, the parking space where Wilber's car should have been was empty.

"¡Mi hermano no está!" Ernesto said angrily. He got out of the car and kicked the curb.

"My brother's not here!" Raúl repeated.

We walked along the side of the building to the back courtyard, a narrow, gravel-filled patch surrounded by chain link. A magnolia tree, overhanging from the neighboring yard, was just beginning to bloom its fleshy petals.

The twins didn't have a key—they'd never been given one—so we were locked out. After ten minutes of intermittent banging on the door, it opened, and Rosalinda, who was talking on the phone, beckoned us in.

"Hi!" she said, covering the receiver and holding the door open before disappearing back into the kitchen. Nicky came bounding up to our feet, jumping at my skirt and running frenetic circles around the twins.

When Wilber showed up about forty minutes later, he was apologetic. "Oh, hi," he said, shaking my hand. We'd met in person only once before, though we'd spoken on the phone a few times. He surveyed the room: Rosalinda in the kitchen, the twins on the sofa with the dog.

"Want to talk outside?" he said. It was a nice night, and Wilber pulled two swiveling chairs beneath their window and asked me to sit down as though inviting me into his office. There, in the lawn chairs, distant sirens sounding and the stars faint above the city's ambient light, we reviewed the conundrum: the twins had a trusted, low-fee lawyer willing to take their case, but she did cost money, and the status she could help them apply for was something of a long shot—or at the very least, not a sure bet. On the other hand, they could apply for asylum, but we hadn't found any lawyer willing to take their case for free or, for that matter, at all. And if we missed their eighteenth birthday, the first option—Special Immigrant Juvenile Status—would be off the table.

"What do *you* think?" he asked.

I had to admit I really didn't know.

"I can help with the lawyer's fees. If she accepts a payment plan, I can help pay it, and they can pay me back," he said.

I reminded him that there was no guarantee they'd win.

He nodded. "But it seems like the only chance, right?" he said.

"As far as I know."

"So."

"You want to give it a try?"

"What else can we do?" he said.

We sat for a while in the quiet. I told him I admired how hard he was trying to support the boys.

"I worry about them," he said.

"Me, too," I said. "Especially Ernesto."

"Yeah," he said. "He has bad dreams sometimes. He wakes the whole house up screaming." He paused. "The desert—it's bad."

"Have you talked to them about what happened?"

"A little," he said. "But I know how it is. They'll just cry—and I really hate to see them cry."

I had another question for Wilber, one that had been nagging at me since the twins first told me about why they'd left El Salvador. "The boys said they had to leave because their uncle wanted to kill them. Is that really true?" It seemed outlandish to me.

"Yeah," he said in English. "That's what happened."

"And the tree? He was that mad over a tree?"

Just then their neighbor, an African American woman in her early twenties wearing slippers and short shorts, walked past us on the gravel, carrying a trash bag. Wilber followed her slow walk with his eyes, then turned back to me.

"The thing is," he said, "that's how it is in El Salvador." He picked up a pebble. "There they'll kill you just for doing this"—and by way of demonstration, he pitched the pebble across the lot. We watched it rattle over the other rocks and come to a stop, lost among the rest. The neighbor walked by again and he nodded her way.

"That's how it is in El Salvador," he repeated. "And that's why they're here."

I thanked him and said goodnight, then poked my head inside the door to tell the twins I'd see them in the morning.

They shot up out of their seats. "We'll walk you to the car," Raúl offered.

"What did Wilber say?" they asked when we were out of earshot of the house. A homeless man sidled by us, pushing a squeaking shopping cart down the empty street.

"He said it was worth a try."

The block outside San Salvador's Policía Nacional Civil station, the federal police, is cordoned off. A yellow school bus with a shattered back window rests in the middle of the street, and officers in balaclavas stand guard in front of the station's entrance, where a crowd has gathered.

A teary woman in an apron approaches one of the officers.

"He didn't do anything!" she pleads, mascara smudged beneath her lower lids.

"*Señora,* we're just searching them," the officer replies gruffly, a machine gun gripped between both hands.

"You have to let him go, he didn't do anything, please, you have to let me see him!"

The crowd behind her begins to murmur. She takes a step toward the guard.

"*¡Señora!*" he shouts. "Please step away!" He takes a heavy pace in her direction. Her cries only build as he marches her to the block's perimeter.

"*¡Por favor!*" he shouts, and the crowd retreats a few shuffle-steps more.

Inside the station, a group of twelve or so shirtless young men kneel facing the wall as an armed guard walks back and forth behind them. Most of them look like they could be high school students. They are silent and still, hands behind their heads. The only motion in the shadowy, cement-floored garage is the pacing guard and the beads of sweat that drip down the young men's backs.

"They were using that bus to extort money from people," a police officer explains, nodding to the bus with his chin. In recent years, Salvadoran individuals and businesses, from market vendors to *pupusa* shops to hotels, have paid an estimated $756 million in *renta*—about 3 percent of the country's GDP. The increments are often small—$20, $50, $200 every two weeks—paid for protection from the very people who collect it. And still most gangsters remain small-time, barely eking out a living. ("El Salvador has been brought to its knees by an army of flies.")

These kneeling boys are evidence of a Salvadoran law called *agrupación ilícita,* or illicit congregation. It allows law enforcement to arrest anyone who looks suspicious, which often means youth dressed stylishly and hanging out together in public spaces. In the flailing war on gangs, guilt is often presumed.

These efforts are part of an Iron Fist campaign, the third incarnation in El Salvador since 2003, and a reaction, in part, to the failed truce of 2012, which began to unravel in 2014. Police patrols are on the rise, and several illicit killings of suspected gang members—extrajudicial massacres that smack of the death squad atrocities of the civil war years—have been exposed by dogged local press, who risk retribution from both the police and the gangs. A Salvadoran young person risks becoming a target on both sides of the law.

The violence has increased over the years, and the sheer number of gang members seems to be growing, too, though it's complicated to count. In 2013, a thorough but unscientific study by the Salvadoran government estimated that, including loved ones, family members, and other close associations, there were 470,000 Salvadorans—more than 7 percent of the population—with direct ties to gangs.

El Salvador has nowhere to put all the suspected criminals. In 2015 prisons reached 310 percent of intended capacity; holding cells that were meant for temporary confinement are crammed with suspects like these young men, who can spend months and even years awaiting trial.

The officer claims they haven't been arrested, yet here they are. Later in the day they will still be held in this garage—hands still behind their heads, same guard marching back and forth, same crowd outside, waiting.

CHAPTER 7

Wilber was overwhelmed.

The sponsor agreement he'd signed with the Office of Refugee Resettlement had seemed far less formal than the document he was now faced with, which outlined the responsibilities of a court-appointed guardian. He read through it again. It wasn't that the individual points seemed unreasonable. "As guardian, you are responsible for providing for food, clothing, shelter, education, and all the medical and dental needs of the child," the paperwork read. He was already more or less doing these things. "You must provide for the safety, protection, and physical and emotional growth of the child." But in Spanish legalese they felt alarmingly official. He had no papers, after all, and here he was placing himself once again on the government's radar.

"A guardian, like a parent, is liable for the harm and damages caused by the willful misconduct of a child." How could he be sure his younger brothers didn't fuck up? If they did, would he be punished or risk deportation himself? Already they were going to school late or skipping it entirely, not only to babysit Rosalinda's daughter Silvia but sometimes just to stay home and do God knew what, while he worked his long hours and shuttled back and forth along the highway, minding the speed limit.

To have a shot at Special Immigrant Juvenile Status, they had to move fast. First they'd have to file a petition in probate court arguing that going back to El Salvador was against their best interests as children—and since they were technically children only until they turned eighteen in mid-April, they'd need to file a special motion to get an expedited court date. The judge would have full discretion on whether to grant the motion, and if he or she didn't, they'd be ineligible by the time their appointment did come around. Given the time crunch, the judge woud be deciding whether to grant the guardianship and the Special Immigrant Juvenile Status on the same day.

If the probate court judge determined that the Flores twins had experienced abuse, abandonment, or neglect, they would issue something called a predicate order for SIJS, and Amy would then file an SIJS application, along with the state court's findings, with U.S. Citizenship and Immigration Services. Once the predicate order was granted, the twins could apply to become legal permanent residents—in other words, get their green cards.

But without Wilber, none of this would be possible.

Wilber spoke to Amy over the phone. Yes, she explained, his name would be entered into official government records (as it had when he'd signed on to take the twins from the shelter in Texas), but the courts had no established procedure for handing over his information to immigration officials. And though he'd be responsible for the twins, his obligation would last only until they turned eighteen.

He'd got them this far. "All right," he told the twins that night. "I'll do it." He signed the paperwork with Amy.

Still, they wondered whether he would actually go through with being their guardian. What if he was saying yes now just to seem like the good guy, because he was afraid of how saying no would look to Ms. Amy, to the school, and to his family back home? He had the power to yank away his promise, and their prospect of gaining legal status, at any time. The twins knew that until he showed up at court with them—a legal necessity—there were no guarantees.

A few days later he asked the boys for help moving in a new bed he'd picked up from a friend. Wilber and Ernesto, on opposite ends of the heavy, jiggling mattress, bickered about how to best maneuver it around the back courtyard and through the front door. Ernesto hated how Wilber snapped at his suggestions, as though he were a stupid kid. He snapped back, and soon they were shouting over the mattress, the sounds partially muffled by the foam. "Motherfucker," Wilber said in English. Ernesto knew what that word meant.

"Fuck you," he spat, also in English, though more heavily accented, and dropped the mattress on the gravel. In Spanish he called Wilber an asshole. They didn't speak for several days after that.

It rattled Raúl. "He's taking care of us," he said. "Give him a break."

"Taking care of who? He doesn't give a shit about us," Ernesto said. "He wished we never came."

Amy, meanwhile, who was working day and night to prep their case, managed to secure them a court date on April 8, three days before their birthday. This was great news—but there'd be no time to appeal if they were turned down.

WILBER signed the papers three weeks before April 8. To complete the transfer of guardianship, their parents also had to sign off. Amy and the boys somehow had to get the papers to La Colonia, where their parents had no computer and only an intermittently working phone. Mail was tricky—even if it reached the family, which could take weeks, it would be complicated and expensive to send back. Emailing a scanned copy of the paperwork would be faster (the family could go to the town's copy shop, where the proprietor could help them), but this wasn't ideal. The document would be less reliable in the eyes of the court because it would be hard to prove its origin. Fax was preferable because the transmission carried a marker of the date, time, and phone number from which the fax was sent, which would prove, at least, that the document originated in El Salvador. Amy devised a plan with the twins to email the papers to Maricela, who would print it at the copy shop, bring it to her parents to sign, and then fax it back to Amy from the shop.

The Internet and printer worked fine, but then came a hitch.

"There's no fax," Maricela reported via Facebook. La Colonia's one fax machine was on the fritz, with no prospect of being fixed soon.

The next best option was in a neighboring town, a thirty-minute bus ride away.

"I don't want her to go," Ernesto said. He knew bus travel in the area had become dangerous; even performing the short errand, he insisted, would put his sister at risk. April 8 was fast approaching, but he was vehement.

THINGS were indeed getting worse around La Colonia. The nearby town had jumped to the sixteenth most dangerous municipality in the country, with fifty-nine homicides that year out of a population of about seventy thousand, and one of the highest disappearance rates in the country. The gangs' ground troops—still mostly poor local kids—were more and more visible to those who knew to look for them, posted on the streets, tracking the movements of daily life. Small as the town was, it was easy enough for gangs to notice people who didn't belong or deviations in the townspeople's routines. Little things like going to the bank, or bigger things like boarding a bus, offered good potential for a money pickup for any profiteer who happened to be paying attention. As a resident, to deviate from routine was to put yourself at potential risk.

Maricela knew that the sooner her brothers got papers, the sooner they could start paying back the debt. And in truth, she always relished the opportunity to leave La Colonia. She was going to find the fax machine, she told Ernesto over Facebook. That was that.

She hitched a ride to the end of the serpentine road that led to the town at the foot of the hill and the crossroads with the main highway, Lupita in tow. Now almost two, Lupita was leaving the cooing baby stage and becoming a serious little girl, with a wide, flat forehead like her twin uncles' and, like Ernesto, brows that were almost perpetually furrowed. Despite living in a small, packed house—her grandparents, her six aunts and uncles, her mom, the chickens, and the dogs—she was shy around almost anyone besides her mom. Whenever Maricela left to spend the day with Cesar, even if she just walked to the door with her purse slung on her shoulder, Lupita launched herself into a paroxysm of grief, flinging herself toward her mother with wails and screeching. Her aunts and grandmother would scoop her up while Maricela hurried out the door, both guilty and irritated. She adored her daughter, but didn't she, too, need a life apart? Aside from her weekly visits to Cesar, she rarely went anywhere without her.

They rode a bus to the neighboring town without incident. Once there, she hoisted Lupita onto her hip, marched through the bustle to the copy shop, and faxed the paperwork to her brothers.

On the ride back to La Colonia, she was triumphant. She'd done something useful, she felt, and they owed her now.

Along the main road, three men boarded the bus and walked toward the back, where they drew knives from their pockets. The bus driver either didn't notice or didn't care, and drove on. "Excuse us," they said tensely, brandishing their weapons. They walked the aisles like boys carrying the alms baskets at church. The passengers knew what to do—heads down, they offered up dollar bills, phones. She knew that as long as she handed something over, nothing was likely to go wrong. Maricela held out a few dollars from her worn wallet, along with her cellphone—the one phone the family had.

The guy attending her aisle grabbed the money and the phone and noticed the gleam of her daughter's gold chain, a gift from Lupita's father in the United States. The guy looped his finger between the bracelet and the girl's soft skin and yanked. It broke against her wrist, and she began screaming. Maricela grabbed her and held her close, trying to lull her to quiet. The thieves got off the bus, and the driver shifted it into gear. They chugged up the road as if nothing had happened.

"I knew she shouldn't have gone," said Ernesto when he heard from Maricela on Facebook. "I knew something would happen." Once again, someone he cared about had suffered on account of him.

But they had the fax. They were ready to go to court.

ERNESTO'S bad dreams continued to bleed into his waking hours. Raúl could sense when an attack was coming the same way he knew it was about to rain. It was something between a seizure, a trance, and a fit of rage. Suddenly his brother would seem possessed by a demon. Raúl thought of the corpse in the desert; touch a dead person, he knew, and you could be fouled by their spirit. When Ernesto got like that, hot and rigid, it was no use trying to soothe him. Put your hand on his shoulder, and he'd buck and shake his head, jaw wired shut. What, really, was going on?

"You okay?" Raúl asked from time to time.

"Leave me alone," Ernesto would reply. Or "Mind your own business."

There was still something Ernesto wasn't telling him.

At school, we finally persuaded Ernesto to meet with a counselor, but in the small, quiet room, he refused to talk. The counselor suggested music therapy, and together they pounded the skins of two tall drums for half an hour. Ernesto's hands tingled for the rest of the day. After school he crawled into bed and slept fourteen hours straight.

After the following session, Ernesto fired his counselor. "*Brujería*," he said by way of explanation. Witchcraft.

EVER since Ernesto had started at Oakland International, he'd shown up every couple of days in the Bob Marley T-shirt Wilber had bought him—the one with Marley in profile, sucking on a joint. He'd been told multiple times not to wear it; drug-related clothing was against school policy. When Cormac, the dean of discipline, finally told him he had to change, Ernesto flipped.

"No," he said, walking away from Cormac. "No way. I'm not changing." But until he changed, he couldn't go to class. He sat in my office in protest. We showed him a stack of T-shirts we kept for this sort of occasion—he could choose any of them to wear for the day. "If you make me change my shirt, I'm going home," he threatened, dart-eyed. He stayed in my office as other students came and went, teeth clenched.

"Just change your shirt," we pleaded. We weren't taking it away from him, or telling him he couldn't wear it elsewhere—just not at school. But he wouldn't budge.

We called Raúl into the office, thinking he might be able to help.

"They want me to change my fucking shirt," Ernesto said. "It's a free country, isn't it? I can do what I want."

I went next door for a meeting in the library, hoping Raúl could calm his twin down. Every now and then through the window into my office, I caught a glimpse of Raúl holding up another T-shirt option, like a street vendor hawking the latest fashions. *What about this one? Or this one? Look how cool this one is!*

When I walked back in fifteen minutes later, the pile of shirts was gone. Raúl had put on every one, shirt over shirt over shirt, trying to make his brother laugh. The last was a big white tourist tee, the kind you'd buy at the airport or in a crappy beachfront shop, MEXICO spelled out in neon block letters balanced on the webbed hand of a sombrero-clad gecko.

"Come on, how about this one?!" he said, taking a spin. He giggled. "Really cool, this one."

"Fuck you," Ernesto mouthed silently. "I will fucking kill you." He slapped a tight fist into his palm. Raúl giggled some more.

Ernesto stood and stormed out of my office, out of the library, and through the school's front door.

"*Fucking!*" he shouted on his way to the street.

He waited for the bus, brooding, and took it all the way back to East Oakland. He returned to school with only an hour left in the day, wearing a sweatshirt. When the last bell rang, he walked outside and pulled off the sweatshirt, to reveal the Bob Marley shirt. He lit a cigarette.

"Do you think evil spirits are real?" Raúl asked me several days later, a rare moment when it was just him and me. Then he answered his own question: "I know for sure that they are."

Then: "Do you think I'm crazy?" he added.

MOST of the boys' friends at school were also unaccompanied minors. Alfredo, from Guatemala, was big and muscly, with slick-backed hair, a cowboy belt, and silver rings on his fingers. He had been nabbed by *la migra* in Texas along with his cousin Brenda, who was short and demure, with thick curly hair, apple cheeks, and a full smile that showed three silver-capped teeth. She took to following the twins around campus like a shy fan. The twins feigned lack of interest, but when she wasn't around, they sought her out and flirted with little jabs about someone's accent, or their funny Spanish sayings, suggestive pushes of the shoulder.

As in El Salvador, Ernesto fell into socializing easily, and when he was around other people, his attacks stayed at bay. They'd go watch soccer games at their friend Douglas's house, also an unaccompanied minor—he lived near Fruitvale with his uncle, who was strict but rarely around. Sometimes at Alfredo's, his mom would make them food, and they'd play video games or watch Spanish movies on his couch. When they could, which wasn't often, they'd get ahold of alcohol, passing the bottle around. One day their small crew took the bus to the woods to take a walk that devolved into a boyish sword battle with sticks. They hit each other hard, as if playing the parts of ancient warriors. Ernesto videoed it, the phone camera shaking with his laughter.

Ernesto controlled the cellphone, making plans that Raúl was free to join or not. Raúl always went along, cautiously—he had learned the hard way that friends often came with a price. His new classmates seemed to be good people, but you never could tell. A few class clowns encouraged him to mess with their English teacher by throwing pencils; he was the one caught in the act and sent to the main office. He was so repentant and ashamed we wondered if he hadn't done something more serious.

"I need to choose better friends," he proclaimed that day.

Ernesto secured himself a girlfriend from another school, named Marie. They met at a park near Hillside where he and Raúl sometimes went to smoke. She was only fifteen, a bit chubby, with long, straight hair and a tea-stain birthmark that spread from her lower eyelid to above her brow. He thought she was beautiful, birthmark and all.

Like Gabby's, Marie's family was Salvadoran, but she was born in the United States, which made her a U.S. citizen. She spoke perfect English and Spanish, which impressed Ernesto. He and Raúl still hardly spoke any English at all, defaulting to Spanish and afraid to speak up at all in class lest they make any mistakes. Marie is an English name, Ernesto explained to Raúl, pronouncing it phonetically in Spanish: *Mar-i-yay*.

The first time they kissed, days after they first met, Raúl sat off to the side smoking a cigarette. He pretended not to be paying attention. Ernesto talked and texted with Marie late into the night, and in just over a week he used up all their phone minutes for the month. So for the rest of March they could only text, meaning they couldn't accept calls from Amy. Raúl scolded him, but for Ernesto, it had been worth it.

Marie introduced him to her family and to the nicely decorated living room in their home a few blocks away. She and Ernesto would sit and watch TV with her parents, who would serve him sodas and chat with him about El Salvador, about school, like a real family. Ernesto loved it over there. But nothing beat their afternoons at Arroyo Viejo Park, when he could sit with Marie and feel her up until nightfall. Given the crime in his neighborhood, it was best to be home before dark.

"Are you going to the park today?" he'd text her from class, hiding the phone underneath his desk.

"Maybe," Marie would reply coyly. "You?" As if there were some reason, other than each other, that they'd end up there.

"Definitely," he'd say. And after school, he'd race off campus. If Raúl was taking too long, Ernesto jumped on the bus without him.

"Does Marie know about your court case?" I asked Ernesto.

"No," he said. "No way. I don't want to bother her with all that." Marie's role for Ernesto was to help him forget.

Raúl feigned indifference to his brother's activities. "Who needs a girlfriend?" he called from the backseat while we were driving to a meeting with Amy. "They take up too much time."

"Jealous," Ernesto said.

"No, seriously," Raúl said, "I don't even care."

A few days before the court date, the probate court investigator left an urgent message for Amy. She had been assigned to investigate the twins' living situation and proposed guardian—standard practice in SIJS cases—and Wilber's background checks had raised some red flags. When she ran his name through the computer, something came up that he hadn't disclosed.

"It didn't sound super serious, but you never know," Amy said. Had he been arrested for something, the boys worried, before they'd arrived in the United States, and never told them?

Wilber would have to go for an in-person interview at the courthouse, and soon, before the court appointment the following week. It unnerved Wilber to learn that after a night in jail and hours of community service and thousands of dollars in fines, his record wasn't clean. The additional meeting meant he'd have to take yet another day off work. "I'll have to ask my boss," he told Amy.

Paperless people like him had only so many job opportunities— things that paid in cash, or that accepted phony Social Security cards. In this city, construction, restaurant work, and landscaping were the big three. In the Central Valley, people worked in the fields, but he'd left El Salvador to avoid that life. Worse than forgoing a day's pay was the shame of walking up to his boss, head hung, to ask for leeway and special favors. He wanted to be the reliable guy, the guy who showed up to work every day with no needs and no drama and worked his ass off. That's how you got ahead, he knew, when you had to work double time, triple time, just to stay afloat.

Wilber waited until the day before the interview to ask for the time off. "I'll be there," he told the twins.

THE Berkeley courthouse was an unassuming building, a beige box lined with windows and set back slightly from busy Martin Luther King Jr. Way. It was directly across from where a farmer's market was held each Saturday, ever packed with Central Valley fruits and vegetables, overpriced vegan chocolates, and raw cheeses, weighed and sold by grizzled older farmers and young hipsters alike. Today the streets were quiet, their well-manicured gardens in bloom.

"Berkeley's nice," Raúl said nervously as we walked inside.

The investigator, a tall Caucasian woman with thick-framed red glasses, ushered the Flores brothers through a door and told Gabby and me to wait outside.

I'd been asked to accompany them to make sure they found the building and got there on time. Gabby had tagged along, I gathered, to support Wilber. We took a seat in a bright, windowed alcove and made small talk. She was excited to finish up her high school credits at the local community college so she could transition to being a full-fledged undergraduate. Wilber was really supportive of her, she said.

She told me how they'd met. "It kind of started on Facebook. We had friends of friends in common, and we just kind of got talking." Her voice had a friendly lilt, and she stuck out her chin to emphasize her points, keeping her hands folded in her lap. She was sweet-faced in a childlike way, dressed somewhere between fashionable and don't-notice-me plain. "It was pretty awkward at first, like, when we met? But then we just sort of really liked each other, and that was that." At nineteen, she seemed comfortable being in it for the long haul with Wilber.

"It was nice of you to come and support the boys," I said.

"Oh, it's no problem. I didn't have nothing better to do."

"Wilber's doing a really good job," I said.

"Yeah. It's hard. But it's good. They're nice kids." Wilber had really done a lot for them, she said, but "that's family."

We sat for a while in silence. Then the doors opened and the three Flores brothers emerged with matching strides. All had gone well, their looks told me. "We're all set," the investigator said.

"I guess there was some traffic ticket I never told them about," Wilber explained, whitewashing the story of the DUI as we walked down the street back toward the car. "I didn't realize they needed to know stuff like that." The ghost of that night would haunt him forever, it seemed; he hadn't quite grasped that the arrest meant he now had a permanent record. "But she said it's okay, and that it won't affect the case." There was nothing to do now but wait.

———

IT was April 8, three days before the twins' birthday: their day in court.

Though Wilber had now been to the courthouse, rather than risk him getting lost in Berkeley, I suggested we drive together from the school. The appointment was at 12:00 p.m., and the boys still doubted whether he'd show up. Eleven a.m., when he said he'd arrive, passed. We sat in the courtyard, the thin springtime sun spilling down on us, not saying much. The boys passed their phone back and forth, checked their phone, and repositioned their seats on the long green benches that surrounded a patch of plants. Ernesto wore large navy blue fake plugs in his ears. Remembering them, he quickly snatched them out of his ears and stuffed them into his pockets, to make sure he looked serious. Raúl began tapping his feet.

"He'll be here," I said.

"Yeah, he will," said Raúl.

Twelve minutes later, in walked Wilber, wearing high-tops and a flat-brimmed baseball cap. The boys stood up. Ernesto ran to deposit his earrings in his locker, and we climbed into the car for a quiet ride to Berkeley.

The courtroom's metal detector unnerved the boys—they felt frantic surrendering their backpacks and emptying their pockets. No one had warned Ernesto about removing his belt, so the alarm blared as he passed through the gate. He and Raúl both startled. The guard patiently instructed him, in exaggerated pantomime, to return through the metal detector, yank off his belt, and place it on the conveyor belt. Walking back through the gate, Ernesto was just boy and cloth: no earrings, no wallet or phone, none of the trappings of almost-adulthood that he wore as both badges of honor and armor.

Upstairs, Amy briefed them again on what was going to happen. When the judge called their names, they would walk to the front of the courtroom. The judge would ask them questions. Amy didn't expect the questions to be hard or complicated, but the boys should know that there was no wrong answer, that they only had to tell the truth. They laughed, nervously, their eyes alternating between her face and the floor.

They waited in the pews while several other family cases played out. A young woman was there to give up custody of her two young children to the children's father and his new girlfriend. On the other side of the aisle, a curly-haired toddler rested her head against her stepmother's shoulder, sucking on her pacifier.

"I love my children, and I want to support them, but I know I'm not able to do so at this time," the mother told the judge.

The Flores case was next up. The boys looked at each other, then at Amy, and stood, adjusting their shirts. We pushed through the low, swinging gates and took our seats to the judge's right. Ernesto and Raúl sat like soldiers at attention, willing themselves to make eye contact with the judge.

The judge confirmed who was there, then smiled down at the boys.

"I'm granting the guardianship to Mr. Wilber Flores," she said. "And I've read over the petition, and I'm going to approve that, too."

"Thank you, Your Honor," Amy said. She looked at us, smiled, and nodded toward the exit.

That was it.

The Flores brothers walked back down the aisle between the pews of waiting children, first Raúl, then Ernesto, then Wilber. Once out in the bright hallway, they turned and looked pleadingly at Amy, not sure what they had heard.

She broke into a smile. "This is great!" she said. "She granted it!" meaning both the guardianship and the order establishing their eligibility for Special Immigrant Juvenile Status. The judge had given no verbal explanation—but she'd deemed, based on the twins' written testimonies, that it was in their best interest to be allowed to stay in the United States.

Raúl started laughing and stamped his foot. Ernesto's eyes shone with almost-tears. The twins looked at each other for an extended moment. The group exchanged celebratory hugs.

"Wow," said Wilber. "Wow. So lucky. So great."

"Now," Amy reminded us, "immigration still has to approve this, and you'll have to do another interview, but this is a really good sign. They rarely go against what this court recommends." For today, they'd had a victory.

The afternoon was bright and warm as the brothers walked to the car, past the lush Berkeley yards decorated with succulents and fruit trees.

"You know what my dream is?" said Wilber after a while. "I actually want to join the army. The U.S. Army. As soon as I get my papers, I'm going to join. It's a good job with good pay, and I love the desert." All the wars and many of the military bases, he knew, were in deserts—Iraq, Afghanistan, Texas, southern California.

"Not me," said Raúl. "I hate the desert."

"I'd love to go to Iraq. And I think I'd be a good soldier. I want to help America fight."

They walked by a patch of roses. "That's my dream," Wilber said, smiling faintly in his reverie. The twins were unsmiling now. "Once I get my papers," Wilber said, "that's my dream."

On the way back to school, the boys watched Berkeley turn into Oakland, and the red lights shift to green, as families of all colors walked across streets and bicycles rattled by, as lunatics raved on corners and homeless wheeled their carts beneath the California sun.

Back at school, the boys ambled across the courtyard until Ernesto peeled right and sprinted back to his locker. "My earrings," he said. He fastened them back into his ears and went to class.

THAT night Wilber entered the twins' room and sat down on the edge of the bed. "I'm happy for you guys," he said. "I really am. But it's been so easy for you." They'd been here only a few months and had already got their papers. "I've been here for seven years." He knew it didn't work that way, papers falling from the sky once you'd been here long enough, but still, he wished.

Ever since the twins had come to live with Wilber, jealousy, that slender snake, had twisted through him on and off—when he dropped them off at school, or when he met with their lawyer today in court. He knew the journey had been hard for them, but it wasn't easy for anyone.

For seven years he had commuted to work, scared of being stopped by police again for speeding or for a knocked-out taillight, worried that *la migra* would raid his workplace, run his prints, and send him home. For seven years he had felt the everyday racism: a Latino like him could show up in a suit and tie at the nicest restaurant in town and still be treated differently than a grubby white guy in jeans and a T-shirt. Life for an undocumented person was better in Oakland than in lots of other places; in Arizona, for instance, he'd once heard the police stopped Latinos just to check their papers, not even with another pretense, and that their politicians wanted to get rid of immigrants altogether. California was better, but still, it wasn't easy. Racism, he knew, was everywhere on earth but perhaps strongest in the United States, this place home to so many different kinds of people.

He'd felt it that night in the parking lot, the cop's smug gaze, the way he approached Wilber in the car, which wasn't even turned on. He would have found any reason to arrest him and his friends. There was the way people looked at him when he was one of the only Latino guys in the store, and a fear that a person could never fully kick, a hum of *you don't belong.* The problem with being paperless in Oakland was that you could almost forget you were an outsider, if only for a flickering moment; when the truth kicked back in, it was all the worse. Gabby, her family, now his own brothers—they all could legally call this place home. But he still lingered among the eleven million in the shadow zone. Those dreams he had—joining the army, going to Iraq, getting papers of his own—were just fantasies.

The twins sat on the bed listening to Wilber, the Spanish rap thudding through the scratchy computer speakers. They didn't know what to say, other than they were sorry.

"Don't worry," Ernesto said, in a rare showing of tenderness.

"You'll get papers someday," Raúl said.

"Yeah," Wilber said, "I guess everything comes in its own time."

For the rest of that week, the boys showed up at school on time, did their homework, and took home books to read at night. After nearly a year of struggle, they now saw the warm potential of the life on this side of the border.

The evil spirits went into hibernation, by Raúl's estimation, and Ernesto slept well.

THE twins kept their celebrations between the two of them, out of respect for Wilber and their undocumented friends. They were even shy about telling their teachers they'd taken their first step toward papers. They did tell their parents, and Wilber Sr. and Esperanza knew that the prayers they'd murmured at church and while holding the statue of the Virgin and Child had worked. The twins didn't plan any celebration on their eighteenth birthday, either. Birthdays back home were never a big to-do; there'd been eleven of them and no extra money. Raúl celebrated by going to a neighboring high school's soccer game, where a friend had arranged for them to meet up with some cute emo girls from another school. He smoked cigarettes, assuming an air of cool as the girls, at a staggered distance, chattered with one another, stealing glances at their male companions. One of them asked him for a cigarette; he felt the thrill of brushing her hand with his, then bringing the flame to her black painted lips. Nothing came of the outing, but he came back well after dark with a confidence he hadn't felt since he'd left home. He had papers, he was eighteen—officially a man: the whole world was unlatched.

Ernesto, too, spent that first week on a cloud, but the dreams came back.

It was just Raúl there to shake his twin back to himself, sit with him while he calmed his quickened breaths, and wait until his brother fell back asleep before allowing himself to shut his own eyes.

Eventually, he asked his brother point-blank: "Why do you have so many bad dreams?"

For whatever reason, Ernesto finally felt like talking. "All right," he said, "I'll tell you."

Raúl perked up, surprised.

"Remember in Reynosa when you went to the bathroom?"

In the safe house, when Raúl had gone upstairs to splash himself with water, Ernesto had sat, avoiding eye contact, on the small mattress they shared on the floor. One of the coyotes, the guy who acted like the boss, opened the door. "Come help me out back?" he'd said. Ernesto looked up and realized the guy was talking to him.

He followed him to the outdoor area where women were cooking food for the migrants shacked up inside. One of the migrants, who had been complaining about how long he'd been there, was back there, too.

"Why haven't we moved?" he was shouting. "When are we going to get out of this fucking hellhole?"

It was stressful, the waiting—Ernesto had been there only two days, and it had got to him, too.

"What am I paying you thousands of dollars for," the man shouted to the boss, "to just sit here and wait forever?"

The boss slapped him across the face. "We move when I say so, asshole."

Instead of silencing him, the slap turned the man hysterical. He flailed, kicked, and shouted. Ernesto backed up against the cinder-block wall, trying to disappear.

"I've been here for two months!" he cried, spit flying from his mouth. "I paid you people to get me there!"

At this, one of the guides took out a machete, sliced the guy along the side of his torso, then jabbed the long blade deep into his stomach. He fell to the floor shouting, blood pooling out of him.

"Help!" he said, and looked at Ernesto, right in the eyes. "Help me!" he pleaded, but Ernesto was frozen still. He did nothing.

The leader, the one who'd ordered Ernesto back here, took out his gun and shot the dying man in the head. His body relaxed into its final slump on the cement. Ernesto turned around and hurried back inside.

"I saw all this, right in front of me," he told Raúl. He never found out what the coyote had wanted from him.

"Why didn't you tell me?" asked Raúl. As far as he knew, it was the first big secret his twin had ever kept from him.

Ernesto hadn't told him back in Reynosa because he couldn't unlock his throat to talk. And also to protect him. To protect them both, really—if Ernesto had blabbed about the murder, what would stop the coyotes from offing him, too? After that, it was just too much to talk about, as if the words might bring it all back to life. When they were caught in Texas, the *migra* officer had asked, in his one-on-one interview, whether he'd seen the coyotes do anything illegal, whether anyone in their group had been mistreated. Cooperating with the authorities against human smugglers and crime rings could help a person get immigration status through a U visa, available "for victims of certain crimes who have suffered mental or physical abuse and are helpful to law enforcement or government officials in the investigation or prosecution of criminal activity." It's questionable whether this would have qualified him for a U Visa. But, either way, all Ernesto had said was no, as the memory of the bullet puncturing the migrant's head swamped the space behind his eyes.

When he'd fallen on the corpse in the desert the following week, onto some poor, miserable migrant just like them, it was God's way of reminding him: *A man died, and you did nothing, you did nothing, you did nothing.*

And it wouldn't all go away because his life here was becoming more permanent. In fact, after the initial post-court reprieve, the luckier he was, the worse Ernesto's dreams seemed to become. That's what penance looked like.

That night they stayed up talking and hardly slept. The next morning they arrived late at school.

THE GIRLS

Politicians claim that the majority of those killed are gangsters, but I know for a fact that's not true," says the director of the Instituto de Medicina Legal, Dr. Fortín Magaña. His office is like that of an eccentric movie mortician: tile floors, classical music keening through speakers, an immaculate desk bearing a neat stack of papers, a snakeskin letter opener and matching magnifying glass. He turns to his computer. "Look at this," he orders, fiddling with the mouse. He pulls up a photograph of two young women dressed in blue medical scrubs, smiling against a backdrop of greenery.

"These two girls were about to graduate from nursing school. This was taken the day before they were killed." He shows another picture—a rotting hand, skin swollen against a thin silver ring. He switches back again to the original image. "See that? Same ring, same hand." He points to a picture of scraps of muddy blue cloth—the scrubs—found beside her naked body.

"Do these look like gangsters? No. These were young women, innocent young people who would have been absolutely valuable to this society. And they killed them."

In 2012, El Salvador had the highest rate of femicide—the gender-motivated killing of women—in the world. High femicide rates persist and reports of rape and domestic violence are also on the rise. The vast majority of victims are poor young women living in rural areas or urban slums, like the girls from the doctor's pictures. In 2015 the government registered 575 femicides, nearly twice the number of femicides in 2014, and the highest since 2011, right before the gang truce. In 2016, there were 524.

Is it so surprising that more and more girls are joining the gangs, wresting a tiny hunk of power from the male-dominated world—of gangs, of police, of the trials and tribulations of their own families—around them?

During the weekly visitors' day in El Salvador's Centro de Inserción Social Femenino, the young inmates—minors convicted of gang-related crimes, including robbery, extortion, prostitution, drug trafficking, and murder—are dressed in their best clothes. A U.S. church group is rumored to be coming by today. Two girls drape themselves against the bars on the MS-13 side of the prison. One of them, tall and thin with dirty blond hair, smooths her locks with one hand as though to increase their shine, holding the bar with the other.

"Are they coming?" she asks.

"Will there be boys?" her friend says. They fall over laughing, each with a fist still gripping one of the metal bars.

The girls lower in the gang pecking order congregate in the overgrown courtyard while the higher-ups remain upstairs in the dingy, eighty-bed dormitory, keeping watch on the activity below.

Carmelina, a chubby seventeen-year-old wearing hot pink spandex shorts, pink Converse, pigtails, and heavy eyeliner, sits hunched on a cement bench and texts on the contraband cellphone she only half-conceals between her knees. None of the guards seem to notice.

"I'm in for extortion," she says, licking a blue ice cream cone, the special treat handed out by the missionary group. She was the one who went around collecting rent. "I got ten years, but my lawyer says if I'm good, I'll only get four."

"You know Paseo del Carmen?" she asks a visitor who happens to be staying in Santa Tecla, a well-known strip of locally owned shops, bars, and restaurants. "That was my territory!" she exclaims with pride.

Gang members reserve the right to claim any girl in the neighborhood as a girlfriend, threatening her or her family with physical harm if she refuses to comply. Gang members' mothers, sisters, aunts, grandmothers, and spouses, who wash their clothes, cook their food, keep house, are linked to the gangs sometimes without meaning or asking to be.

"Women often take the same risks for crimes as the men do," explains Silvia Juárez, of the Organization of Salvadoran Women for Peace, "but they don't receive the same revenue or benefit of the crime."

Girls like Carmelina don't look the part of gang members, so they can more easily evade the police: perfectly disguised for doing the dirty work, they become cannon fodder.

"The problem in Santa Tecla," Carmelina explained with a what-can-you-do shrug, "was the cameras." They caught her on film going door to door.

The fact is that young women in El Salvador don't have a lot of options. According to a 2015 study by the United Nations Population Fund, 25,132 of the 83,468 registered pregnancies in El Salvador, around a third of all pregnancies, were girls or young women between the ages of ten and nineteen. Twenty-five percent of girls are married before they are eighteen, and abortion is illegal; women in El Salvador have even been jailed for miscarriage. Salvadoran girls attend school at approximately the same rates as boys, yet schooling is subpar for all; according to a 2016 USAID report, though more and more youth are attending elementary school, only about half of Salvadoran youth enroll in seventh to ninth grades, and only about half of those matriculate into high school. More than three hundred thousand youth in El Salvador are currently out of school and without a job.

Is it so surprising that more and more girls are going north, fleeing the odds?

In 2012, at the height of the first surge of unaccompanied minors, 23 percent were girls. In 2015 some 32 percent were girls, and in 2016 it was 33 percent. And in the first six months of 2016, more than 32,000 cases of parents traveling with their children—mostly young mothers—were apprehended along the southern border, more than twice the number of that same time period the year before.

A paralegal working with unaccompanied minors in the Rio Grande Valley of Texas explains that girls know what they're risking on the trip north. "They take the pill or get a birth control shot so that, if they are raped, they won't get pregnant." A 2010 Amnesty International Report cited research that six out of ten migrant women and girls were sexually assaulted en route to the United States—other estimates are even higher. It's just considered part of the payment, the paralegal says, of the passage north.

CHAPTER 8

Ernesto's story was out. After he told Raúl, he told me, then even Wilber, in a flash of intimacy after the court date. But liberating the secret didn't make things any better. In fact, it might have made things worse. To tell what had happened was to reify it, to give it shape and weight outside his memory.

Alcohol was a balm, and Ernesto started to drink more. The week after he told Raúl about the Reynosa murder, Ernesto was caught drinking at school. It was a twelfth grader's birthday, and to celebrate, the older boy had smuggled in a bottle of vodka. The boys met in the bathroom and siphoned the vodka into juice and Gatorade bottles. Ernesto guzzled down the sweet, bitter mix amid his new pals and the urinals. Within the hour, he was bleary-eyed and slurring his words in class, then stumbling around the courtyard. He was sent home and suspended for two days.

Ernesto loved that the booze made him feel like a bubble, iridescent and weightless. The first drink smudged the sharp edges of memory and brightened the world around him as though he'd applied an Instagram filter: life was nicer-looking through tipsy eyes.

Unfortunately, that feeling was hard to sustain. The levity would wear off, and the world would suddenly fall back out of kilter. He'd smoke to calm himself, but booze fractured a critical valve in him, unloosing grim thoughts in a rush. Then the only remedy was sleep, though then he risked bad dreams. He'd wake up the next day feeling heavy and full of remorse yet wanting to chase that lightness, again, that lifted him off the sad fact of being human, even for a few moments.

"THE money?" Maricela wrote to the twins through Facebook. The debt was nearly $19,000 now. They didn't write back to her.

Through friends from school, the twins—first Ernesto and, with his recommendation, Raúl—got a job moving boxes. They worked one day a week after school, driving around Oakland and picking up parcels, stacking them in the back of the truck. The rate fluctuated, but they usually made one hundred dollars for four hours of work—a ton of money, in cash. Making money meant they were moving forward.

Their earnings added up to about $640 a month, which they pledged to save until the end of the month, when they would send it back to El Salvador. Except just ten dollars for cigarettes—no big deal. And an occasional stop at McDonald's—but you could get a meal there for five dollars, a filling one. And they needed new jackets, and their shoes were beginning to pull apart at the seams. Since they were working, Wilber didn't give them pocket money anymore, so all this had to come out of their wages.

By the end of the first month, they had hardly saved any money at all. They'd do better next month, they promised themselves. Ernesto scored another gig, deep-cleaning a Japanese restaurant in the tony Montclair district of Oakland once a week. He'd be paid nine dollars per hour, then the minimum wage in Oakland, using a borrowed Social Security number. But by the end of the second month, they still only had about $150 to send home—which didn't even pay off the interest accrued that month.

The disconnect between the life they were building and their family's dire situation overwhelmed them. Yet, they worked hard, and didn't

they need food and shoes? The good things here, big and small—the little triumphs like a girl flirting with them at school, or the good fortune
of winning the first part of their case and finding jobs to help sustain
them—were ringed with a halo of guilt.

As a distraction, the twins redoubled their efforts to amass friends,
to inch their way into a cooler crowd while still keeping more innocent
friends like Brenda and Alfredo. They plotted over who could get ahold
of booze (more money gone), they made more connections over Facebook, and they sneaked out of class and even smoked pot a few times
on the corners after school. They got fancier phones, first Ernesto, then
Raúl: iPhones, a previously unimaginable luxury. They needed them
to find their way around Oakland, they reasoned. They would pay seventy dollars a month each on an unlimited phone plan. They bought
bottled water from Walgreens and dropped five dollars on street tacos
after work.

Our school didn't let students out for lunch because four hundred
students released into the neighborhood invited a chaos the adults found
unwelcome. Ernesto would text Raúl during fourth period, right before
the lunch bell rang: "Raúl, where do you want to eat lunch today?"
Raúl's phone wasn't connected, but he could receive texts over the
school's Wi-Fi, whose contraband code circulated among students. The
security guard or Cormac would catch them in a relaxed amble back to
campus, sipping fountain sodas in the middle of fifth period. The boys
winced when the adults spotted them, but they wouldn't quicken their
pace. It was too nice, that feeling of walking along in the sun, a few
minutes of no one needing them to move something or lift something or
read something or pay something. Sometimes they just walked out the
front door of the school unnoticed, but often they slipped out a student-
size hole in the chain link, cut out like a door and easily pushed back
into place.

After school one day, Ernesto was emptying his backpack, preparing
to rush out the door. Out came his binder, a crumple of math and sci-
ence worksheets, and some books his teacher was encouraging him to
try reading. He shoved these into a locker already filled with work he'd
never turned in, papers stuffed and scattered. Also inside was a pair

of soccer cleats the school's soccer coach had given him his first weeks here, back when he had time to play at school and before he decided he wasn't any good. On the top shelf of his locker were four McChickens, wrapped in the yellow and orange paper. He'd bought extras, to share.

"*Dame uno,*" said a Honduran student as he walked by. Gimme one. He wasn't a good friend of Ernesto's, but he knew him well enough. Ernesto tossed one of the sandwiches over, laughing.

"*Gracias, maje,*" the kid said with a smile. Thanks, bro.

AT Oakland International, regular classes ended three weeks before the end of the semester, just before Memorial Day. The final three weeks were spent in a single intensive class, with a mixed-grade group of students. I, along with the twins' math teacher, Mr. David, taught a hiking and camping class that earned students PE credits. Ernesto was one of twenty-six students in our group.

The first day we gave an overview of the class. We'd take two trips, the first to a local teaching farm, the second a two-day hike where we'd be backpacking. That meant, we told them, carrying all our food—along with tents, clothing, sleeping bags, and kitchen supplies—throughout. If they skipped one of the camping trips, they failed the class.

Ernesto skipped the orientation day, having slept in. He'd been coming to school less and less; when he slept during the day, he seemed to have fewer nightmares. He showed up on the second day just as we were getting into the cars to leave on the first trip. He didn't know anyone in our group apart from Diego, his first friend and former tablemate, who had plenty of other friends in the class, and he'd missed the icebreakers and get-to-know-you games, as well as the long hike we'd taken up the bald peak above the UC Berkeley campus. He plugged his ears with headphones and faced the window as we crossed the Richmond–San Rafael Bridge toward the Marin headlands. We wound up Mount Tamalpais and moved through a dappled tunnel of oak and manzanita before the road pitched us out into the golden hills and the wide vista of the Pacific. Ernesto could count on his hand the number of times he'd seen the ocean.

We spent the afternoon milking goats and turning compost, walking across the tidal zones in search of starfish and sea cucumbers, watching the sea collide against the craggy edge of the continent. While the other students shrieked giddily as the goats bucked or a rogue wave soaked their feet, Ernesto stood off to the side, his face a mask of indifference.

A beetle ambled slowly across our paths. Its black armor had an iridescent green sheen, and we bent to inspect it.

"Look how beautiful!" one of the girls said.

"Wow!" another cooed.

Ernesto walked over to the bug and stomped on it. Then he laughed and walked away.

THAT night at the campfire, the students roasted marshmallows and played "I Spy," with surprising enthusiasm for teenagers. Ernesto insisted we skip his turn. He played on his phone until it ran out of charge and asked repeatedly when we'd get back to camp. Night fell. We cleaned up bits of burnt marshmallow, glinting Hershey wrappers, and pieces of gum, then doused the fire with a bucket of water that made a soft hiss. As we walked back to camp through the coastal scrub, Ernesto scratched himself, becoming increasingly agitated. "Something's wrong," he said, "something's wrong, I don't know what's going on." He raked his fingernails against his arms so hard, I thought he might draw blood.

"Maybe you're allergic to one of the plants?" There was no swelling or marks apart from where he'd scratched himself raw. We had him soak his arms in tubs of cold water, and he'd be still for a few moments, eyes closed while he took deep breaths. Then he'd flare back up into panic. He finally calmed down after we gave him some Benadryl and opted to sleep it off.

When he crawled into his tent, he smelled smoke. "Cigarettes?" he asked the boys who were lounging in their sleeping bags, listening to music. He'd left his pack at home with Raúl and, with the cars pulling out right when he got to school, hadn't had a chance to buy more.

"Yeah man, you want one?" asked Ibrahim, a skinny senior from

Iraq who drove a gold rattle-trap Mercedes, dressed hip-hop, and smiled often.

"Yeah," Ernesto said. They turned out their lights and walked across the moonlit field to an outcropping out of sight of camp.

Ibrahim offered him a cigarette and a light. Ernesto inhaled deep into his lungs and exhaled into the dark. Newer students generally stuck to friends from their own language group, but older students like Ibrahim, who had learned more English, often branched out. He wanted to learn some Spanish, too, because he had a Mexican girlfriend from another school.

Ernesto thanked him for the cigarette. They could hardly see each other in the dark and didn't talk—Ibrahim didn't speak much Spanish yet, and Ernesto still barely spoke English. They just sat in each other's company, watching the disembodied glow of their cherries move through the air and listening to the exhales against the shattering of waves. Ernesto's invisible rash was gone.

THE following week we left for the backpacking trip, which was in Big Basin Redwoods State Park, a thick swath of redwoods that plunged from the Santa Cruz Mountains to the sea. Our bus snaked slowly up the narrow roads to the park entrance while the students whooped and hollered from the backseats. Ernesto, by now, had made multiple friends in the class, including an older Salvadoran girl and two Guatemalan sisters who called him Ernestito, or "My Ernesto." Most of them didn't realize he had a twin, and Ernesto rarely mentioned it.

The first hike was an eight-mile trek that culminated in a steep ascent up a cliff alongside a waterfall. Ernesto didn't complain as we scrambled over rocks and up ladders, and he offered repeatedly to take some of the weight from other students, particularly the girls. He carried an extra jug of water on behalf of the group, he took on another cooking pot, and he stuffed extra clothing and water bottles in the spare pockets and corners of his backpack. His face seemed to loosen as he hiked; he started to look more like Raúl. At one point I turned around to check on the group, and I saw him walking alone in silence, smiling.

At night he and Ibrahim went off for a cigarette along with Diego, who also spoke near-perfect English and so could translate. They found a good place to hide, crouching next to the adjacent camp's latrines.

"You have a twin brother?" Ibrahim asked.

Ernesto nodded—*twin* was an English word he'd learned early on. Ibrahim had realized this, he explained, when he said hi to a kid who he thought was Ernesto and had been ignored.

"I was like, 'What the hell, man, I'm your friend, Ibrahim!' And you didn't say nothing. And then I figured it out!" Diego translated, and Ernesto laughed.

"That's crazy, man, a twin."

The three smoked in silence for a while, and then Ernesto, in English, asked Ibrahim where he was from.

"Iraq," Ibrahim said.

"Damn," Ernesto said in English. Then, in Spanish: "Why you here?"

Ibrahim explained he'd had to leave Iraq because his dad had worked with the U.S. government. He had a sister, Sara, who was a tenth grader at our school. "One day my sister walked out the door to go to school." The family had drivers, he said, because it wasn't safe for them to drive their own cars. "She got outside and the driver was screaming at her, 'Go back! Go back!' But she didn't know what to do or what was going on, so she couldn't move. And he pointed, and there was a bomb right there. Right next to her." If she had knocked against the bomb, it would have detonated, killing her and, possibly, the whole family.

"So we had to come here," Ibrahim said. "Refugees."

"Wow," Ernesto said after Diego finished translating, and shook his head. "Damn." They took long drags from their cigarettes. "I'm sorry." Then, after a while: "Me too. I had to come here because they were going to kill me, too."

"Shit, man," Ibrahim said. "See, Arab, Latino, white, black—we're all the same. Same shit, good shit, bad shit—same shit."

The three decided to smoke another, this time one of the slim Iraqi cigarettes Ibrahim bought at the halal market near school. "Much better than that American crap," he said and doled them out with a smile.

THE second day's hike was far less strenuous, but we were all sore from the day before and had to carry more water because there were no sources along this stretch of trail. Ernesto still moved like a billy goat, keeping up with Ibrahim and some of the older boys from Yemen. When we got to camp, the students collapsed, barely able to muster the energy to put up their tents and cook dinner.

After camp settled down, a commotion arose.

The Guatemalan sisters ran out of their tent shouting, spewing curses in Spanish, threatening to beat the shit out of another group of girls who were sleeping. "It was them!" they were shouting. "I know it was them! They were talking shit about us before! It was them! They fucking did this!" The sisters' tent, off to the side, had fallen into a messy pile of nylon. Someone had collapsed it on top of them. But the girls they were accusing appeared to be fast asleep in their own tent.

Ernesto sat off to the side, shaking his head and muttering. A female friend had her arm around him, cooing at him to calm down, calm down.

"They're not going to get away with this!" he suddenly shouted. "Fucking bitches, messing with my friends!" He stood up and stamped over to the other girls' tent. He kicked it, then yanked out one of the poles, ripping a long gash in the tent's side. The girls inside gasped and screamed.

Ernesto backed away. Someone shone a light on him; his eyes were unfocused, and he was swaying on his feet.

I pulled Ernesto aside, and David went to deal with the girls.

"You've been drinking," I said. "You need to calm down."

"I don't care!" he shouted so his friends could hear. "I don't care about the tent, I'll pay for it, I don't care. Those girls have to pay for what they did to my friends."

His crew had smuggled Four Lokos in his backpack, the saccharine tall-boy alcoholic drink whose colorful can resembled an iced tea or energy drink, marketed implicitly toward young people like them. The girls had apparently drunk them the night before at the first camp without making a scene. Today Ernesto had taken one down to the trickling stream, along with one of Ibrahim's cigarettes, and sipped it leisurely. In the past he'd drunk to blur his own edges, but today he was drinking in celebration. Today he was happy with the world as it was.

The problem was, as always, that the celebratory feeling didn't last. Now he sat off to the side of the outhouse, head between his knees, swaying. He'd had too much, he said, and didn't feel good.

"Why did you drink?" I asked. He'd been doing so well, I'd thought.

He picked up his head and looked at me, the beam of his headlamp shining into my eyes. "Why do you think?" he spat. "Because! Because! Because of my family!" He dropped his head to his knees and began sobbing. "Because of everything that happened, everything."

His cries came out dry and deep from his midsection. For twenty minutes he let out yells that became sobs, quaking and rocking himself forward and back. There, in the middle of the redwoods, we were four miles from the nearest road. Every few moments he'd stop, sit up as though he'd heard some sound in the woods, then shake his head back and forth, knocking his hand against his temple over and over.

He eventually quieted into a state of heavy breathing and slow rocking.

"I could have stopped him," he said. "You know? I could have." Reynosa, he meant, the restless migrant with the bullet in his head.

"You would have risked your own life," I said. "There was nothing you could do."

"I could have tried." He spoke softly now. "I could have tried to do something."

"Then you'd be dead, too."

"Maybe better."

He went to stand up. I helped him to his feet, but he shook me off and turned away. He took four steps, then halted, swaying back and forth like a leaf in a light breeze, and fell over into a mess of brambles on the side of the path.

There, lying in the brush, he laughed, then cackled, shaking his head until he was out of breath. "Whoa!" he said, trying to stand again. He fell right back down.

We sat for over an hour while he drank water and, inevitably, vomited alongside the latrine.

"Sorry about the tent," he said finally, the chemical outhouse smell mingling with that of his vomit. "Sorry, sorry, sorry."

WHEN Ernesto got back to school, the first thing he did was text Marie. "I missed you," he said. "I missed you so much. You miss me?" "Want to go to the park?"

Their meet-up that afternoon turned his hangover around. "I love you," he crooned into her ear as she sucked a hickey into his neck. "I love you."

"How was camping?" Raúl asked later that night.

"Fine," Ernesto said. He went to sleep without saying anything else.

Raúl, for his part, had been assigned to a day-hiking class. He often missed field trips because he came late to school, and he hadn't made any friends in the class. He wished he'd got to sleep outside and spend time in the woods, as he and Ernesto had back home guarding the animals.

The semester ended, and there were two weeks off before summer school began. The boys stayed home mostly and slept, or they played video games and helped watch Rosalinda's kid. Ernesto hung out with Marie. He texted her the minute he woke up and the minute before he went to sleep. "My angel." "My baby." "I love you." "Your lips, mmm, I love your lips." "Sleep tight, my love."

MEANWHILE they were starting to see on Univision and hear at school about a new flood of immigrants. Kids, mostly, like them. In May 2014 alone authorities caught over 9,000 unaccompanied minors along the southern border. That made 47,000 since the beginning of the fiscal year in October, up from 38,759 in 2013, and with four months of the year still to go. Salvadorans were on the rise both proportionally and in absolute numbers. In 2011 the Office of Refugee Resettlement detained 1,394 unaccompanied minors from El Salvador; in 2014 that number was 16,404.

And it wasn't only kids; families, often mothers with small children, were being apprehended in hordes. Many of them, road weary, were turning themselves in just across the border, sometimes at the advice of loved ones or smugglers. By year's end, Customs and Border Protection had apprehended 68,684 "family case" individuals, a 356 percent increase over the year before.

As always, the migrants came for a host of reasons, but increasingly they were claiming their primary motivation as fear of gang violence. Immigrant rights advocates like the Women's Refugee Commission and the national organization Kids in Need of Defense claimed that these children were, and should be considered under the eyes of the law, refugees. But would deeming Central Americans in the United States "refugees" encourage more children like them to come climbing our fences and splashing through that exacting river? For reasons perhaps more political than legal, the tens of thousands of new migrants would not be named refugees en masse as they almost always are abroad, from Syrians in Turkey to Eastern Congolese in Uganda to Eritreans in Ethiopia. Central Americans in the United States would continue to have to apply for immigration relief one by one—and hope they qualified.

Ernesto took to leaving the room when the news came on the TV at Hillside. Raúl, though, thought about the crisis more and more. He didn't like how people talked about immigrants like they were some kind of parasite. Sure they crossed the border illegally, but no one wanted to leave home, their parents, for no good reason. He searched pictures online of kids sleeping in too-small rooms under reflective blankets on the floor, as they had, little kids steadied on the tops of Mexican trains.

The U.S. government ran out of shelter beds. During a major unaccompanied minor spike in 2012, authorities had been unprepared; now too they raced to catch up, shacking children up in former nursing homes and military bases and releasing families from overcrowded, austere detention facilities with a court summons. *Hielera* conditions were no longer just for temporary holding stations; they were now, in many places, the detention norm. In June the Federal Emergency Management Agency was called in to help manage the situation—it sent a mass email through national advocacy networks seeking potential short-term shelters that were "within 50 miles of major city (Pop ~200K)/airport; available for lease; able to be fenced or have adequate security." Showers and toilets were preferable but not necessary so long as there was outdoor space for "staging areas for shower/restroom/laundry/kitchen trailers, etc." Their suggestions for potentially workable locations included "office space, warehouse, big box store, shopping mall with interior concourse, event venues, hotel or dorms, aircraft hangers [sic]"—provided that they were vacant and able to be leased. The kids would be housed here until a sponsor like Wilber could be found, willing to take them in and make sure they got to court.

President Barack Obama deemed what was happening at the border "an urgent humanitarian situation." He requested billions of dollars in additional funding from Congress, largely for housing and related costs. The original $494 million that the president had allocated for housing in 2013 didn't even come close to footing the year's bill. In July 2014, during the thick of the crisis, the Obama administration authorized $3.7 billion in emergency supplemental funding, $1.8 billion of which was earmarked for nonprofit housing contractors and medical providers. That year Southwest Key received over $156 million in government grants.

The rest of the funding was earmarked for border security, funds to support repatriation efforts of deportees, and a massive multimedia *quedate,* or "stay home," campaign. Through leaflets, documentaries, billboards, radio announcements, and television ads, the United States, in collaboration with Central American governments, launched a massive PR campaign to warn families of the great dangers of sending their kids north. Secretary of Homeland Security Jeh Johnson penned an open letter to Central American parents that ran in Spanish in newspapers throughout the region. "It is dangerous to send a child on the long journey from Central America to the United States," he wrote.

The criminal smuggling networks that you pay to deliver your child to the United States have no regard for his or her safety and well-being—to them, your child is a commodity to be exchanged for a payment. In the hands of smugglers, many children are traumatized and psychologically abused by their journey, or worse, beaten, starved, sexually assaulted, or sold into the sex trade; they are exposed to psychological abuse at the hands of criminals. Conditions for an attempt to cross our southern border illegally will become much worse as it gets hotter in July and August.

The conditions Johnson was describing were not news in the Northern Triangle. Like many families sending kids north in the new wave, the Flores family had known what the risks were.

Johnson did address some important misinformation: rumors were circulating through Central America that children and parents with young kids were being offered *permisos,* papers to stay in the United States, if they turned themselves in. In fact, the lack of beds was pushing people out of detention centers more quickly, and once they transferred their cases to their new home jurisdiction, they received a piece of paper summoning them to court sometimes months or even years down the line. This form was sometimes confused with a *permiso.*

There are no "permisos," "permits," or free passes at the end. . . . That means that if your child is caught crossing the border illegally, he or she will be charged with violating United States immigration laws, and placed in deportation proceedings—a situation no one wants. The document issued to your child is not a "permiso," but a Notice To Appear in a deportation proceeding before an immigration judge.

"The desire to see a child have a better life in the United States is understandable," his letter continued. "But, the risks of illegal migration by an unaccompanied child to achieve that dream are far too great."

The more they watched and heard, the more scared the twins felt for their family. The same things that were pushing out all these people were bearing down on them, too.

MARICELA was feeling tired and a bit nauseous, and her breasts were swollen and sore. But Cesar was sterile; it was impossible. She bought a home pregnancy test. Sure enough, she was pregnant.

She wanted to tell Cesar in person. "I'm coming there," she texted. On the bus she rehearsed what she might say. She expected him to be mad, or to disappear as Sebastian had, to buck and run at the onset of new responsibility. But when she told him, voice unsteady, he hugged her.

"This is the best news I've ever gotten," he said. He had thought himself unable to make a kid after his accident, and all this time he'd never got anyone pregnant. He couldn't wait to have a flesh-and-blood child of their own, he told Maricela. He already knew she was a good mom. He had no job, but he loved her, and he'd get a job—he'd be a good dad and husband to her, he promised. She knew other people would question his commitment, but she believed in him. They talked about him moving out of his parents' house, her moving in once he could get settled.

She prepared to tell her parents. She wasn't a girl this time; she was a mature adult, in a mature adult relationship. This child, unlike Lupita, would have a dad. Still, she wasn't married, and though her parents had met and liked Cesar, how could they be sure he was really committed? The baby would be another mouth to feed, another expense at the hospital. And they relied on Maricela to help with the finances, the phone calls, to manage the situation with the lender.

She got the worry and disappointment she'd been expecting, but she hadn't been expecting Ricardo's reaction, far worse than it had been with Lupita. He stormed into her room, screamed at her that she was a fucking idiot, a damned whore, and she better get the fuck out of the house.

"If you don't leave," he told her, "I'll join a gang to take care of the family." This didn't feel like an empty threat.

Once again she found herself on the run. She went with Lupita to her maternal grandmother's house, but it was only buying time; there wasn't space to stay long term, and anyway, how would she support herself? She could have gone and lived with Cesar's family, but they were fighting a lot, and she needed to earn money to take care of herself and her daughter. Her parents may not have known what Ricardo had said to her, but they understood that he had run her out of the house—and they'd done nothing to stop him. To her it seemed that they were scared of their own son.

After a couple of days some friends connected her with a job as a live-in maid for an elderly woman outside San Salvador. She'd have a place to live and a small income, but she couldn't bring Lupita with her. Maricela packed a bag and returned to her parents' house when she knew Ricardo would be away. Her little sisters would take care of her daughter until she figured out a longer-term plan. Maricela kissed Lupita goodbye, shut the door against her wails, boarded the bus, and left.

WHEN the twins found out about Maricela from Ricardo, Ernesto took to Facebook to scold her. Didn't she know, he wrote, that you had to think about the consequences before you acted? Raúl flopped onto the mattress and sighed. They were certain what kind of guy had knocked up their sister: some wayward gangster wannabe, someone with no future, who'd do nothing to take care of her or her second born. They could hear in Ricardo's messages that he was furious. It seemed like a good thing that Maricela had gone away for a while.

The twins enrolled in summer school to improve their English and recoup credits from the classes they'd failed that spring—largely, from absences—but they missed the first day and came late to the second. They knew they should go, and they didn't much want to be at home, either. But the first morning they showed up, they were already sick of being stuck inside the school walls. They spent the rest of the week devising schemes to ditch.

One afternoon they sneaked out of class, and Ernesto spotted an empty brown lunch sack. He picked it up, crumpled it, and threw it at Raúl, who chucked it back. Soon they were volleying the trash like cats with a ball of yarn. Ernesto pulled his lighter out and lit the edge of the bag, and Raúl laughed hysterically as the bag rose into the air, burning itself to smoke and a few black embers that settled back to the ground. The twins looked around nervously, but no one, it seemed, had seen them.

Wrong. The incident got them suspended from summer school. The district had a strict missed-class policy for summer school, and since they'd already missed so much, after the paper bag antics they weren't allowed to come back. This austere policy meant that Raúl and Ernesto missed out on three weeks of coursework that they both needed to graduate and, more urgently, to improve their English.

Over the following weeks, Ernesto saw Marie as much as he could. She was in summer school so had less time than he did, but he worried she wasn't as interested in him anymore. She took a while to respond to his texts now and sometimes didn't respond at all.

One restless afternoon he took a walk to Arrojo Viejo and lit a cigarette. In the corner of the park he saw a girl with long hair sitting next to a guy. It was hard to be sure, because right as he arrived, the two began making out, the boy's hand reaching around her neck, but her sleek, dark hair had to be Marie's.

Ernesto froze for a moment, then turned around. He stormed home in a state of compressed fury. He immediately blocked her on Facebook and Instagram. "You're a traitor," he texted her. "You don't give a shit about me. Never talk to me again."

All night Raúl got texts and phone calls from Marie. *What was wrong with Ernesto? What happened? Why won't your brother talk to me?* Raúl didn't know how to answer her—Ernesto wasn't telling him anything, either—but twin code meant he was on his brother's side.

Ernesto changed his profile picture to a photo he took in the bathroom, sunglasses and hat on, no shirt, flexing his muscles. His banner photo changed, too, to an image of a pretty girl in underwear and a Raiders cap crouched suggestively on a bed. The picture was mirrored, such that two identical girls in Raiders caps faced each other, looking at the camera. Twins.

When Ernesto and Raúl first started school in February, there had been around forty unaccompanied minors at Oakland International.

There were sixty by the end of the school year. When school started back up again in late August, there were over ninety, out of a population of 375. Many had had problems back home and were shackled with debt, and all had bad memories of their trips north. And they all needed lawyers. September 30 marked the end of the 2014 fiscal year, during which 57,496 minors were placed into custody in the United States—an increase of over 700 percent from what was once the annual norm. Children numbering the entire population of White Plains, New York, were caught crossing the southern border without their parents that year and placed in ORR detention.

In a way, seeing all these other kids in his same shoes fortified Ernesto, as when Ibrahim had told him about fleeing Iraq. He and Raúl made a pact to not drink so much this year and to really focus on school: eleventh grade.

And they'd focus on the debt. No amount of cash they managed to send home—$100, $200, $500—made a dent, because the interest was growing faster than they could pay it off. They called home every couple of weeks, and every time their father asked: Did they still need to be going to school for their case? Could they leave and start working? Their mother didn't pressure them so much. "I'm glad you're in school," she said. It was Maricela who had pressured them the most, but then she'd fucked up her own situation, so she wasn't hassling them anymore.

"Once we get our papers," Ernesto said each time to his father, "we'll be able to pay it off easy." They called home less and less often.

In order for their Special Immigrant Juvenile Status visa to be approved by the U.S. immigration authorities, the twins had to attend an interview with an immigration official in downtown San Francisco, where they'd be questioned both separately and together (and could answer in Spanish, thank goodness). They would be asked simple questions, mostly: who their father was, how many siblings they had, what life was like for them with their families, when they left El Salvador, when and how they'd entered the United States, where they lived now, and whether they went to school.

Amy practiced with the boys. "Just answer honestly," she said. "And don't worry—don't be nervous." But what if they gave answers the interviewer didn't like? And what if they had to talk about what had happened in the desert, or in Reynosa, or in Guatemala, in front of a stranger?

The twins' English class was writing newspaper articles about the border crisis. The day before his SIJS interview, Ernesto turned in his paper:

Unaccompanied Minors
By: Ernesto Flores

Many children are crossing the border for a better life. In 2012 police caught 13,000. And 2013 there were even more 2014. Many young people come to the U.S. without parents. They are leaving from Central America. Many come because the gangs make their life very difficult. Many of them are arrested by the police officer.

The government can less the problem by, helping the children considered, as refugees because in their home country many times. They don't have enough help to protect everyone to the gangs. For this reason I think the government from the U.S can help them. The president he can make a law to, protect every children who come to the United States without parent. I know in this country we have a lot of opportunities to a better life, for begin a professional, no can think for many reasons how protect immigrants children.

I think the government can work how, they can protect the immigrant children here in the United States. The police officer and the government they can not stop the children to cross the border, every children know that it's dangerous, but they want a better life for them, and for their family.

The article wasn't nearly at the eleventh-grade level, and he'd got help from more advanced students, but after mediocre schooling in El Salvador and a spotty six months of American high school, this report was considered an accomplishment for Ernesto, though he still had a long way to go. The biggest improvement was in his effort.

The next day the boys walked out of the interview in downtown San

Francisco with doubts about how it had gone. Amy assured them that they'd done great, but they weren't so sure.

AT the old woman's house, Maricela worked until she was about to burst, cooking and mopping, washing and folding the laundry. A little over a month before her due date, she gave up: it was time to go home. She couldn't stay here forever, and Ricardo must have cooled off by now, she figured. Plus, she missed her daughter.

The labor of the second child was much easier than the first, and it helped that she had not just her mother but Cesar at her side. After laboring for a while, they wheeled her to the operating room. It was another girl. She'd been hoping for a boy, which would make Cesar happy and her father, too, but this baby—Maria Elena, they named her, or Leiny—was perfect.

While Maricela was in the hospital, one of the nurses offered her a birth control option: if she wasn't hoping to have more children, she could opt to be sterilized for free before she was discharged. She thought it over, nursing her newborn. When Cesar came in to check on her, she asked, "Would we ever want to have more children?"

"I don't know," he said. "Children are expensive." He'd just got a job putting together electronics on a factory assembly line, and he'd moved out of his parents' house. When she was ready and they had enough starting money, plus money for a ring and a wedding, Maricela could move in with him.

"I think two is enough," he said. Two—because he was counting Lupita.

She smiled. "Yeah, I think two is enough," she agreed. She had the procedure done before checking out of the hospital.

She didn't tell her parents, because she knew they would think choosing to sterilize herself, as she put it, was a sin. She was nervous about God being disappointed in her, but she didn't want to carry the weight of a huge family as her parents had. Her daughters would have everything—a father, financial stability, everything.

Up north the Flores twins were growing up and settling into an unaccustomed permanence, while their sister was, with this new baby and with Cesar, dropping the anchor into her Salvadoran life. All the elder Flores siblings were setting roots into circumstances they hadn't fully chosen. But the baby offered a wink of optimism, family wide.

"You have another niece," their mom announced proudly the next time the twins phoned. During that call, no one mentioned the debt.

I borrowed a van and drove a group of eight students to the city council meeting, holding signs they'd made. "Support Oakland's Immigrant Children." "We need lawyers." The twins had agreed to come along.

Our school was full by mid-September—the earliest we'd ever been full in our history. By October, the Oakland Unified School District had run out of spaces for newcomer students in high school. About three-quarters of the new influx were unaccompanied minors.

Thanks in part to the media attention of that summer, several legal agencies—in particular, Centro Legal de la Raza and the East Bay Sanctuary Covenant—had stepped up, heroically offering free legal services to hundreds of unaccompanied minors and family cases in Oakland. Despite limited staffing, they weren't turning any students away. They had convened a consortium of legal agencies and social justice organizations to advocate for these children: they were refugees, the group contended, and as children, they should not face deportation proceedings without counsel. Just as the school district was trying to gather resources to open more newcomer programs and support unaccompanied minors in school, this group had put together several proposals to advocate for funding from the philanthropic community as well as from city and county bodies, particularly for mental health and legal services.

Tonight, Oakland's City Council was accepting public comment on one of the consortium's proposals. The consortium wanted to pack the meeting with supporters, especially those who could testify to how important legal services were, hence their request for a group of students from Oakland International to come. The students, from El Salvador, Guatemala, and Honduras, were eager, if also apprehensive, to speak out on behalf of their communities. They sat in the front row for over an hour while the council ran through its agenda. They watched as Mayor Jean Quan awarded commendations, and then as Oakland residents stood in line to make public comments on a variety of topics. While many had genuine grievances, some regulars rattled off conspiracy theories and impossible demands. Raider Nation, the die-hard football fan club whose members dressed like they were in a heavy metal band, recited a poem about their beloved team and toasted a deceased member of their group. During the spectacle the students looked to me in search of explanation. "Anyone gets a chance to talk to their representatives," I said. Just like the students, including the twins, would get a chance to stand up when their classmate explained how important it was for him to have a lawyer from Centro Legal de la Raza, which had helped him gain status here after fleeing Guatemala's gangs.

The meeting was democracy in action, in all its messy glory. The City Council decided to fund the legal services proposal, earmarking several hundred thousand dollars for pro-bono counsel so that, for the time being, no more unaccompanied minors in Oakland would have to go to immigration court alone.

THE twins' green card approval notice arrived at the end of September. Amy called me early in the morning—the twins weren't answering their cellphones, so she was hoping to track them down at school. They'd showed up in class that day, their teachers informed me, but had suddenly walked out. I got in the car and drove around the neighborhood hoping to find them, and sure enough there they were, two blocks from school on the corner of Forty-eighth and Telegraph, Ernesto squatting on the sidewalk and Raúl leaning against a pole, smoking cigarettes with furrowed brows. I told them Amy had news.

"We know," Raúl spat, shaking his head. "We already know."

I was confused. "What do you mean?"

"We got the letter," he said, pulling it from his backpack. The approval notice had arrived in the Hillside mailbox last night.

"It's bad, right?" Raúl said.

I looked at them in disbelief. "What? No! It's good news. It's really good news!"

"Don't joke around with us," Raúl said gravely. "Just tell us the truth."

I told them. The twins looked at each other, then back at me.

"Are you sure?" Ernesto snapped.

"*Sure?*" repeated Raúl.

"Yes," I said. "Your applications were approved!"

They looked at each other again, then smiled. Their smiles became embarrassed laughter. Raúl shook the letter.

The paper, a slim ornament of bureaucracy that resembled a juror summons or a DMV receipt, was crowded with austere, automated-looking text. They hadn't been able to read it. "We thought it said we'd been rejected."

I looked at the paper. "Why did you think that?"

They shrugged. "Just didn't look like good news."

THE FAILED

It's the summer of 2015, and the failed migrants disembark from the line of buses looking haggard. The driver tosses their belongings onto the sidewalk: backpacks, dusty duffel bags, plastic sacks secured with double knots. It's early afternoon, and the day's first five buses have arrived at the San Salvador reception center carrying more than 175 people from Siglo XXI, the massive detention center in Tapachula, Chiapas, Mexico. Buses from another detention center farther north will arrive later today. The authorities in Tapachula have phoned most of the migrants' relatives to let them know when to expect their loved ones. The families congregate beneath tents in the front of the San Salvador compound, waiting.

"The migrants are very vulnerable," says Ana Solorzano, director of the reception center run by the Salvadoran government. "What you see in some of their eyes when they get off the bus . . ."

The migrants walk into the center, bags slung over shoulders. All their shoelaces were removed in detention to prevent anyone from harming him- or herself, so the tongues of their sneakers flap free as they walk. Under a tent donated by Save the Children, reception center staff greet them with snacks and soda, then point them into an air-conditioned room. In the front row, a plump woman in a bright orange blouse opens snack boxes for her two young children. She takes a compact out of her purse while they eat and slowly powders the sheen off of her face.

The immigration officials explain the registration process, which must take place before they are released: *We'll fingerprint*

*you, let you call home, ask you some questions, make sure you're safe and
healthy and have everything you need.*

"Yeah, yeah, we know how it all works, we've done this a hundred times already!" a guy shouts, laughing.

The woman in orange laughs, too. She snaps the compact back
into her purse. "Come on," she says to her kids. They stand and
join the line to be fingerprinted.

Children traveling alone are brought into a separate room
to meet with a child-welfare worker. The twenty or so children
today are fourteen, fifteen, sixteen, seventeen. If they're caught
farther north in Mexico, they're sent home by plane. Those under
twelve will come by plane regardless of where in Mexico they
were caught.

The majority of deportations to El Salvador used to come from
the United States, but now they come from Mexico: in June only
1,900 came from the United States but 3,000 from Mexico. The
Mexican immigration crackdown is part of Mexico's Programa
Frontera Sur, an operation to secure its southern border from
drugs and migrants. The United States encourages and has heavily funded these efforts, even more so since the migrant crisis last
summer. If migrants can be stopped and deported from Mexico,
they won't become the United States' problem.

This year the number of unaccompanied minors making it to
the United States is already down; 57,496 were taken into federal
ORR custody in 2014 whereas there were 33,726 by the end of
2015, largely because of the Mexican crackdown. It was a decrease
of more than 40 percent, while Mexico's apprehensions increased
by 67 percent.

The group of children begin their interviews. Where were
they from? Why did they leave? Would they feel safe going home?
Were they being mistreated? Would they try to go north again?

"After my birthday," one boy says, which is in a couple of
weeks. He wants to spend his birthday at home.

"You see," an immigration official says, referring to the

almost-birthday boy. "He can't be all that worried about whatever is going on at home if he can wait a few more weeks to spend his birthday with his mommy."

Nearly all the children, according to officials, say they will try again: "We've seen children who've tried six, seven times."

Returnees have been a part of El Salvador's social fabric for decades, since even before the civil war days in the eighties. But not on this scale. Everyone—from bus drivers and immigration officials in El Salvador to the Salvadoran consul in Mexico to the migrants themselves—will tell you the migration "emergency" in El Salvador is not going to stop. In response to the crackdown in southern Mexico, people are simply changing their routes: moving on foot through the mountains, boarding too-packed boats in the middle of the night. These same buses will be back next week with more.

CHAPTER 9

Ernesto began working five nights a week at the Japanese restaurant in upscale Montclair, and shortly thereafter Raúl was offered a job at an Italian restaurant down the road. This was big money: together they'd be making several hundred dollars every week.

They both spent evenings busing tables, and after the customers left, they emptied the trash, scrubbed the industrial sinks, stovetops, and counters, and mopped the floors. Whoever got out from work first would text the other, then walk to the bus stop to smoke until his brother arrived. Downtown Montclair emptied early, and late at night on the dark streets only the sounds of the nearby highway and the closing of the restaurants could be heard—final customers straggling to their cars, busboys swinging garbage bags into Dumpsters, lights shutting off, and keys jangling into locks. They'd take the bus back into the Temescal neighborhood, where OIHS was located, then wait for the number-one bus to take them back east through the late-night International Corridor, where, at this hour, the sex workers in their high heels cruised for customers. They walked the ten blocks home guardedly.

Once, while waiting for Raúl outside the corner store near their house, a guy Ernesto had never seen before came up and slugged him full force in the face. He fell down onto the pavement, his vision going dark. Before he could say anything, the guy helped him up.

"Whoa, sorry, man," he said. "I thought you were someone else." He walked away. Ernesto's mouth was bleeding, and a hunk of a back molar had broken off. He ran home, hoping not to come across the guy again, and cleaned himself up.

A few weeks later Raúl was taking the bus home one night from work alone, which was rare. As he waited for the bus, a group of six guys, covered in hoods and low-slung skullcaps, ran up to him.

One grabbed him from behind. "Give us your fucking money!" another one shouted.

He froze. It was like he was back in Guatemala, head in the dirt.

"Give it to us!"

He couldn't move. They frisked him, grabbed his wallet out of his jeans—it had about fifty dollars—rifled through his backpack, and took his phone. They ran off and left him there in the vacant street where he stood, immobilized, until the bus came.

From then on, they came home from work on psychological tiptoe, vigilant of their surroundings while pretending to be fully at ease. Oakland was a great city but not without its problems. Over the years, dozens of Oakland International students had been jumped or mugged on their way to and from school—a few times even at gunpoint within a few-block radius of OIHS, a much safer neighborhood than where many of the students lived. Though increasingly safe, in 2013 Oakland was home to the most violent crime, by far, of any California city over ten thousand people. In 2014 aggravated assault was up 5 percent and possession of weapons was up 14 percent from the year before, though robbery was down 31 percent.

Crime happened at all times of day, but the twins were really wary only at night. From the bus stop, they walked briskly together, trying to appear determined, fearless, and simultaneously fearsome, assuming this armor as they marched each night, puffing cigarettes with counterfeit "don't fuck with me" expressions, past the corner stores and the guys chilling on the stoops, the barking dogs, the howling babies, the occasional car doing doughnuts in the street, their own little mini-sideshow.

They might stop for a minute and watch the commotion with the rest of the onlookers, momentarily joining in the ecstatic, late-night urban thrill of ragtag strangers assembled before a common spectacle, until they remembered themselves again, stiffened, and hightailed it home.

WHILE their new niece had brought a moment of calm to the La Colonia household, tensions were building again at Hillside, and not just between Ernesto and Wilber. Rosalinda's new boyfriend had moved in with them and had invited two of his friends to rent the fourth room. The already full house now had three more grown men living in it, whom the twins referred to as "the Mexicans." Sober, they were nice enough people, but in the evenings they became rowdy. They guzzled Coronas and Negro Modelos and cranked music, twanging *corridos,* their voices growing louder as the night went on. The twins almost never left their room, now.

Only Rosalinda seemed to like the new arrangement, happy to have a man by her side and people her own age—late thirties—to hang out with. The cheaper rent helped, too. The twins got used to avoiding the living room; they'd walk in the front door, nod hello to the trio of men drinking beer, and head straight to their bedroom—no more watching family movies with the kids stretched out on the living room's couches, wrapped up in pilled blankets.

One night they overheard the Mexicans talking shit about them: about Wilber's bad attitude, about the mess the boys made in the kitchen and the bathroom. Another day one of them accused Ernesto and Raúl of eating all his cornflakes. That wasn't their fucking food, he scolded. They had clearly been badly brought up to think they could steal other people's stuff.

The twins insisted they hadn't touched the cornflakes.

"Who did it, then?" he wanted to know.

A few days earlier they'd watched José scarf down several bowls with milk that also wasn't his. But pointing the finger at Rosalinda's son felt like it would violate the necessary kid code of the apartment. They shrugged.

Within weeks their self-imposed exile became full-blown, their bedroom a homemade fortress. They'd scoop up Nicky and lounge in the bed texting girls and friends from school, glugging down the Red Bulls and generic colas Wilber bought by the pallet at Costco and Mi Pueblo, watching movies and listening to music, posting photos of themselves in flat-billed hats and sunglasses and of their tennis shoes. Ernesto was still heartbroken about Marie, but he didn't talk about it, even with Raúl. He hoped she'd see his photos online and feel jealous. When José came over, he'd knock on the door and hop into the pile on the bed or sprawl out on the dank carpet.

The Mexicans' presence was unmooring to Wilber, too, though he kept quiet. But then Gabby overheard them accusing Wilber and his brothers again of eating all their food. "I'm gonna beat the shit out of that fucker," one of them slurred, referring to Wilber.

"How am I supposed to live with these guys when they want to fight me?" he demanded to Gabby.

"Oh, relax," Rosalinda told her daughter. "Don't take it seriously." They were just drunk, she said, waving him off.

Wilber and the other men began to toughen up in each other's presence, holding their ground. Wilber, too, was used to this peacocking and feigned lack of intimidation, this tightrope game of trying to appear strong while never outwardly copping to one's own fear. It wasn't unlike how it had been in El Salvador at times, though it seemed more complex here on account of all the colliding cultures. But this was no way to feel in one's own home.

Wilber talked to Rosalinda—this wasn't what he'd bargained for when he opted to move in with Gabby's family. But she shut him down. Did he know what it was like to be a single mom of three kids? What was his problem?

Gabby took her mom's side. "Just ignore them." Much as she could have done without the Mexicans, in her eyes Wilber's attitude just made it worse. The couple fought about it, and once the seal was broken on this dynamic, they fought about other things, too. Money was one. Wilber needed to push his little brothers to help out more, she said. Wilber didn't disagree, but he didn't like her butting in. The twins could hear them arguing through the walls in low, tense murmurs, then in shouts. Gabby felt Wilber was putting her in the middle, forcing her to choose between her boyfriend and her mother. Wilber would exit the house in a fury and speed out of the driveway in his car, his own fortress, the one place he had to be alone.

ONE day on the way to school, a tenth grader named Franklin stepped onto the twins' bus. He was also from El Salvador, baby-faced but nearly six feet tall with a bulky build. He seemed to smoke pot constantly—out of joints, glass bowls, even cafeteria apples that he carved into pipes. The boys sat with their headphones in, tuning the music low enough that they could still hear what was going on around them. As the bus rolled north along Telegraph, Raúl nudged Ernesto. Franklin was talking about them. Ernesto listened and, sure enough, heard Franklin say the word *twins* a couple of times.

They got off the bus a few blocks early and walked off their rage. Franklin was big, but the two of them could take him, they thought. They made it to school and went to class. But the next period, when Ernesto went to the bathroom, he recognized Franklin at the sink.

"If you're going to talk shit about me and my brother," Ernesto said, "don't talk behind our backs."

Franklin turned around, drying his hands. "What?" he said.

"You know what I'm talking about," Ernesto said, marching toward him. He stood nearly a foot shorter but puffed up his chest to appear, or at least feel, intimidating. "If you have something to say to me, say it to my face."

"Bitch," Franklin said, taking a step toward Ernesto.

Ernesto pushed him, and Franklin stumbled backward out the bathroom door. They were in the hallway now, where a crowd of kids quickly formed and began cheering. Ernesto punched him in the face, just as an adult came running to break up the fight.

Back in the office, Franklin insisted he hadn't been saying anything about the twins—he didn't even know their names. But Ernesto knew what he had heard. Since Ernesto had started the fight, he was suspended for the day to cool off.

The twins had made accidental enemies like Franklin and their Mexican housemates all their lives. But the cause was more than just the fighting words, the bad looks, the accusations that they thought were directed at them. It was what was beneath them, Ernesto and Raúl felt. Those looks accused the boys of being nothing.

ONE night a few weeks later the Mexicans, drinking Modelos and eating a bucket of chicken with the TV blaring, dropped a plate of bones on the carpet next to Nicky. Wilber and Gabby weren't home yet, and the twins were tucked quietly into their room. The Chihuahua spent the rest of the evening chewing at the bones, which cracked and split between her tiny teeth.

The next morning Nicky seemed distressed, trembling more than usual. Gabby and Wilber figured she just had the dog flu.

That evening when the boys came home from school, they found Gabby in her room hunched over, crying. Wilber was rubbing her back, trying to soothe her while holding back tears of his own. They went in, and there was Nicky, splayed out on her little blue dog bed, unmoving. Dead.

Later that night Gabby and Wilber scooped up Nicky's body, wrapped it in a blanket, and brought it out to the car. They drove to a vet, who took X-rays that showed splinters of bone stuck in her stomach and throat.

"It ripped open her stomach," Raúl said, jaw clenched, snapping his head as if to buck the memory.

"Those fuckers killed her," Ernesto spat.

The next day Wilber and Gabby dug a hole on the parched hill that cast a morning shadow over their apartment. They held a private burial for Nicky.

Wilber held Gabby while she shook with sobs. "We have to move," she told him.

The twins agreed. "We're moving," they told me gravely the next day. They'd sooner sleep on the streets than spend another night with those fucking Mexicans, they said.

"*Mucha falta* Nicky," Ernesto told me in my office a few days later, when they could bring themselves to talk about it.

"*Mucha falta* Nicky," Raúl repeated. "I really miss Nicky," though the direct translation is less personal, more factual: "Nicky is really missed."

Gabby confronted her mom about what the Mexicans had done, but Rosalinda defended them, insisting that they were only trying to feed Nicky. Gabby accused Rosalinda of choosing her boyfriend's stupid friends over her own daughter. Rosalinda was furious—after all she'd done to support her daughter, after taking in her boyfriend and his needy little cornflake-stealing brothers?

"Go ahead, move out with your boyfriend!" Rosalinda said. Gabby called her mother's bluff and left.

THROUGH co-workers at the landscaping company, Wilber found them another apartment, a two-bedroom in a building closer to Fruitvale and downtown Oakland (and closer to school). Wilber, Gabby, Ernesto, and Raúl loaded their stuff into Wilber's car, ready to start over. It was February 2015, just over a year since they'd moved to Oakland.

Gabby bought another dog from the pound, a little white fluffball mutt they named Nicky Two. The twins showed off pictures of her seated in the front seat of a car with a red bandanna tied around her neck—a gang symbol. Raúl posted on his Facebook wall:

My dog's an Oakland gangsta.

It was just a joke, he insisted.

The main room of the new apartment was an adjoined kitchen and living room, off of which were the two bedrooms—one for Wilber and Gabby, one for the twins—and a bathroom. Gabby's brother took up residence on the couch a few nights a week. The house was newly renovated and let in more light than the apartment on Hillside had, which gave the space an air of possibility, notwithstanding the nuggets of dog shit that quickly littered the tile floor.

The new place was more expensive, though, so the twins ramped up their hours at the restaurants, working five to six days a week to pay their five-hundred-dollar share of the rent. They also needed to pay off their legal fees. Though Amy never once pressed them for the money, it was another financial obligation, and they wanted to make sure they kept their promise. They weren't actually paying monthly, but every now and again they delivered some money to her.

There still wasn't much left over for paying down the debt in El Salvador.

"You need to be sending at least a thousand dollars a month," Maricela told them over the phone. Now that she was home again, new baby in tow, she was back to nagging them. They knew she was right; the interest was compounding the debt so much that anything much less than a thousand wouldn't even begin to hack away at the principal. But she was stuck in that mentality that the North fulfilled its promises. "It's not as easy as it seems," Ernesto said. She had no idea of all the things they were trying to balance.

From Maricela's perspective, her brothers had it great: jobs, school, freedom from the gangs and from their family—everything she didn't have. Cesar was working and helping to support her and Leiny (and, by extension, Lupita), which helped, but as Leiny grew, she needed more diapers and more milk. He still didn't have enough for a ring for her or for a wedding; she would have moved in with him anyway, but he felt he still didn't have enough stability, and things with his parents continued to sour. She waited patiently. Though he had less energy and time to make the trip to La Colonia these days, she still felt confident, if a bit shakier than before, that they'd be together.

She wasn't so confident when it came to her brothers. She'd seen the pictures they posted online. She knew that Ernesto had bought an iPhone. Beyond the rent and fees, the twins felt they spent relatively little on themselves and that what they did was justified. Raúl needed a new pair of shoes because his were falling apart again, and they had got wet one day and smelled so moldy, he couldn't keep them in his room. Ernesto needed a jacket—it was cold at night, waiting for the bus after work.

Raúl picked out hundred-dollar Nikes; Ernesto's jacket was Nike, too, costing seventy-five. From what Maricela could glean on Facebook, these were massive purchases, showing what they prioritized over all else: themselves. Wilber had left promising to help the family; he hadn't done much, but at least he'd paid off the debt. The twins had dug a deep hole for the family and scrambled out themselves. "Ask them," their father pleaded, "to not buy so many clothes."

Maricela thought the threat of losing the land might kill her father. "Why are you still in school?" she wrote to the twins. Surely they could work full time at least for a while, to make sure they weren't responsible for destroying their family.

THE twins didn't want to leave school—they wanted to learn English and graduate. The irony was that the after-hours jobs they had taken, to make school possible, were ruining their grades. The first year they had earned mostly Cs, but now they were getting almost all Fs and Ds, and every class that they missed put them further behind. By four o'clock they had to run out the door for work. Mostly they had no time for homework. They got home at eleven p.m. on a good night, but with bus delays and on busier nights at the restaurants, they often weren't home until after midnight. On a good day they woke up around eight a.m.; the school, an hourlong bus ride away, rang its bell at 8:20. And though the new apartment was forty blocks closer to school, the buses were often full by the time they reached the twins' stop and passed them by. They stood there morning after morning, waiting with their backpacks while drinking Monsters and drawing down their morning cigarettes.

It didn't help that they'd insisted on enrolling in eleventh grade—which was more advanced than they were ready for. When they'd registered in August, the teachers had suggested they repeat tenth grade, since they'd missed so much school and had only enrolled in February. But the suggestion that the twins couldn't hack it was unacceptable to them—they'd nearly graduated high school in El Salvador, after all. Yet now, due to their spotty attendance, they were woefully behind their classmates in eleventh grade, even other newcomers and unaccompanied minors like themselves.

Ernesto could come up with enough answers to complete the homework when he tried, and to appear not lost on the days he showed up to class. But when he saw clearly how far behind most of the other students he was, he felt they must all think he was stupid. "I hate my class," he announced one day, and marched out of school. He was used to being the smart one, and now, after nearly a year without Raúl by his side in class, he felt anything but. Raúl, though he had weaker English and fewer academic skills after years of deferring to his brother for answers, fared much better. Because he was used to needing extra help from Ernesto, he had no trouble asking questions.

Yet neither was even close to passing the eleventh grade. The twins wouldn't leave school yet, but they did have to make decisions. Their teachers wanted them to create an action plan to right the ship, some kind of agreement about what they could do to improve things at school. But they were tired of people—Wilber, Maricela, their parents, me— trying to force them into doing things. They wouldn't make any more agreements they couldn't keep.

"We've come to an agreement," Raúl announced to me, "which is that we're not going to make any agreement." What they did decide was that things would be better if they were in the same class. Ernesto took to walking out of his classroom early on in the period and wandering over to Raúl's classroom, where he'd pull up a chair next to his brother. The teachers repeatedly asked him to leave, but they noticed that—as long as the twins weren't spending too much time giggling with each other—they got more work done when they were together. Ernesto, especially: no longer did he put his head down on the table or refuse to work with other students.

As the spring semester drew on, things did get better. They almost never made it to school on time and their grades were still subpar, but they weren't entirely failing. The teachers saw what the twins had long felt: they were better as a duo than apart.

Ernesto started work on his final portfolio, a presentation to be made to a group of his peers and teachers at the end of the semester. An early slide was titled "One Struggle." "My struggle was that i am absent in the every day in the school," he wrote in white letters against a blue backdrop. "I try to come every day. I had to work in the afternoon, finished in the night."

He was proud, looking back. Last year he had been a scared boy: a drunk, stricken with night terrors and guilt. Now, almost a year and a half after breaking down on the camping trip, he had papers, friends, a job, and an apartment, and he knew his way around Oakland. Okay, his grades weren't good, but they weren't all failures. Look at him now—presenting in English, raggedy as it was, in front of the whole class.

When he was in the right frame of mind, he could see that his life had righted itself, somewhat, and in spite of all the challenges, his future was, when the light caught it just right, one of potential, again.

THESE days they barely saw Wilber, returning home late as they did and waking up after he'd already left for his shift. Weekends they sometimes saw him before their shifts began at four p.m., but rarely—the twins tended to use those days to catch up on sleep and then some, as though storing it up for the week ahead.

Occasionally Wilber planned day trips for the family. The brothers sometimes went with Gabby and José to the beach in Half Moon Bay, or the waterfront in Alameda, or for a hike. But Ernesto usually either declined these outings or wasn't invited. Wilber drove Raúl up to the hills one day, where they walked around and came across a gated-in pack of goats. Like boys at a petting zoo, they stroked them and fed them apples, laughing at the creatures' diabolical faces. So charmed were they by the goats, so surprised to see them up on these lonely hills, that a passerby might not know that these young men in skinny jeans and flat-brimmed caps had been skilled farmers and shepherds when they were no taller than goats themselves. Raúl filmed the herd munching grass on his phone (he'd bought a replacement after he was robbed, sacrificing a couple hundred dollars), getting as close as he could before they lunged at the camera, and he had to jump back, laughing. When Raúl showed Ernesto the video, his twin rolled his eyes.

Though things had got better between him and Wilber once they moved out of the tension-laden Hillside apartment, after a few months they were back at each other's throats: Ernesto didn't clean up his dishes, Wilber didn't drive him somewhere he'd promised, Ernesto had a bad attitude, and on and on. He and Wilber avoided each other both by accident and by choice.

Things came to a head in May. Convinced that Wilber had taken a stack of his cash, Ernesto exploded, telling his older brother to fuck off, that he didn't need him, that he was leaving. A few days later he heard from friends at work about an available bedroom that would cost five hundred dollars a month, and it was settled. He moved out the next day.

Raúl, as usual, was in the middle. If he left with his twin, he would piss Wilber off, and his big brother would be stuck with a two-bedroom apartment that he and Gabby couldn't afford. "He found this place so we could all live together," Raúl reasoned. But he didn't like the idea of living apart from his twin or taking on Ernesto's share of the rent.

Ernesto, prideful and eager to get away from Wilber, told Raúl he didn't care if he came or not. "Do what you want, doesn't matter to me," Ernesto said as he crammed his stuff into his backpack and shopping bags.

"It's just for now," said Raúl, "until we figure things out."

"You're messy," he snapped at Raúl, pointing to the soda cans and piles of dirty clothes.

Raúl laughed, but Ernesto didn't.

Ernesto's new place was in the three-bedroom lower level of a duplex farther east. He shared it with a middle-aged couple and a single guy in his thirties. He put a lock on his bedroom door so he could come and go as he pleased. After a few days, he decided he liked having a place of his own, apart from Raúl—something he'd never had before. He could keep his things organized, and he didn't have to worry about family, like Wilber, being all up in his business. Apart from the line in the morning for the shower, it felt like a pretty good place for Ernesto. And anyway, he saw his twin every day at school.

On Tuesdays, their day off from work, Raúl spent the night at Ernesto's. Sometimes on other days, too. They'd stay up late, listening to low music and texting and falling asleep on the same small bed.

WHEN Raúl wasn't at Ernesto's, he was spending a lot of time alone: in his room, on the way to school, on the way home from work. He was lonesome there at the sink, scrubbing the detritus of meals. He hung out with friends during lunch sometimes, and in class, but there wasn't really time after school to socialize. He had more time alone, to think and to remember.

Through a friend at work, Raúl found a girlfriend, who lived in San Jose. He skipped a few days of school that spring to go down and see her, taking the bus from the East Oakland terminal. They understood each other, Raúl felt, and texting her all night, he felt less lonely.

Was Raúl in love? "I guess so," he said. "We must be, since we fight so much." But with his schedule and her living in San Jose, they rarely saw each other.

They liked to play a game where he pretended to be her dad and get her in trouble. "I'm mad at you, *mija!*" he'd say or write in Spanish. "I'm going to punish you."

"Papa, I'm sorry, I'll never do it again!" she'd respond. "I promise!" She'd act hurt and scared, and he'd forgive her for whatever transgression, real or imagined, she'd committed.

One night she admitted to Raúl that she'd smoked pot that day at school. This upset him. It wasn't good for girls to smoke pot, and he didn't like that she was doing those kinds of things without him around. Who knew what she did when she smoked pot, who could take advantage of her, or who she was hanging out with?

"Papa, I'm sorry!" she wrote.

"It's not funny," he said.

"Papa, don't be mad! Forgive me!"

But it wasn't a game this time. Raúl brooded. He wanted to get back at her.

The next day he asked a friend to buy him vodka, which he mixed into a blue Gatorade and drank down. By third period, he was stumbling around campus alone. There had been a party in his class that day, and someone had brought Taki chips; now his lips were covered in red powder, giving him the look of a washed-up drag queen who'd misapplied her lipstick.

I found him sitting on the sidewalk outside school, waiting for Ernesto to be finished with class and take him home. He swayed and rambled like a small-town drunk. "It's because of my friends!" he said of his drinking. "My ex-friends!"

"Do you realize," he said, finger pointed up toward the sky, gaze veering left, "that my parents, they pray for me? They do prayers every week at church for me." He paused, almost dramatically. "Prayers," he said. "For me. And for my brother.

"I just want to show them," he said. "I want to prove to them . . ." He trailed off.

"To the ex-friends, or to your parents?" I asked.

"Yes," he said. "Yes.

"I can't explain. What those fuckers did to me. But they pray. Every Sunday at church! My parents pray for me to be okay."

A couple of weeks later Raúl and his girlfriend had another big fight, a permanent one, and broke up.

The twins' girlfriends came and went that year. They found most of them through friends of friends on Facebook, or WhatsApp or Kik, where their profiles were public. They'd strike up a flirtation, and eventually, if things went well, they'd agree to meet in person. The connections rarely lasted long, though, or got very physical. They never had the time.

Raúl posted on Facebook in English:

I'm fucking single.

MONEY was tight, and Wilber, Gabby, and Raúl did not pay their rent on time. After four months living there, they thought they'd get some leeway, but the landlord ordered them evicted: they had two weeks to move.

Once they got the eviction notice, Raúl and Wilber decided to part ways. Temporarily, anyway. At least now he wouldn't have to choose between Wilber and Ernesto, Raúl thought—the eviction had given him a clean break, a good reason for moving in with his twin.

But suddenly Ernesto didn't seem so sure about welcoming him. "You're too messy," he said the week before move-out day, biting into an apple he'd swiped from a friend's cafeteria tray. "My room's too small, there's no space. You'll have to find some place of your own."

"Fine," Raúl said, cementing his gaze. "Whatever."

Ernesto chucked the apple core into the trash can.

Raúl shook the conversation off and laughed at a joke a friend made in passing. Ernesto was just playing around, was all.

But when Ernesto said the same thing later that afternoon, Raúl took it harder. "You think I want to live with your stupid ass?" Raúl said. "Fucking animal."

After the final afternoon bell rang, Raúl sat outside school on the cement retaining wall, waiting for Ernesto. His shoulders were hunched, his head hung over his phone.

Passing by, I stopped and sat down next to him. "How are things?" I asked.

"Fine," he said. I asked if he wasn't worried about the eviction; he didn't answer right away. I told him about short-term shelter options in Oakland, where he could go anytime if we couldn't find him a more permanent place to stay.

"Shelter?" he said. "Like in Texas? No, Miss, thank you, but I can't go to a place like that."

Just then Ernesto exited a side door, spotted us, and came over.

Raúl bolted up. "Gotta go to work," he said, and walked toward the bus stop.

I asked Ernesto how things were going. "Oh, fine," he said. "Things are good, Miss. Remember how bad they were last year? It's not like that anymore. Things are really starting to get good."

Was he not worried about his brother, with all the stress of the move?

"No," he said. In his eyes, they were getting along great.

They didn't talk much about the eviction for the next couple of days, but for Raúl, it was the subtext of every conversation. "I guess I'll be homeless," he said one afternoon.

Ernesto just shrugged. *Not my problem.*

"Who wants to live with an animal like you anyway?" Raúl said. "I want my own space. I'll get a place of my own."

Every time one of them spoke about housing, it was like a chess move. Ernesto controlled the game, and Raúl's defensive strategy was to avoid the position of begging, feigning indifference to what Ernesto had to offer: a room with a bed. The clock kept ticking, the drop-dead date approaching. They both knew Raúl had nowhere to go.

When push came to shove, a few days before eviction day, Ernesto relented. "Of course, I wanted my brother to come live with me," he told me. "Obviously." He'd just been kidding all along, and he was sure Raúl had known that.

WE stuffed Raúl's possessions into garbage bags and grocery totes. One bag held a cracked DVD, batteries, a razor, a tub of Nivea skin cream, a battered stick of deodorant, and a large wooden plaque with an old-fashioned schooner, embossed in metal, with a message below that read, ENJOY, LIVE, RELAX. Raúl scooped up a pile of thin, polished wooden sticks—a disassembled easel, he explained, for the paintings he would like to start doing. It had stood in his room ready at attention, empty. "You should have seen the paintings I used to do in El Salvador," he said. "I was really, really good."

We were taking his things to Ernesto's before school. In the watery early-morning light of spring, East Oakland was just getting going: the highway was thickening with commuters a few blocks west of us, cars were sputtering into action, people were shaking off sleep on the way to the bus stop. We lifted the easel and bags into the car, which was now blocking an idling minivan. A little girl with pigtails and pink shorts rode in circles on a kick scooter as her friend, to whom she called and waved, approached the car whose path I was blocking.

"It's time for school, time for school!" the girl's mother cajoled in Spanish. She was heavyset and wore gray sweatshorts, her hair up in a messy knot. "Let's go, *mija!*" She held out her daughter's lunchbox until she climbed into the minivan. The pigtailed girl pedaled to her door, dropped her scooter inside, and ran to her own waiting mother. We slung the last of Raúl's things into the trunk and buckled ourselves in.

"Say goodbye to your house!" I said cheerily, trying to lighten the mood.

"I'm coming back later today to clean it," he replied in monotone, "before work."

I reversed, getting out of everyone's way. We drove slowly by the ordinary yet spectacular sight of mothers taking their kids to school.

It's a Monday, July 27, 2015, early morning, and commuters wait along the road for their rides. The cars and trucks and brightly painted buses hurtle down Avenida San Martín in Santa Tecla, a thriving town in San Salvador's ragged fringe. A bus stops on the corner, and as the passengers board, a muscular military official with a balaclava over his face and a lustrous semiautomatic in hand looks each one of them in the eye.

Over the weekend, country-wide murmurings began: there was going to be a *paro,* halt—a forced bus strike. The Revolucionarios branch of the Barrio 18 gang has worked its networks to convey that any bus driver who goes to work on Monday risks being shot and killed. The government has mobilized police and army officials to guard the buses that do run.

Many bus drivers stay home. The news reports filter in through the radio and television and streetside buzz: by day's end, five bus drivers and one transit worker are dead.

There are even fewer buses in the evening commute. The traffic thickens and slows into a coagulated mass. People scramble and push to get on board, and others cram into taxis, onto truck beds, and into the backseats and trunks of cars. Thousands of commuters who'd made it to work that morning have no way to get home to their families.

The gangs have targeted the transit system for years, extorting money out of drivers and killing those who don't pay. But this is the first country-wide action of this kind. They want the government to ease up on its antigang crackdown. The Barrio 18 splinter group is sending a message: *We own you. We can rip out the roots of commerce in an instant.*

"They do these things so everyone can see how powerful they are," proclaims a stone-faced twelve-year-old boy.

It continues like this on Tuesday, Wednesday. Businesses close since people can't come to work. And the people whose family economy relies on hawking to the bus commuters—bags of fruit, bottles of water, tortillas, chips, packages of fried plantains—have no one to sell to. Some schools and universities suspend classes. The Salvadoran newspaper *El Diario de Hoy* reported that $12 million in commerce was lost each day of the strike, from roadside *pupusa* vendors all the way up to the country's largest companies. The newspaper industry is one of the hardest hit.

Tuesday evening: President Salvador Sánchez Cerén makes a public address, promising more security forces to bolster the transportation workers and civil society against the gangs' threats. They won't negotiate anymore, Sánchez Cerén insists. "The criminals want to hold talks, but we can't talk with those who live by killing and extortion," he says.

Wednesday morning: President Sánchez Cerén leaves on a preplanned trip to get medical care in Cuba and is not scheduled to return for nearly two weeks. He does not change his plans.

Early that morning traffic is particularly bad coming into the city limits from the east. There's been an accident, it seems: a bus has hit a tree, perhaps, rolled onto its side. The area is roped off by caution tape, blocking most of the inbound lanes. Later it's announced on the news that the bus accident was, in fact, a crime scene. A Barrio 18 gangster had boarded the bus at a popular stop and fired a round of bullets at the twenty-one-year-old driver, killing him on the spot.

Rumors tremble through the streets, everyone grasping for some kind of explanation. Are the rival gangs in fact working together on this strike? Is ARENA, the conservative party and rival to the president's FMLN, actually behind the strike? Might ARENA be encouraging the army to boycott going to work, thus upending the government order? In a cryptic moment of Tuesday's speech, the president asked ARENA to stop destabilizing the government; to what was he referring, or was he just trying to deflect criticism on his handling of the strike onto the opposition? Is the president in fact dying and in need of urgent medical care, hence his trip to Cuba during this crisis? Everyone—from taxi drivers to NGO workers to government officials—has some conspiracy that helps explain the *paro*. None of these is confirmed fact, much of it baseless, but there are suspicions nonetheless. Conspiracy is the stuff of unrest.

Thursday, Friday, the same. By the following Wednesday, it seems the stoppage has come to a close, but then again the news reports trickle in: another bus driver has been shot and killed. That makes eight in total, along with some wounded. The country has lost well over over $60 million in commerce. And the gangs? Everyone can see how powerful they are.

CHAPTER 10

By the summer of 2015, the twins were living on their own, having fully and finally severed from daily life with Wilber. Raúl talked to him on the phone from time to time, but Ernesto refused. Any necessary communication—about sending money back to El Salvador, about their parents—went through Raúl.

Things settled into a rhythm. They had steady jobs, the weather was warm but not too hot, and they were excelling at summer school, earning credits toward graduation that would help make up for some of last year's Fs, which counted for no credits at all. They didn't see Wilber much that summer, but summer school had shorter days, ending at 2:00 instead of 3:30. That extra hour and a half allowed them more time to relax with friends in the uneven shade around school before heading to Montclair. The quiet look-alikes traipsed through Oakland in the early mornings and late nights, ferrying themselves between school and home and work to make enough money to do it all over again the next month.

Raúl, in particular, was grateful for the routine. Those days of uncertainty between the eviction notice and Ernesto allowing him to move in had shaken him deeply. He felt comfortable in the summer's equilibrium, although this time the bad spirits that seemed to stalk him had not so much retreated as lodged inside him—below the surface, dormant, but there.

"I've got a bomb inside my head," he said. "I can feel it in there. It's like I can hear it clicking."

IN August, three months after Raúl moved in, the brothers stopped for tacos at a Mexican restaurant on their way to work. Raúl ordered *carnitas,* while Ernesto, who had been skittish about eating red meat ever since the desert, ordered chicken. They ate in silence until Ernesto looked up and spotted their bus, the northbound number one, slowing to a halt across the street. Missing this bus could leave them stranded for over half an hour. Ernesto shoved one last bite of chicken taco into his mouth and made a run for it. "Come on!" he shouted. Raúl, still working on his *carnitas,* didn't notice the bus until his brother was already out the door. He boarded just before the doors shut behind him.

They rode in silence for twenty minutes, funneling down into the Chinatown thickets of markets and pedestrians, then rounding the bend north toward Berkeley.

Then Raúl felt his pocket. "Shit!" he said. "Shit, shit, shit!"

"What?" Ernesto said.

"My wallet!" It was stolen, he said. Someone had stolen it from him.

"You left it on the table," Ernesto said.

"No, I didn't!" He was sure he remembered putting it into his pocket.

The wallet was black fake leather embossed with the words EL SALVA-DOR and the national seal. It had held a hundred dollars in cash and his school ID. Raúl now had no identification whatsoever, and no money. He couldn't go back to the restaurant now or he risked being fired for lateness, and anyway he was sure someone had pickpocketed him. He spent his shift that night recalling the faces from the bus as though they were a police lineup.

The next day he went back to the restaurant. "Sorry," the lady behind the counter said, and shrugged. She hadn't seen a wallet. "Good luck."

THAT was money they had been planning to send home, and their parents needed it worse than ever. The debt was nearly $20,000 now, and things had got bad in the fields. "There's a drought," his father explained. The drought had been slowly building for a few years—too little rain, rain coming at the wrong time—but the summer of 2015 was a terribly dry one in El Salvador. In just June and July, over $100 million in revenue from corn alone was lost, affecting about 211,000 acres, mostly from small-scale farming operations like the Flores family's. They were almost through the spring's harvest, surviving off what little more they could grow between seasons and purchase when the twins sent money home. They siphoned that money away from the debt payments. There were practically no tomatoes left over to sell in town to have money for other things.

Wilber Sr. worried about the rest of the year. "We're suffering, *mijo*," he said to Raúl. "We just haven't had any rain." Since living alone, the twins had sent $200, $500, and $750 installments, but they still couldn't crack the goal of a thousand a month. One week Ernesto had given Wilber $650 to send home, but according to Maricela it never came. Was she lying, or Wilber? He suspected Wilber—whether he'd forgotten, or hadn't had the time, or had pocketed it to fill one of the frequent holes in his own finances, Ernesto wasn't sure. Furious but unwilling to wage another battle, Ernesto added it to the list of ways his brother had let him down.

Every month Maricela walked hangdog to visit the moneylender and offer the latest excuses. Sometimes Wilber Sr. went along with her, sometimes he didn't—but since he couldn't read that well, and his math was limited, Maricela was the family ambassador. It was shameful, admitting again and again that they couldn't pay.

Raúl and Ernesto remembered the time after Wilber Jr. left, when the whole family had huddled together in the kitchen, stomachs rumbling, eight children listening to their mother and father spin lies about how they were all good, just fine, that Wilber shouldn't worry, no problem if he couldn't send money that month, may God bless him. That now his parents were openly telling Raúl and Ernesto about their woes meant it had to be bad—really bad. He and Ernesto scrounged together what they could and sent seventy-five dollars the next day. It wasn't much, but it was something. Their guilt ate away at them in pieces.

THE twins didn't know much about the U.S. government, but ever since the rich guy who wanted to be president started talking about building a wall and deporting immigrants home, the Spanish news stations, and the whole Latino community they knew—from their friends at school to their co-workers to the guy who pierced their face to the lady who cut their hair for cheap—were talking about Donald Trump.

"Do you know he said Mexicans were rapists and criminals?" Raúl said.

"Asshole," said Ernesto. They took this comment to mean that all Latino immigrants were criminals or were suspected as such. In the evenings, the restaurant kitchens were filled with chatter about this guy, his bold racism. The kitchen crews at both restaurants laughed about the things he'd said as they scrubbed the pans and stacked the dishes into the sinks—"We'll all go home, boys! Donald Trump's on his way!" but, both twins noted, real fear underlay the joking.

A lot of people on the news and at school said he wouldn't win the nomination, but most of their friends and co-workers weren't so sure.

"I think he'll win," Raúl said. "Definitely." People were racist, he knew, and lots of people in the United States—even in Oakland—disliked immigrants. They could feel it, sometimes, in the gazes of people in the pizza shop or the *taquería* by school, that look reserved for people thought of as outsiders and even as threats. He didn't understand why. What had immigrants ever done to them, besides build their houses, pick their food in the fields, serve it to them in restaurants, wash their plates, then do it all over again?

"He will be the president," Raúl insisted, and then "we'll all have to watch out."

THE twins had a three-week break between the end of summer classes and the start of the 2015 school year, which offered a gift of time: they could sleep in as late as they wanted and see friends in the mornings and afternoons. But soon enough it was back to long nights and too-early mornings. After a week in the twelfth grade, where they understood little and couldn't keep up with the work, they made a decision: they wanted to try eleventh grade over again.

"We want to focus this time," Ernesto told the school counselor.

A week later the twins received the good news, right on time given their political anxiety: their green cards, said Amy, had finally arrived. Learning a few months back that they'd been approved was one thing, but the victory had been abstract, not something they could fully trust. That Amy now had the cards in her office, with their names and their photos, was something different altogether.

"I'll believe it when I have it in my own hands," Raúl said.

Ernesto worked seven days a week while Raúl worked only five, so it was Raúl who went into San Francisco to pick up the cards. He was giddy. What would they look like?

In her office, Amy handed the cards over with a smile. "You don't want to lose this," she said. "But you really should carry it around with you, just in case you're ever picked up for any reason." It was rare but wasn't unheard of, she explained, for the authorities to put someone in immigration detention, only to later figure out that that person had papers.

Raúl nodded, but he knew he would never lose his green card. It wasn't unlike the bike they'd traded for with his father's corn, a prize that bestowed freedom and also, because it was rare and costly, a little guilt.

It deserved a proper home, but Raúl still had no wallet. On Mission Street he ducked into a small outpost that advertised cheap shipping to El Salvador. Inside were stalls carrying key chains, statuettes of the Virgin, and phone cards. "Excuse me, *señora,* but do you have any wallets from El Salvador?" he asked a bored-looking woman sitting behind a glass case.

"Let's see, *mijo,*" she said. She pulled out wallets one by one. "Guatemala," she said, pausing, "Guatemala, Guatemala, Guatemala. Aha! *Sí!* El Salvador." Onto the glass counter she placed a brown horsehair wallet with EL SALVADOR burned into its skin.

"No, not that one," he said. "That's not my style."

"What's your style, then?" she asked, amused.

"I don't know." He shook his head. "I'll know it when I see it." They rifled through the rest of her collection but came up empty. Raúl was disappointed. For all his disdain for the conditions back home, he brandished his Salvadoran-ness as if it were his sponsor: a hat with the 503 country code, a key chain in the shape of El Salvador, a Salvadoran T-shirt.

He opted for a plain black wallet, like the one Ernesto had: faux leather, plenty of slots for the cards and photos he might one day need to store, boring maybe, but also professional looking—the kind carried by a permanent resident of the United States. By a man. In the safety of the store, he slipped his green card into one of the slots: a perfect fit.

THE fact of their permanent residency answered, once and for all, the question of whether Raúl and Ernesto were allowed to stay in the United States. Yet in the same stroke it forced the twins to confront another question: whether they wanted to go back home. Now that they had their *papeles,* they could get passports, which meant they would legally be able to travel—which allowed them to think, in real terms, about visiting El Salvador. This was an option Wilber had never had (and still didn't), and while they were waiting on the outcome of their case, it had seemed the most distant of hypotheticals.

On the one hand, things back home were terrible and getting worse. In addition to the debt and the drought, homicides were higher than even before the 2012 truce. The MS-13 and Barrio 18 factions were at war as always, but now the government was ramping up its side of things. Following the bus strike, El Salvador's Supreme Court ruled that any gang member was to be, in the eyes of the law, considered a terrorist and thus subject to even harsher prison sentences. The street wars were out of control, with nearly thirty homicides a day in August—higher even than during the civil war.

On the other hand, the twins missed their family.

But perhaps the notion of going home was an abstraction anyway.

They asked around about plane fare; the absurdity of spending a single dollar for tickets, let alone over a grand, to visit those still burdened by their leaving felt paralyzing. It would have to be a consideration only for that magic, future time when their debt would be settled and their lives along with it.

The twins argued over which place was better: the United States or El Salvador. Raúl insisted the United States was better, but Ernesto, the one who had lusted for life up north, now wasn't so sure.

"It's safe here," Raúl insisted, throwing his hands up. "I'll never go back there, not ever!"

"It's dangerous here, too!" Ernesto reminded him. Oakland had plenty of violence of its own; they had both been jumped, after all.

Yes, there was violence in Oakland, allowed Raúl, but nothing like in El Salvador.

"Things are fine," Esperanza told her boys when they next called, back to whitewashing the narrative. "Things are fine. We pray for you, my angels."

THE first practical order of business, after getting their green cards, was to apply for Social Security cards. That would mean they could start working for full minimum wage.

They took their birth certificates, their completed applications, and their green cards to the commercial office building in downtown Oakland, where the doorman directed them to the third floor. The guards pointed them over to the check-in kiosk, which spat out a number: A063. They sat down to wait among the rows of gray metal seats. Next to them was a young woman dressed in pink velour pants, who muttered to herself while laying out the contents of her purse on the empty chair next to Ernesto—a packet of gum, headphones, several tubes of lipstick and mascara—then placing each item back in her purse, only to take it all out again.

"Motherfuckers," she said each time a new number was called. "How the fuck we supposed to hear what the fuck they're even saying, shit?" Ernesto and Raúl exchanged tense smiles.

An hour later, when their number was finally called, they handed their paperwork over to the officer behind the counter.

"Twins, huh?" the woman said, looking them over. Same faces, both dressed in their common uniform of black shirts, jeans, and red and black Nikes. She scanned their paperwork.

"Okay, whose is this?" she asked, waving Ernesto's birth certificate.

"Mine," he said.

"This one I can do, but yours," she said, pointing to Raúl, "I need an original." She shook his birth certificate. "An original," she repeated, a little louder. Ernesto had a tattered color copy with a new stamp, so it looked original, whereas Raúl's was a black and white facsimile, the duplication slightly askew.

"Come back when you have it," she said matter-of-factly, and thrust the copy back, moving on with Ernesto's application. Raúl nodded and stepped away from the counter, not daring to argue.

When Ernesto's Social Security card arrived at school six days later, he laughed as he tore open the envelope. Raúl watched from the office doorway. Ernesto pulled out the blue card stock and flung it aside on the desk, peering into the envelope. "Where is it?" he said.

Then he picked up the document from the desk and saw the small card attached by perforation. "That's it?" he said. This thing everyone wanted, that people bought and traded on the black market, that ensured fair wages and employability in this great northern beast of a country, looked like something he could have made in computer class. He smiled and gently tore the card from the rest of the sheet. He'd take it that night to his boss and get on the official payroll.

Raúl left the room.

ERNESTO was doing well at work. He did less dishwashing and more busing now, working invisibly around the customers. He even answered the phone every now and then, something he secretly loved to do. "Hello, how can I help you?" he'd say in English that, though his vocabulary remained limited, was less and less accented each day. His boss complimented him on his work ethic and made sure he was tipped out at the end of each night. Wilber Sr. had taught his children to work hard. It wasn't easy, said Ernesto, to find such hard workers as he and his brother.

The customers liked him, too. A few regulars would slip his tips into the pocket of his apron, something that made him nervous because one of the cooks, who rolled sushi from behind the bar, would scowl when he saw it.

"I get a lot of attention from women customers," Ernesto explained to me. "I think it's because I wear a shirt with short sleeves, and I carry a lot of things, which flexes my muscles so it makes me look like I'm really strong."

He felt welcome, needed, and capable at the sushi restaurant. In most other Montclair establishments, he felt out of place. They were *gabacho* restaurants, restaurants for white people, for Americans—not for people like him and his brother. "I'm embarrassed," he said, just walking into a *gabacho* place. "I don't feel comfortable in places like that." Gringos, he put it in a clear display of internalized racism, were more "refined" than they—more sensitive and delicate.

"It's just true," Raúl agreed. Not that they were born different, but they grew up different and therefore were different—it was a cultural thing. "Places like that," from the twins' point of view, were where people like them worked, not where they were patrons. Their comfort in the affluent parts of Oakland wasn't an issue of either language or legality. Living on the margins of a gentrifying city only underlined to Ernesto what the twins had been told and had fought during their whole lives: that they were less than, and that they didn't, and shouldn't expect to, belong.

One night Ernesto's boss made a big deal about someone who had just walked into the restaurant. Everyone from the kitchen leaned out to look. It was an older guy, bald with thick white eyebrows, dressed in a black long-sleeved shirt. A movie star, maybe?

"That's the governor," his co-worker said. Jerry Brown. The head, someone explained to him, of the state of California.

Governor Brown came in a few more times that fall. One night he came in by himself, and Ernesto felt the urge to ask for a picture with him, to have some proof of his proximity to an Important Person. But he was too nervous to ask.

His co-worker asked for him. "Sure," replied the governor gamely.

Ernesto was legal now; he had nothing to fear posing with the leader of California in front of the restaurant's health board certifications. He thanked Brown in English and turned toward the kitchen, right then posting the photo to Instagram and Snapchat, overlaid with a caption, "With the governor," followed by a blushing emoji.

On a busy night a few weeks later, Ernesto was busing the table of a couple in their twenties, perspiring in his smeared black apron. The table was a mess of splattered soy sauce and sushi remnants, and Ernesto did his best to be inconspicuous as he cleared the plates. The guy had ordered several large beers already. He gesticulated just as Ernesto went to take one of his empty bottles, inadvertently swatting it out of Ernesto's hands and into his own lap.

"Fucking Latino!" he shouted.

Ernesto narrowed his eyes and said back, "Fuck you!"

The guy moved as if to hit Ernesto, who didn't flinch, but then his girlfriend calmed him down. Ernesto turned around and walked toward the kitchen. He punched a wall in the back of the restaurant and dented it slightly, ripping the skin off his knuckles. His boss didn't reprimand him but didn't seem to sympathize much, either. "Stay in the back," she said, "until he's gone."

ERNESTO still dreamed of going home.

He knew he couldn't go to La Colonia—too dangerous—but he could at least get to the capital and meet his mother there, maybe his father and some of his siblings, too. *Someday,* he thought.

It couldn't hurt to apply for a Salvadoran passport. He'd been on a winning streak with bureaucracy lately, and the process seemed simple enough: go to the Salvadoran consulate in San Francisco, fill out the paperwork, show his green card, and pay the fee. But after waiting on line at the consulate, a dim-lit, low-ceilinged office suite in San Francisco's Tenderloin district, he learned that to get a passport he'd first need a

DUI—a Salvadoran ID. He could apply for that here in San Francisco, but he'd need not only an original birth certificate but one that had been printed and stamped by his local mayor's office sometime in the past year. This he didn't have.

Assuming Ernesto could even get his birth certificate, the DUI and passport process would take months. Going home receded even farther into the horizon.

Raúl, for his part, still had no interest in going back. El Salvador had gone sour, like food left out too long. He had been dwelling in the past again; if he allowed himself to think too much, his whole body began to shake. That place had kicked him out on his ass, far away from his family, his loved ones, his place, his future. "My friends, my ex-friends, are with the devil. I never want to see their faces again, never, *ni en una pintura*" or "not at all"—literally, "not even in a painting." Just picturing them in his mind made him want to punch his own hole in the wall.

He felt this anger, but also, he could admit sometimes, a fear. "I'm scared," he said, to go back. People he'd trusted had let him down spectacularly.

He finally received his Social Security card, which brought temporary relief, but as the fall dragged on, his anxiety mounted. He had a hard time sleeping, and even when he was awake, thoughts rose to the surface that for over a year had been pretty well tamped down. He'd be sitting on a bus or in class, and it would suddenly go black all around him, as if he were there on the cold roadside in Guatemala, head throbbing and listening to the *coyota* scream. Now that he was truly "safe" in the United States, all the old worries and soiled memories came flooding back in.

MEANWHILE Ernesto fell in love. Love, as he'd learned last year with Marie, was a good distraction from both homesickness and bad memories. His new girlfriend was a ninth grader; too young for him, Ernesto knew, but she had pursued him, shooting him glances in PE class and hanging on to his arm while the teacher shouted instructions. Sofía was her name. Ernesto loved her eyes, sultry but also kind and soft. Though she was only fourteen, she had a lot of responsibilities at home, where she had to cook and clean and take care of little kids. She understood him, he felt—not all the way, but she could grasp that he had a lot on his plate.

Best of all, she was from El Salvador.

Raúl was jealous that his twin had someone at school to loiter with in the courtyard, to kiss, jealous of the fact that he was in love. He also wasn't sure about Sofía. She'd give long hugs to other classmates, or be chatting with a group of younger students—mostly boys—and not even acknowledge the twins as they passed. And then she'd go accusing Ernesto of flirting with other girls on Facebook and complaining about how he spent too much time at work.

Sofía buddied up to Raúl at first, calling him her *cuñado,* her in-law, and nestling up to him sometimes purring, *"Hola, cuñado, qué tal?"* Sofía didn't seem to have a hard time telling them apart, even from the beginning. Raúl liked that about her. But Sofía monopolized his brother's attention. Just days after they'd started going out, gone were the twins' off-campus lunches. Ernesto and Sofía would snuggle on the couch in the back corner of the library while Raúl sat alone with the company of his earbuds and phone. Often, when he sneaked out to go buy something, Ernesto noticed him leaving and yelled him over.

"Raúl!" he'd shout. Raúl would saunter over, feigning uncaring. "Buy me a taco."

"And a soda!" Sofía would add. Sometimes he did their bidding, other times he didn't.

Raúl could feel the bomb in his head making him jittery and withdrawn, but his brother didn't seem to notice. He had been there for Ernesto the year before when he was unraveling, all those nightmares and breakdowns. Now his twin was off with this fourteen-year-old, and he'd become invisible.

MARICELA continued to hound her brothers. "How much can you send this month?" "We're worried they're going to take away the land for real this time." She asked them about school—how much longer until they graduated? Could they take a break?

"We only go to school a couple of hours a day," Raúl told her, which was a lie. "We're doing everything we can."

But Cesar remained a steadfast father and boyfriend, sending the seventy dollars each month, visiting as often as he could, meeting Maricela outside the factory on his lunch break, crooning into his wriggling baby's ear as he gobbled down the food Maricela brought him. She'd ride over an hour each way to see him for this fleeting break, but it was worth it.

Cesar complained all the time about how bad his job was. He worked like a donkey in that factory, tiring his body and wasting his mind, all for practically no money in the grand scheme. After a few months, the owners cut everyone's hours, and thus their wages, so he only made $350. He was starting to think that the way out was the United States.

A neighbor said she could connect him to someone in the United States who would, for a price, marry him so he could immigrate legally. When he shared this idea with Maricela, she was furious. The notion of her man, the father of her children, leaving her—and worse, marrying someone else? Cesar protested that the American contact was a sixty-something old lady, no one he'd ever actually be interested in, only a business arrangement. It would be good for the family, he promised, and after two or three years, once he got his papers sorted out, he'd divorce the lady, come back to El Salvador to marry Maricela, and apply for papers for her and the kids.

In the United States, marriage fraud for immigration purposes is a felony punishable by up to five years in jail and a fine of up to $250,000. Over the past decade, several fraud rings have been busted for coaching couples on how to make their marriage appear legitimate. In part to combat arrangements of the kind Cesar was considering, the Department of Homeland Security created a special Document and Benefit Task Force and, in 2014, launched an aggressive ad campaign. ("If you walk down this aisle for the wrong reasons," an ICE brochure reads over an image of a church altar, ". . . you could end up walking down this aisle," over a photograph of a prison hall.) Marrying someone with papers in the United States is a lengthy and expensive process that receives much government scrutiny. Immigration officers ask to see wedding pictures and proof of a past relationship, and they can even conduct home visits to ascertain a marriage's legitimacy.

Cesar's plan, then, was a risky one, if not an outright scam. It was unlikely that the marriage would seem plausible to the U.S. government, if his contact actually married him instead of walking away with his money. A marriage visa had to be initiated before the spouse entered the United States; Cesar's plan to just show up and get married wasn't how it worked, and the older woman likely knew that.

But Cesar didn't. Nor did Maricela. In spite of her jealousy, the way Cesar spoke about the plan seemed to her to make some sense.

Recently, both Wilber Sr. and Esperanza had contracted chikungunya, a mosquito-borne virus not unlike dengue fever that wipes people out for weeks with a fever, sore muscles, and aching joints. They are barely able to get out of bed to use the bathroom. Though rarely fatal, the greatest risk of chikungunya is to infants and the elderly—like Wilber Sr., only in his sixties, but frail and weakened, it seemed, by his fears around losing the land. Maricela sponged their brows and spoon-fed them soup and *atole* as she thought over Cesar's plan. Her father had grown alarmingly frail. At times, staring at him on the bed like that, sweating, stiff, his chest hardly rising and falling, she worried he might die. And what would happen to their family then?

Maricela gave Cesar her blessing to go; she was convinced because he was convinced. She also started to think about going north herself—not in a dreamy way but for real this time.

She'd heard that women traveling with children were being set free when they crossed the border. (This was a later mutation of the rumor Homeland Security secretary Jeh Johnson had tried to discredit nearly two years prior in the *quedate* campaigns, a misunderstanding stemming from the U.S. government's practice of releasing women from overcrowded detention facilities while they awaited removal proceedings. The future court dates, the prospect of deportation, and the ankle bracelet tracking devices that ensured these women didn't disappear were facts that had been lost in the game of telephone that brought immigration news to La Colonia.)

Going all that way by herself without a coyote would be too risky: many women, she knew, were raped, kidnapped, and even killed. She knew girls often took birth control before they left to make sure they didn't get pregnant if—when, even—they were raped. Plus, she doubted her ability to find her own way. She'd have to go with a coyote, which cost about $8,000 these days. Could she take out another loan, this time in her own name?

Cesar loved the idea. In his plan, he would go live with the lady and get official papers while Maricela made it across the border, turned herself in, and was set free. He'd be officially married, but what did that matter? They'd be together, in America, with their daughter. She couldn't travel with both girls, so she'd have to leave Lupita at home—it would be easier to feed and travel with an infant than a toddler—until she could send for her.

No matter who told her—her brothers, especially—that this plan wouldn't work, for a few weeks she couldn't be dissuaded. But then Cesar began to change his mind. He became aware that the marriage plan was quite probably a scam and that it offered no guarantees. They set the plan aside.

Still, Maricela thought about going.

"Don't come," Ernesto messaged her on Facebook. "Seriously. Don't do it." She scrolled through their photos again. If she were in their place, everything would be different—not just for her but for the whole family. It should have been she who'd gone.

"We'll see," she replied.

IN October, Raúl decided that he wouldn't go to school anymore. A few of their friends, like Ibrahim and Diego, had graduated, and others, like Brenda, Douglas, and Alfredo, had dropped out or changed schools. They hadn't really kept in touch. Being around people, friends new and old, now made him anxious, and besides, he wanted to be with his own girlfriend. He'd found her on Kik, the chatting app, two weeks after Ernesto and Sofía got together. Marleny was her name. She was a senior at a high school downtown, and though she was born in the United States, she was Mexican American and had grown up speaking Spanish. Like him, she was tired of school, and like him, she was lonely.

"I love you," she texted early on, with three red hearts.

"Me too I love you" he replied.

"I love you I love you."

"Damn," typed Raúl. "I love you so much."

The Monday after they started going out, Raúl and Marleny ditched together. They met up in downtown Oakland and walked the streets, intoxicated with the waking up of the city, the freedom of having nowhere to be, and being in love. They sat on the benches in Jefferson Square Park, halfway between the city center and the highway, and hopped another bus to the lake, where they walked its perimeter, holding hands. They swung on the swings as homeless men sat hunched on benches and elderly men pulled cans from the municipal trash bins. They made out and he felt her up before they hopped on the bus and ate tacos on International. He kept his body as close to hers as possible, and they kissed for a long time before he had to leave for work in Montclair, promising to see her tomorrow.

Around the time he met Marleny, he began cutting himself. He'd heard of other kids at school doing this, how sometimes people felt better with a little bit of pain. He tried it once, and the feeling of the blood seeping from his skin was like the release of a pressure valve. He liked the way the stripe of red-brown looked on his arms after the blood dried.

As Ernesto was sleeping one night, Raúl took out the small knife, hunched over by the light of a lamp on his bed, and sliced.

Ernesto woke to his twin's low grunts of pain and satisfaction. "What are you doing?" he hissed.

"Leave me alone. It makes me feel better." But he was glad Ernesto was awake as he cut more slashes into his arm, digging just deep enough to let out a satisfying bit of blood, just enough to start beading on the skin. The accumulation would linger a moment and then burst its own dam, dripping down his arm in a stream just red and thick enough to be impressive.

For a week he passed the time like this: leaving with Ernesto in the morning with the promise of going back to school, getting on the bus, then jumping off downtown to meet Marleny before Ernesto could stop him. Raúl didn't care that he was lying to Ernesto every time he promised to go to school. If Ernesto got to spend all day with his girlfriend, then Raúl should get to, too. He and Marleny wandered the streets together, wounded by the world and in love. She stroked the raised accumulation of scars on his lower arm, moving lightly over the freshest ones, still red, like hash marks to chart the passage of days.

But after that first week, she insisted she needed to go back to class—it was her senior year, and she loved him, of course she loved him, but she had to be in school. For her *future*. So after their morning meet-up, he began dropping her off in front of her school, then chose a bus to hop on. One took him to Alameda, where he stared out the window as the bus crossed the Oakland estuary and meandered through the quiet, tree-lined streets full of big houses. Another took him to the base of the Oakland hills, where he looked up at the hillsides balding from thirst—the same drought, he knew, that was afflicting his family back in El Salvador. For another week he rode AC Transit to new places, not answering his brothers' phone calls, not answering anyone's calls, just staring out the window, feeling his arm throb, listening to the tick-tock in his head.

Marleny was the only one he wanted to talk to, but after not too long, their relationship turned volatile. He resented her for not skipping with him and accused her of having another boyfriend in school; she accused him of flirting with other girls. Twice that third week they broke up and got back together again.

Raúl spent nearly two weeks under the radar, avoiding school and his twin. He added more piercings to his face like more and more of his friends had at school, loving the way the needle felt when it pushed through his skin. He changed the barbell of the eyebrow piercing on his right side to a peg with black shiny barbs on each end, then added a twin piercing on the right side, which gave the impression of horns.

Ernesto already had an eyebrow piercing, but now Raúl had two. Ernesto had pierced his upper cheek, but Raúl bested him again, piercing a pinch of flesh on his temple, opting for barbed ends of that one, too. The last and most expensive piercing was a little circle that clipped into his cheek like a small, sparkling shield. Ernesto didn't have anything like that.

On the bus after each piercing, Raúl would polish the screen of his phone and hold it up as a mirror, admiring the work. He felt proud of the way he was designing himself. It was a free country here. No one would bother him for these piercings or assume he was a gang member, as they might back home—just as they might for his Nikes, his hip-hop clothes, and his nice phone. It was his face, his money, he'd think, passing the hours as the pain in his face dulled.

He never once missed work. He'd end each sojourn at the Italian restaurant, always showing up just before his five o'clock shift so he could change into his work clothes—a T-shirt stained and stretched at the neckline, dishwater-soiled pants—pull on his thick white apron, and get to work on the dishes.

The Italian restaurant, tucked back into a second-rate strip mall, was a nice place where diners often came to celebrate birthdays and graduations. Raúl impressed the kitchen with his quick work and resolve. He scoured the industrial metal pans with vigor, dislodging every meatball remnant, hosing them down, replacing the clean pans under the counter as the line cooks filled more trays with newly shaped meatballs. Raúl had tired of the food there, but he didn't mind the washing—the physicality and pace seemed to stave off his anxiety. The marks on his arms grew sodden and red with the dirty water.

The older guys at the restaurant called him Pepito and poked fun at him for being the youngest, but he didn't care. He knew he was the best worker, and for those six hours every night, he took refuge in efficiency—every moment meant more of a dollar he could take home, every dish a concrete task. It was when he was walking, or lying in bed, or looking out the window on the bus, that the bomb came back into his head. Maricela had called a few nights into his hooky spree to report that Esperanza and Wilber Sr. had come down with chikungunya; he hated that he wasn't there to help them. He was stuck here in Oakland where he didn't really want to be, but he would never go back, either. When his sense of injustice welled to the breaking point, he'd take out his little knife and slice into his arm, as if he was slitting his ex-friends' throats.

"WHAT the fuck?" Ernesto said in English when he saw Raúl's new piercings.

"I can do whatever I want. It's my face," said Raúl.

"You're always following what I'm doing," Ernesto replied.

"Fuck you. I make my own choices." They didn't talk the rest of that night.

They were careful not to post too many close-ups on Facebook so their sister and brother wouldn't see their piercings and tattle to their parents. Wilber Sr. and Esperanza would think it was devil work, if not proof that they'd become gangsters up north.

That weekend Ernesto got a new barb on his eyebrow, then a half ring on his lip. Sofía thought they were cool, but after the lip ring, she thought things had gone far enough. "No more," she said.

After a month of going out together, Ernesto decided it was time to ask Sofía's parents for permission to date her. This was a common custom: a young man courting a girl must ask her parents as a prerequisite to getting their approval for it. The last girl he'd asked about was Marie, his only other real girlfriend. "Going out without permission," he said, "that's fine, but it's a different thing." It was less serious, that is, than what he felt for Sofía.

He hadn't approached Sofía's mother yet because Sofía wasn't allowed to date anyone until her fifteenth birthday, which was coming up. Ernesto was planning to ask soon afterward, but he was nervous. He rehearsed in his head: he'd take out all his piercings, visit Sofía's home, and look her parents in the eye with stiff formality: "I am your daughter's boyfriend, and I want to ask your permission to keep seeing her. I love her very much, and it's not right for us to go on without your permission." What worried him was the questions they might ask—about his age, his family, where he lived, whom he lived with, his grades in school. He knew he couldn't give reassuring answers to these.

She wanted him to be at her *quinceañera,* but it was a Saturday on Halloween weekend, and getting off work would be hard. She vacillated between understanding and being annoyed that her boyfriend couldn't come to her party, her big day. He'd do his best, he told her.

He focused on her real birthday, two weeks before the party. That day he carried an aerial bouquet of Happy Birthday balloons to school, along with a necklace and matching earrings that he'd picked out with painstaking deliberation from Forever 21. He felt sure she'd like the attention of getting jewelry and a bunch of iridescent balloons from her boyfriend in public. But he was over an hour late to school, and before he could find her, she sent an angry string of texts: "You're not a responsible person." "It's my birthday and you don't even come on time to see me." "You don't take school seriously."

They spent the day in a fight. He shoved the balloons toward her and walked off. She snatched their ribbons before they floated away.

"Maybe we'll break up," he said, shrugging. He didn't want that. But he was too tired to fight. After hours of back-and-forth texting that night, they made up. "Thank you for my balloons," she said. The next day he gave her the jewelry. When she untied the bow and lifted the top of the box, she squealed and hugged him. He gently hung the necklace around her, fastening it from behind, and she clipped on the earrings eagerly. They were good again.

RAÚL and Marleny broke up for good. By ditching school so many days in a row, Raúl had gotten his brother's attention. Ernesto worried about what Raúl did all day, and also about his parents laid up back home, shaking with fever. They'd been sick now for over two weeks—standard for chikungunya but ominous all the same. "You don't understand," he told me when I tried to reassure him. "They're old, and frail. This could kill them."

Ernesto monitored his twin's social media, where Raúl posted photographs of his cut-up arms. "What the fuck is he doing to himself?" Ernesto said. "If my mother knew, she'd just—I don't know what, she'd die."

One morning when he couldn't take it anymore, he left school to go look for Raúl downtown. Ernesto dialed his twin's number on repeat in hopes of driving him crazy enough to answer, but he wouldn't pick up. Ernesto pictured him watching the phone ring and ring and ring, flashing his name. He'd never ignored him like this. Ernesto hardly needed to glance around Jefferson Square Park to know Raúl wasn't there. "I can tell when he's around," he said, "and when he's not."

He'd heard the stories before, in El Salvador and here, the stuff of bad movies and bad dreams: "All of a sudden you get a phone call, and your brother is dead." Suicide, he meant, that sin.

Ernesto took to camping out in my office for extended periods each day, overwhelmed, looking for help tracking down Raúl. One day a group of Yemeni mothers, clad in long, shiny black *abayas* that covered their frames from wrist to neck to ankle, and colorful scarves pinned tightly against their faces, visited the office regarding the parent English class we offered. They noticed Ernesto seated in the corner and murmured to one another in Arabic. They wanted to know what had happened to this sad boy.

"What's wrong?" one of them asked him. "Are you okay?"

Where to start? He shook his head, then replied, "My mom is sick."

"Your mama is sick? Oh, is she in the hospital?" the woman asked.

"No, she's in El Salvador."

"You're here in this country all by yourself without your mama? Where's your dad?"

"He's in El Salvador, too."

"*Habibi,* sorry, you poor baby," the woman said, looking at Ernesto with tenderness. Then all four of the women teared up, seemingly surprised at their own sudden outpouring of emotion, missing their own families at home, perhaps, and dabbing their eyes with tissues and the ends of their headscarves and whispering to one another.

Ernesto tensed his jaw and swiveled his chair toward the corner.

Seeing them there, these four mothers from a far-off place, with their strange gowns and soft, kind faces, made Ernesto miss Esperanza even more, and he began to cry. He hadn't cried in a long time; even when he had been unraveling last spring, when he'd got the racing heart and trouble breathing, he'd never cried—not while sober, anyway. The horrible things that had happened to him had once ruled him, shackled him with anger and hate; now things were relatively good for him, but they had become terrible for everyone else he loved. Was it a zero-sum game? The tears came fast and hard. He twisted his face to stop them, but it was no use, they just kept coming, and the more they came, the more he felt like a boy and remembered crying in his mother's arms, the way he could let his whole body fall into hers.

The truth was, he needed Raúl as much as Raúl needed him. But how could he help him? He didn't want to be crying in the office at school surrounded by a bunch of strangers; he didn't want to be looking for his brother on the streets of downtown Oakland. *Get over it,* he wanted to say to Raúl. *Stop it. Start over.* He wanted to be angry, but cooped up in this tiny dark office with these women, he could feel only the anxious consequence of love. He hunched toward the wall and let it go, filling the room with the echoes of his grief.

The women wiped their faces and stood up to go. "We'll pray for you," said the one who spoke English, "*Habibi,* we'll pray for you."

"Thank you," he managed. She'd spoken in English, and he'd understood what she'd said.

RAÚL had missed nine days in a row of school.

"Do you know what happened today?" Ernesto said to him after work that night. "I was in Ms. Lauren's office, and a bunch of Arab ladies came in and asked about Mom. And I cried. I fucking cried—because of you."

Raúl was surprised. He knew his brother was concerned, but not this much.

"I'm scared you're going to end up dead," Ernesto said. "I don't want to be crying in a room full of strange ladies because I don't know where you are, or what's going on, and you're not even picking up your fucking phone."

"I know," Raúl said. "I'm sorry."

"If you don't quit that shit," Ernesto said, pointing to Raúl's scabby forearms, "I'm going to kick your ass." He told his brother, "I love you," after a pause.

The next day Raúl came back to school.

THE LONG WALK

In the heavy heat of the southern Mexico summer, in Tapachula, a family of three from Honduras sit outside the Belén migrant shelter, lounging on the rocks that form a low perimeter around the front lawn.

The father has his shirt off. He perches on a rock and leans against the flat incline of another, hands above his head.

"Papi!" his nine-year-old daughter screeches, and jumps onto his outstretched legs.

"Careful, girl," he says, scooping her up. She curls up on his lap while her mother, fair-skinned and tired-looking, settles heavily on an adjacent rock.

"My feet hurt," says the girl cheerily, and rubs them. "It was a long walk."

The night before last, the three of them tramped over twenty-five miles from where they crossed the Mexican–Guatemalan border, determined to make it to Belén, one of the southernmost shelters in Mexico, before stopping. There, they had heard, they would find lodging, food, and travel tips—where the newest immigration and police checkpoints were, where rapes and robberies had been reported, what new routes migrants were taking through the mountains. None of the intel was a sure bet, but it would be something to go on.

Shelters like Belén are safe houses run by nonprofits that string north through Mexico along the migrant trail like an underground railroad. According to an agreement between the immigration forces and immigrant advocates, officials leave the shelters alone.

The girl's mother hunches over her to brush her hair. She is just getting over chikungunya, the virus that is spreading like a full-bodied rash throughout Latin America, having mysteriously made its way from Asia to the Caribbean several years ago. The fever and aches are subsiding, though she is still sore, particularly after that long walk, and swollen. The edema plumps her skin such that when her daughter pokes her arm or thigh, the tissue stays indented like putty. It is nice to rest a little before moving again.

Nearby, a drunken, glassy-eyed Salvadoran stumbles around, showing off a stack of paperwork that proves, he insists, that he deserves asylum in the United States. Reclining a few rocks over is a man in his mid-thirties, tattooed and shirtless. He used to live in the United States but was deported. Credit card fraud.

"Bad boy," he says in English, raising his eyebrows. He'd once had a green card, a high school diploma, a family, kids. When he was caught, he'd spent a few years in prison before being deported back to El Salvador.

"You can't even go outside there," he says, because of the gangs. Having spent so much time away, he is now a *desconocido,* an unknown, and outsiders make the *maras,* or gangs, suspicious. Especially tough-looking guys like him. "I can't live there."

"*Tranquilo,*" he says to the drunk man. "Take it easy."

"Any day on the road north," he continues, "you know you might die."

The nine-year-old tires of the scene and heads back into the building, where a trio of adults from El Salvador—a sister, her brother, and her brother's wife, all of whom had left their kids back home—crouch on the tile floor sorting their belongings.

The girl plops cross-legged on the floor among their piles of clothes. The women—one skinny, one heavyset with a deep scar on her temple, both of them mothers—dote on the girl, distracting her from her worn-out mom. The skinny one hands the girl a plate with a tamale, fresh from the shelter's kitchen.

The girl unfolds the banana leaves, and steam spills up toward her face. "Mmm."

Across from her hangs a map of North America outlining distances north from Tapachula: Houston, 2,930 kilometers; New York, 4,375 kilometers; Los Angeles, 4,025.

The Hondurans and the Salvadorans decide to travel from Tapachula together. They'll set out first thing tomorrow morning, moving north until the Salvadorans split west—they're heading for Baja, not the States. It's too dangerous up that way, they say, too many people getting nabbed and sent back to El Salvador. In Baja they have a friend who has a friend who might have some work for them. More and more migrants like them are opting to stay in Mexico.

The woman with the scar places her belongings into piles: things to bring on the road and things to mail ahead to Baja. They shopped for supplies before they left El Salvador, and now they realize they've brought too much. A big blue plastic urn full of beans, for example—it's way too heavy. The migrant shelters have food, and if they get desperate, they can buy beans on the road. A sweater and clean pants are tossed into the "keep" pile; leggings and a satin bra with the tags still attached are stacked alongside the urn of beans. When she gets to Baja, assuming she makes it, she'll have fresh clothes waiting for her there. That'll be nice. She places a jar of cream on the "keep" pile—foot balm to soothe the blisters and cracks.

They plan to hit the road early tomorrow. They'll travel on buses until a checkpoint comes into view, when they'll disembark and skirt the main thoroughfares on foot.

These new checkpoints push people like them into territory where their risk of encountering exploitation and violence is greater. Above them on the shelter wall hangs a bulletin board tacked full of photographs of missing people and of bad guys—rapists, thieves, con men who pretend to be coyotes.

The little girl has picked the banana leaves clean of tamale. "You know I went to the United States once?" she announces, licking her fingers. She speaks as if she's on stage. "We went to

Texas. It was really beautiful, full of snow. I walked there when I was tiny, just a little kid."

The women laugh and shake their heads. "You went all the way there when you were little?" one says, rolling up a pair of pants and pushing them to the bottom of her backpack.

"I went with my grandparents!" says the girl. "My parents have never been before, but I have, so I'm not scared." She is writing the fairy tale as she goes along. "And then we came back!"

"Why did you come back?" the woman asks.

"We, um, we walked," she replies.

The women look at each other. "*No creo,*" one mouths. I don't think so.

The foot cream sits atop the pile of keepers. The girl snatches the jar, pulls off her pink tennis shoes and thin white socks, and unscrews the lid. She dips her fingertips into the cool, white cream, thick like a custard, and begins rubbing it onto her soles.

"It's going to be a lot of walking," the girl says, "but I'm really strong."

She reaches for the jar again, and the women wince. They seem about to say something—they'll need this cream later—but they let her take it anyway.

CHAPTER 11

It was an accident, of course. A broken condom. Sofía and Ernesto had had sex only a few times. They planned to buy the morning-after pill, which they'd learned about in school, but they hadn't made it to the drugstore—they didn't have enough money on hand, and she had no time to slip out of the house unnoticed—until two days later. She took the pill, and they figured it would still work.

During the December holiday break, the twins slept in, relishing the absence of school demands. Some mornings Sofía could sneak out of her house, her family thinking she was still in her room in teenage can't-rouse-me sleep. Those days Ernesto was happy to wake up early. He met up with her in the Fruitvale, and they got food, Ernesto always footing the bill, and walked around the neighborhood holding hands. When they had enough time before he was due at work or she needed to slip back home, he'd take her back to his apartment. She was the first girlfriend with whom he'd had an ongoing intimate relationship, and though he knew their age difference made sex against the law, he couldn't turn down the opportunity. He loved her.

Ernesto and Raúl had taken on more hours at work, and in the final days of 2015, they made a new plan to deal with the debt: every two-week pay period they would each lay away $250 and wouldn't touch it, so that by the end of the month, they would have saved a thousand dollars to send home. Even better was the news that Oakland's minimum wage was going up again: when the clock struck midnight on December 31, they'd be making $12.55 an hour, a thirty-cent increase. That could add up.

"For real?" Maricela wrote when they told her that a large sum was coming their way. Right before the new year, they sent $1,100 back to El Salvador. If they stuck with the plan—difficult but not impossible— they could unburden the family of the whole debt within a couple years.

In mid-January they had five hundred dollars laid away from their January 1 paychecks. School was back in session.

But Sofía wasn't feeling that well. "I think I'm pregnant," she told Ernesto.

She seemed serious. He bought her a test. The pill hadn't worked; Sofía was pregnant.

They didn't talk about their options—they didn't see any other choice but the obvious. "I would never give my baby away to anyone else," Sofía said. And neither of them considered abortion—it was a sin and illegal in El Salvador, something they just wouldn't do. They'd be keeping it.

"We're not stupid," said Ernesto.

"Sofía's pregnant," he told Raúl a few days after finding out, with a tremor in his voice.

Raúl didn't respond at first. "You're a fucking idiot."

Ernesto nodded. He was so overwhelmed, he could do nothing else.

"What the fuck were you thinking?" Raúl laid into Ernesto just as Ernesto had laid into Maricela. Didn't Ernesto know how much harder he had just made everything? "Why didn't you think?"

BACK home, still buoyant from the twins' recent payment and blissfully in the dark about her soon-to-be niece or nephew, Maricela began to develop some suspicions about Cesar. He was growing distant. She knew he was tired at work, that all those hours putting machine parts together over and over and over again at the factory were wearing him down. Still, he used to call her to complain because he knew she'd make him feel better. But he wasn't calling much, wasn't coming to visit.

"What is it? What's wrong?" she asked.

"Nothing. I'm tired. I work, okay? I work hard."

"Where were you last night?"

He always had some excuse.

One day he told her he'd left his parents' house—he'd been fighting with them, she knew, and they'd forced him to pay rent in spite of his challenging financial circumstances. He had moved out.

"Where are you living?"

"With a friend."

What she considered her female intuition wouldn't let it go. Something was up.

Finally he told her. "I'm staying with someone else," he said. A woman.

Cesar had been back in touch with an old girlfriend from long before the day he saw "Daniella's" number on the TV screen. He met up with her one night after work in town, and one thing led to another. She lived on her own, and he stayed over there more often until he decided, lovesick and wanting to get out of his parents' house, to move in with her. That was that. One day he was a devoted father and loving husband-to-be to Maricela, and the next he was shacking up with this bitch from his past.

"I'm in love with her," he said.

Maricela got a message on Facebook from a girl she didn't know— the girl Cesar was very likely leaving her for—calling her a *puta,* telling her that he doubted the baby was even his, just as Sebastian's girls had done when she was pregnant with Lupita. Things were meant to be different this time around, and yet here she was again. The news of the affair knocked the wind out of her, and stuck in La Colonia, she had no way to intervene or to stop them. When she tried to contact Cesar, he either blocked the call or was curt and rushed.

Things happen. People fall in love with other people. A man could vanish from his commitments in a heartbeat, take on a new life. For men, the world was always open. Not so, thought Maricela, for women. Who would love her now? She was barren, after all, since they'd opted—as a duo, a family—for the sterilization procedure at the hospital. What man would take her with two kids from two different men and no chance of having another? She walked around the dark house in La Colonia slumped with heartbreak, checking her phone constantly in hopes that it might offer a reversal of fate.

The phone didn't ring. He'd blocked her online. He didn't respond to her calls, her pleading text messages. It was over.

After a few nights of fitful sleep, she came to the conclusion that this girl must be working witchcraft on Cesar. *Brujería.* How else could a man change like that, on a dime?

She posted an anime image of a man and a woman holding hands, heads cocked askew, hanging from nooses on two separate trees. A photo of Angelina Jolie with a gun resting against her head. Then a photo of a knife slicing into an arm. She changed her profile picture to a stylized image of an eye, set into a dark backdrop of dark clouds, dropping a tear into a vast blue lake.

Cesar's mom was on Maricela's side. "Come down here and we'll talk about it," she said. They'd find a way to get Cesar back in his right mind. Perhaps, she said, they needed to do some witchcraft of their own. Maricela felt reassured as she listened, but as soon as she hung up the phone, the doubt settled in like old dust.

ERNESTO hadn't even asked Sofía's mom and stepdad for permission to date her, and now they had to tell them about the pregnancy.

Sofía didn't want to do it alone. "You're the dad, and you need to be there when I tell them," she said.

Ernesto knew she was right. He hadn't told anyone about the baby besides Raúl.

"We have to do it tomorrow," Sofía texted.

Ernesto agreed. "Will you come with me?" he asked Raúl.

Raúl looked at him like he was crazy.

"Please?" Ernesto said, his tone uncharacteristically pleading.

Raúl was touched but feigned indifference. "Okay," he agreed with a shrug.

Ever since that night Ernesto had laid into him, he had stopped cutting his arms and ditching school, though his fog of depression hadn't lifted. But now that Ernesto had his own personal emergency, Raúl rose to the occasion.

The only time Ernesto had come face-to-face with Sofía's mother before was at the *quinceañera,* which Ernesto had made it to after all. Sofía had been dressed like a cake-top princess, and Ernesto showed up in a flaming red shirt and red Nikes, piercings all over his face. *Puro marero,* the mom had told Sofía after the party. Total gangster.

"He's not!" Sofía had said. "He's a really good person, really responsible." But not responsible enough, it seemed.

The twins took the bus together and followed Sofía through the door. She motioned for them to sit on the couch across from her mother, Katerine, who had been waiting for them.

"Mom," she said, "this is my boyfriend." Ernesto forced himself to look up at Sofía's mother. "And his brother."

"Hello," Ernesto said.

Katerine, sensing something was coming, didn't respond.

"I'm pregnant."

Katerine heaved a throaty sigh and dropped her head into her lap.

Sofía began to cry. "I'm sorry," she said, "I'm sorry."

Ernesto couldn't bring himself to say anything, not a word.

Katerine also began to cry, shaking her head. "You did this," she said, pointing a shaking finger at Ernesto. "You have to take responsibility for what you've done, for this baby, and for your baby's mother."

Ernesto nodded miserably as Katerine shouted her lecture. She had given birth to Sofía at fifteen and had always wanted a different life for her. Sofía's father had abandoned them, and she'd managed to get them to the United States. And now, in spite of all her efforts, the cycle was repeating.

"This is your problem now," Katerine spat at Ernesto. They were in her living room, the TV turned low, an army of stuffed animals looking down from a high shelf. She pointed at Sofía's belly. "You are responsible for her and for your baby."

"I know," he said in a near-whisper. Raúl just sat there, quiet.

Soon Ernesto and Raúl picked themselves up off the couch. Ernesto muttered thin words of apology and followed Raúl out the door.

Once outside, he realized he hadn't even told Katerine his name.

He texted with Sofía during the whole bus ride to work. Her mom was still referring to Ernesto as a gangster, citing his piercings, his clothes, and his clear lack of manners—he hadn't even introduced himself. She had called him *maleducado,* Sofía said. Badly brought up.

This infuriated Raúl. That lady didn't know the Flores family; she couldn't talk that way about his twin. But Ernesto took the hit. He'd made a mistake, and now he had to pay. He straightened in his seat. It was time to grow up, to get down to business, to accept responsibility for what had happened, and to face their uncertain future.

At school, Sofía told Ernesto that her mom was livid, alternating between shouting at her and ignoring her entirely, speaking to her only about logistics like watching her little brother or attending the prenatal appointment she'd booked.

"She told me she wasn't going to support the baby. That I'd have to get a job, and you'd have to pay for everything."

"I will," Ernesto said. "I will, I promise. I'll take care of everything."

He feared her mother would kick her out any minute; but the shit-box room he shared with his twin brother was no place for a girl like Sofía, let alone a baby. He'd need to find a new place. But who would rent to two kids about to have a baby?

His commitment emboldened Sofía, who dug deeper into her feud with her mother. If she wasn't going to help, who needed her? Sofía was full of the delusions of a young woman both in crisis and in love. She concocted a fantasy in which she and her older, employed boyfriend could live together, support a newborn, and create a family without hardship.

"I can cook, I can clean, and I'll learn to take care of my baby," she said confidently. She just wanted a space in which to set up her imagined home.

Ernesto wanted to be swept up in her bright scenario, too, but, as someone who actually lived on his own, he knew it wasn't so easy.

"I don't need much," she insisted. "Not a big house or anything. Just a studio is fine." The average price for a studio at the time in Oakland was over twelve hundred dollars a month, about the entirety of Ernesto's salary. And plus, if they got a studio, where would Raúl go?

"You have to do right by this baby," her mother had said. "It's not the baby's fault that you two are irresponsible, and the baby can't suffer because of it."

It wasn't his baby's fault.

"I have to be responsible," Ernesto repeated to Raúl and to Sofía, like a mantra.

Raúl watched his brother mull over the mess of possibilities and obstacles. His brother had been so stupid, so, so stupid, to add another responsibility, another set of circumstances in which he owed something to someone else. And Sofía was so young. But his fury subsided into concern as he saw how the stress of it all weighed on his twin.

"I'll help you find a place," Raúl told him. "Whatever you do is fine with me."

The twins sent only four hundred dollars home in January. In February they sent nothing.

WILBER Sr. lay in bed and felt himself floating away from his body. All of a sudden he was in the field, his field, surrounded by lilies: the flowers he'd most often seen decorating coffins and the houses of death. The flowers were arranged in a big arc, like a bridge for him to walk under, and the most exquisite soft, white light filtered down from the sky.

"Are you seeing this beautiful field?" he asked out loud to Esperanza, who was lying next to him in bed.

She was startled. "What field?"

Hearing her voice, he knew he could not yet walk through that bridge of flowers to the other side. *You have to go back,* he told himself. He reentered his body, back in his room in La Colonia.

Earlier that day the creditors had told the Flores family that, the following week, they'd put one of the parcels of land up for sale unless they brought in some cash.

Wilber Sr. had made it through chikungunya, but he was still achy and had low energy, and the instability of the land weakened him further. The whole family worried that any minute, he would die from the very idea of losing it. The debt was likely to eat the Flores family, to cover them like dirt and roots surround a coffin.

The twins couldn't tell their parents about the baby—not yet.

MARICELA hadn't received child support from Cesar in two months—he'd abandoned not only her but their daughter, too. She went to file a report so that he would be ordered to resume payments. As a matter of procedure, she had to go to his workplace to get paperwork signed by his employers. She had the jitters as she rode the bus there, terrified at the thought of running into him, masochistically hopeful that she would. She knew the odds were practically none that she'd see him. And yet there, as she walked in the gate, was Cesar.

They both stopped. He stared at her with a wistful, lost expression.

She mustered control of her emotions. She wasn't going to be the first one to talk.

"Aren't you going to hug me?" he asked.

"Why would I do that?" He approached her and opened his arms into an embrace.

She kept her body tight, not reciprocating the hug. Nevertheless, the feel of him destabilized her resolve.

"I'm sorry," he said, letting her go.

She said nothing.

"Forgive me?" he pleaded. "I don't know what I was thinking. Forgive me. I love you. Take me back."

The other woman was now long gone. He regretted everything, he insisted. He'd only really left because he was confused and needed to get out of his parents' house. Maricela—faithful, loving, kind, a good mother—was the only woman in the world for him. It was as though he'd been bucked out of a trance.

"I have to think about it," she said. "How can I ever trust you again?"

If she took him back—and though it was hard to admit, she had no doubt in her mind that she'd take him back eventually if he let her, and take him back again and again—she knew it would never be the same.

"I know," he said. "I'm sorry. I'm so sorry."

She was proud of how stoic she stayed as he told her all the things she'd wanted to hear. She repeated that she'd think it over.

"I'll call you," he said, and she turned and walked away, back toward the bus. She didn't go in for the child support signature after all.

Back home, she took to Facebook.

What an unforgettable day with my love. There will be a wedding soon.

She did it just to see what people might say, to get a reaction, as if crowdsourcing her dilemma. Dozens of people liked her post. "Congratulations!" "You gonna invite me?"

After a few days of that post hanging in the ether, masquerading her pain as joy, she agreed.

They went to San Salvador together to get a promise ring—not an engagement ring, but a pre-engagement ring, a symbol of commitment that, she thought, would help wipe away the shame of having been walked out on. Cesar liked the one she picked; he likely would have bought any one of them for her. It cost ninety dollars, or twenty more than he had sent each month for diapers and milk.

They walked out of the store happy. She couldn't stop stealing glances at her hand: the hand of a loved woman, of an almost wife.

"Thank you," she told him. He kissed her there in the street.

IN Oakland, Sofía and Ernesto went to visit a school for teen moms, where Sofía might transfer once she had the baby—or earlier, even, for summer school. The school, run by the County of Alameda's Office of Education, partnered with Head Start to offer free childcare so that the young mothers could earn their high school credits more quickly while also learning parenting skills. At any one time, the school was home to a dozen or so students from throughout the county. The campus was on the basement level of a commercial building just north of Fruitvale, but in spite of its dim lighting and almost hidden location, it had computers and teachers and kind staff. Two trailers stood behind the main building of the school, which held the daycare center where the babies and toddlers spent their days while their mothers studied. The childcare rooms were full of light and laughter and burbling babies. The staff, Ernesto noted, seemed to really love the little ones, and each kid was being minded. A few of the childcare workers spoke Spanish. Ernesto spotted a boy and a girl dressed the same and holding hands.

"Twins!" one of the ladies told him, laughing.

A good enough sign for Ernesto.

"I like it here," Sofía said. She'd start in the summer session.

On TV at work, and in videos online, they saw seas of white people chanting "Build the wall," over and over again. Wasn't a big wall, they thought, already built? People held up signs: NO AMNESTY FOR ILLEGALS. NO LEGAL = NO JOBS. THE SILENT MAJORITY IS WITH TRUMP. THANK YOU, LORD JESUS, FOR PRESIDENT TRUMP. I'M READY TO WORK ON THE WALL. CLOSE BORDERS NOW. DEPORT ILLEGAL ALIENS. He saw a video from the year before about a homeless Latino man in Boston who was beaten up and pissed on by two brothers. "Trump was right," the alleged perpetrator said. "All these illegals need to be deported."

Wilber had come to the United States when George Bush was president and watched as Obama—the guy who'd campaigned on hope— ramped up his deportations. And now Trump. Wilber told his brothers he wasn't all that surprised that a guy like this was making headlines. To him, Trump represented the dark but very real side of the United States, filled with subtleties of racism and classism and xenophobia that often only immigrants could see. It wasn't so much him but his rallies: those seas of people chanting to build the wall, cheering when he said he would deport millions. Wilber knew he might very well be included in those millions.

The craziest part, to all of them, was that some Latinos were rallying and campaigning for him. He saw a picture of one lady with a shirt that read LATINOS FOR THE WALL.

At least, Ernesto considered, his baby would be born here. His adopted, not-quite-yet home was a better place to start from scratch than El Salvador. And his child would fuse him to the United States for real and for good. His baby would be a citizen, would speak English, would even vote. He'd vote too, one day, if he ever became a citizen—if he got that chance.

ERNESTO skipped classes on Friday to pick up an extra shift at work. He didn't get to see Sofía that day and hold her belly, whisper to the baby. That weekend Sofía avoided his calls and sent only curt texts. What was going on? When he finally got hold of her, she was vague about her whereabouts and distracted, as though she weren't even listening.

"What's up?" he said.

"Nothing," she said. "See you tomorrow."

That afternoon he got a message from a friend of a friend. Sofía had been making out with a kid named Mario, a tenth grader from El Salvador, right in the middle of the courtyard on Friday. Everyone, the snitch assured Ernesto, had seen.

With his child inside her growing belly, she'd cheated on him.

Fuming, he texted her: "You're a cheat, you're a liar."

"What?" she said.

"You know what you did."

They texted furiously until he decided to turn his phone off. He'd avoid her altogether, make her suffer. He'd never, ever forgive her. He'd never take her back.

The next day she confronted him and begged for his forgiveness. "I'm sorry!" she said. "I don't know what I was thinking! I'm just over-whelmed. I'm so sorry. I made a mistake. You have to forgive me."

Holding back tears, he shook his head. "I'm going to talk to your mom and let her know that I'll support the baby," he said with a quiver-ing voice. "But I won't support you." His responsibilities to Sofía be-yond the baby were, as far as he was concerned, over.

He couldn't look at her. He stormed past her and sat on the curb outside school, the same place where his brother had sat dumb-drunk last year, and put his head between his knees. He wailed like a little boy.

He reported to work that night and then went home, phone turned off, refusing to talk to her. He avoided her at school the next day and the next.

"I didn't mean it!" she said, cornering him one day in the office. "I'm so sorry!"

He'd calmed down somewhat and could see that he had the power back in the situation. "I'll talk to you," he said. "It's the right thing for the baby." He'd take her back into his life, but not as his girlfriend.

By that afternoon they were nuzzling each other in the courtyard, holding hands.

From then on Ernesto and Sofía were on-again-off-again. One day Ernesto would post:

Today King Ernest & Queen Sofía LOVE FOR EVER EVER.

Soon afterward he'd post a picture of a homeboy giving a middle finger:

Fuck Relationships, I'm Single.

Tomorrow is the day everything becomes clear: my last day with you.

It was hard for any of their friends to keep track. It was hard for them to keep track, too.

"The relationship changes," Ernesto explained. "Once that trust has been broken, it's hard to put it back together." His heart, too.

But Sofía and his baby needed him, he knew, and this trumped their day-to-day drama. If it was hard for him, he could muster the maturity to see that it was a thousand times worse for her: fifteen years old, carrying a baby. He would never walk away from his child, but he would always have the option to do so. She never would.

AT first Ernesto and Sofía were convinced it was a boy, because Sofía had gained weight in her face. But then she started craving lemons and grapes; sour things like that were definitely the mark of a girl. But if it was a girl, Ernesto would be gaining weight—and he was as skinny as ever, all muscle and bones. He hardly ate a solid meal most days, surviving mostly on chips and Monster drinks.

One day Ernesto was walking down International Boulevard on his way to the restaurant when he saw, in the middle of the sidewalk, a tiny sock. His heart skipped, and he knelt to pick it up. The sock was navy blue with a pink fringe, speckled with little pink hearts. A little girl's sock. It fit neatly in the palm of his hand.

He placed it in his backpack, where he would keep it as a lucky charm.

"We're having a girl," he declared to Sofía. "Definitely."

Though their relationship was more off than on, Ernesto was still devoted to Sofía's well-being as well as to their baby.

"Are you eating enough?" he'd asked. "You sleeping? What does the baby feel like, what's it doing?" He took her to the lake, to get ice cream, and to San Francisco to buy miniature clothes.

Raúl dismissed Ernesto's sidewalk sign—it was just a sock, after all— and soon convinced Ernesto that the baby was a boy. On the bus and at home before sleep, the twins talked about their nephew-son—what they could name him, what he'd look like, what they'd do together—until he became real. Seven years after they'd stopped dressing alike, the twins talked excitedly about buying matching clothes for the three of them, the Flores brothers and their tiny triplet.

ERNESTO decided he wasn't going to go back to school in the fall. Outwardly, he was confident about his choice. He and Raúl had failed several classes because, between the late nights working and the ups and downs of depression, it had been hard to make it to school on time—and sometimes even at all. They each felt ashamed of their failures in their separate ways. Raúl was sure he could make a change, but Ernesto, for his part, knew that things would only get more complicated once the baby came. What was the point of being in school if they weren't getting any closer to graduation? But his decision was a loss. By giving up his boyhood dream of a U.S. education, he was both accepting the reality of his circumstances and falling on his sword. "I have to be responsible," he repeated. Clean hands.

The school counselor helped him enroll in the publicly funded adult school in nearby Alameda. He was an adult, after all. There he could take classes part time to earn credits toward his high school diploma. He'd have more time to work, and he'd be able to pick up another job.

"We need to send money home," said Raúl.

"I have to focus on my family," he said. Sofía, he meant, and the baby.

"What about our family?"

"We just didn't know how hard it was going to be. We thought it was easier to make money." He was almost cavalier, Raúl felt, about abandoning his plans, his promises.

Raúl didn't have that kind of luxury. Now with Ernesto, like Wilber, focusing on his own small world, he'd have to assume the burden of the debt. Of saving the family.

At the baby shower, Raúl sat in the corner, silent. How much had this cost, he wondered, these games, these decorations, all this food? They'd even made special invitations for everyone. How much had Ernesto contributed? People placed bets on the date the baby would be born, and as they opened their presents, Ernesto and Sofía had to guess who had brought which gift. Each time they were wrong, the gift giver got to draw something with marker on their faces. Ernesto was aware that all these people were Sofía's people, that he didn't know anyone except Raúl. And Raúl wondered if anyone would notice if he disappeared.

With Ernesto spending so much time with Sofía, Raúl reached out to Wilber. They hadn't spent much time with Wilber since the fall, and when they did hang out, he made clear that they'd have to pay for their own food or chip in for gas—even though he always paid for Gabby or friends of his who tagged along. The twins didn't mind paying, but it seemed like Wilber was trying to make a point, which made everything feel strained. Raúl called anyway.

"Want to come running?" Wilber asked.

Wilber now ran every day. It calmed him, he said. His new dog came with him and waited in the car. He ran by where he and Gabby had buried Nicky One. Raúl had a hard time keeping up, but he admired his brother's discipline. He, too, had been working out: one hundred push-ups each night, one hundred sit-ups. Running through the hills like that was relaxing, Wilber insisted. His anxiety had built of late: he was working a lot, growing tired of the commute, back in the packed house, fighting with Gabby, worried about what he was hearing on the news.

Ernesto hadn't told Wilber about the baby, and Raúl kept the secret.

WHEN it came time for the four-month ultrasound where they'd find out the sex of the baby, the doctor told Sofía and Ernesto that they could invite people for support.

"Wanna come?" Ernesto asked Raúl. It would be just a couple of days after the twins' twentieth birthday.

The ultrasound room turned out to be too small to let in more than one observer. When Ernesto arrived, right on time, Sofía's mother Katerine left the room to give him her place. She had grown more accepting of the situation and of Ernesto's commitment to becoming a good father. She wanted them to have the moment together. While the monitor skated across the surface of Sofía's growing belly, pictures began to pulse into focus on the screen.

Out in the hallway, Raúl leaned over his phone, not talking to Katerine or her friend who'd come for moral support. They had a bet going on the sex: whoever lost would buy the other lunch. "Who's going to win?" Katerine asked Raúl, trying to engage him.

"It's a boy," he said. "I'm sure of it." He went back to fiddling with his phone.

Sofía and Ernesto burst out of the door, holding the ultrasound copy.

"So, who's betting what? What do you think?" Sofía said, laughing at everyone's hungry faces. Ernesto was silent, shaking slightly.

"Don't mess around!" Katerine scolded her daughter. "Just tell us!"

Sofía smiled and raised her eyebrow.

"Boy!" Katerine said.

"*Girl!*" Sofía shouted.

Ernesto shook his head, smiling, and then began to cry. Knowing the sex had somehow made everything more real.

"Girl?" said Raúl. "Wow."

Sofía unfurled a long scroll-like sheet of images of the baby in utero. The group gathered around, admiring the little foot, the head, what appeared to be an elbow: a series of pictures from all different angles, like a cubist study of the baby-to-be.

Ernesto stood off to the side, breathless. He could hardly speak as they walked out of the hospital. His body had become light, too light, and feeble—he struggled to push open the door.

They walked Sofía to her mother's car.

"You're buying lunch!" their family friend said, gleeful.

"We won't know for *sure* until the baby comes out!" said Katerine. They cackled.

"We're going to take the bus," Ernesto said, referring to himself and Raúl, when they got to the car. Katerine shrugged. He gave Sofía a kiss goodbye and rubbed her stomach.

"Guess we won't all be dressing the same," Raúl said as they reclined against either side of the bus stop pole.

"Yeah." Ernesto shook his head and smiled. He watched Sofía and her mom pull out of the hospital driveway. His baby was in that car: his little girl. How crazy, those ten pictures, printed out like a long receipt. *Me, me this way, me this other way, me again,* his daughter announced from each one. He wanted to tell his parents but was still afraid. It would mean announcing one more financial obstacle. It would also, he felt deeply, renew their sense of loss—the thought of their sons living so far away and now making a new family they might never know.

The twins stared into the distance, waiting for the bus, dragging their cigarettes in near rhythm with each other. They had nothing to say, and that was fine. Here on the sidewalk, no one knew them, no one wanted to smash their heads in with rocks, no one loved them—people just passed them by. And though there was something forlorn about Oakland's sea of anonymity, being alone together, just the two of them, had a refreshing weightlessness: no one quite yet a father, no new trag-edy having yet struck. They soaked in the sunlight and nicotine, hoping the bus would take a little longer to come.

Later that week Ernesto got up the guts to call home. "My girlfriend is having a baby," he said to his mother. "A baby girl."

"Oh," Esperanza said. She began to cry, then collected herself.

"Just make sure you bring the baby home someday so I can meet it," she said.

"Okay," he promised. "I will."

THE LAND

Sometimes there was no rain; sometimes the rain came at the wrong time. The land was thirsty. All over the country, the cattle were dying, and the corn was drying on its withered stalks. In April 2016 the president of El Salvador declared a national water shortage emergency. That had never happened before. Some 3.5 million people in Central America were at risk of food insecurity or were already hungry.

The old man with thirteen children—three up north, six here in El Salvador, four buried in the churchyard—sometimes went out to the land to pray.

That summer his tomato crop was bad, due to a problem he'd never seen before. The tomatoes, though they had a good enough flavor—not his best, but good—were pallid in color, their skin a mottled orange-yellow. Seen from far away, they were easily mistaken for citrus. He couldn't figure out what had gone wrong. His wife took them into town anyway, but she couldn't make the sale. "Sweet flavor, good price!" she crooned to the crowds of the roadside market. But who wanted to buy the wrong-color fruit?

Then there was the dust. A dust cloud from the Sahara, as he understood it, had flown in and settled onto his crops. Who knew what damage it might be doing to the soil? And last year there had been the problem with the coffee—rust, they called it. Every crop had its own plague.

Wilber Sr. was still feeble from sickness, from age. His sons weren't helping much anymore, so he was mostly on his own out there in the sun, harvesting the forlorn tomatoes. He hadn't been a perfect father, a perfect husband, but he'd tried.

A thought came to him, as it often did after prayer: beets.

"I came up with an idea," he announced to his family—the members who remained—that evening. "The tomatoes don't have the right color, and they aren't sweet enough. So my solution is as follows. You know that in some places they use beets to make sugar? Yes, exactly. Well," he paused, "my plan is to grow beets, take the juice from the beets, and pour the juice at the base of the tomato plants."

That way, he reasoned, the roots would suck up the deep dark color as well as the sweet flavor. Either it would bring life back to the farm, or it would work otherwise. Whatever God's will.

A person could slip out of this world so easily. But this project with the beets made him want to stay at least a little longer. Every plan was a Hail Mary for the faithful, after all. Even if the rain never came again, even if he was forced to sell his land, his inheritance, he'd work until he no longer could.

CHAPTER 12

After learning that Ernesto was having a kid, Maricela couldn't sleep. She was visiting a friend in San Salvador, and Leiny had dropped off into easy slumber. Not Maricela. A mosquito had got into the room and buzzed like a miniature curse. She'd dreamed of having a niece for her daughters to play with. How nice, to be an aunt, to no longer be the only one of the nine with a kid. But Ernesto? Why not Wilber or Ricardo—the ones who were actually ready, or at least older? She'd heard the girl was younger, that poor thing. She knew what it would be like for her. Girls had so few options. Her younger sister, Lucia, had recently left home to go to school at the convent. She was going to become a nun. Another of Maricela's people, gone. She knew her brother was a good guy, but guys, like Cesar, couldn't be trusted to stay good. And being good to the girl almost certainly meant leaving his own family behind. Her brother had set roots in the United States: his phones, his sneakers, his clothes, his education, and now his baby. She swatted at the mosquito, and it quieted for a moment, then came right back buzzing.

A few weeks later Maricela woke up to a hard kick into her stomach. It nearly knocked the wind out of her. Ricardo.

"What the fuck were you thinking?" he said, practically spitting. She had forgotten to turn the light off in the house's main room. She could smell the liquor on him, and he was swaying. "Stupid bitch." He left the room.

Her little sister rushed to her side. "You okay?" she asked.

The baby now was crying. Maricela hushed it and lay still until she was sure that Ricardo had fallen asleep.

He came home drunk again a few nights later, but this time he confided in her. "They want me to join," he said. Meaning the gangs. "But they told me I'd have to kill Dad."

Maricela was too stunned to respond.

"And I don't have the courage to do that."

It was a rare moment of closeness, this confiding, and it didn't last. Ricardo still hadn't forgiven Maricela for her second pregnancy; he pinned everything on her, it seemed, from the family's financial circumstances to his own lack of options in life. After that night, he grew even more vitriolic, as if he were punishing her for knowing his secrets.

Another night she took the remote and changed the TV station.

"What are you doing?" her younger brother Pablo said. More and more he'd been parroting his older brother, taking on a bullying masculine stance. She wondered if he, too, was considering joining the gangs. She didn't respond.

Ricardo stood up and looked at her menacingly.

"I can change the channel if I want," Maricela responded.

At that, Pablo got up and socked her in the face. Ricardo laughed hard, and harder still as Maricela ran into her room holding her cheek. She stayed there with her girls until the next morning.

She told Ernesto and Raúl over Facebook, "Ricardo's out of control." She couldn't tell their father, because he'd confront Ricardo, and then Ricardo would find another way to punish her. So like a battered wife, she stayed fearfully quiet, avoided eye contact, and whisked the kids away when they were fussy lest they enrage one of their uncles. She tried to become invisible in her own house.

THEN, in August, after more than three years, Sebastian's brother was released from a jail sentence for his affiliation with Barrio 18 and came back to La Colonia. Rumors went that he was hunting down people all over the region—rival gang members who he thought had something to do with why he ended up in jail.

Maricela knew nothing of this until Ricardo came home one night and pulled her into a room. She stiffened, expecting another beating.

"Don't go outside," he said. Someone had passed word to him that, to avenge the death of the people he'd killed, the local MS-13 guys were looking to kill not just Sebastian's brother but a member of his family. Sebastian lived in Houston now, so they couldn't get to him.

"They want to kill you and Lupita," he said.

"Lupita?"

The three-year-old was, after all, part of Sebastian's bloodline.

"Don't go outside," Ricardo repeated. That was all he had to offer, and he did so with a gruff tenderness, despite all that had passed between them. She believed he was telling the truth or, anyway, what he knew of the truth. As always, who knew what word on the street was real and what was fabrication or misinformation? The only way to confirm the rumor was to see if Maricela or her three-year-old daughter ended up in a body bag.

She stayed inside with her daughters for a few days. She couldn't call the police about the threats—one never knew whom they were working for, and how such a call might fan the flames. Finally, she risked taking the bus to go talk to Cesar.

In his tiny place in town, she told him what happened. He just looked at her and kept quiet. Then he started to cry. He wanted to help, he told her, he wanted to protect her, and it drove him crazy that there was nothing he could do. He couldn't even help with money; as he'd shame-facedly told her weeks earlier, he'd taken out a credit card and racked up $3,000 in debt, such that the company was garnishing his wages until he paid it back—which, at this rate, would take years.

"I think the only thing I can do is go north," she said. Cesar barely earned enough now to cover his rent, much less pay her way, but she thought her brothers would be willing to help.

After a pause, Cesar said, "Don't go." That he really didn't want her to leave delighted her, but she didn't show it.

She called Sebastian to tell him what was going on. He hadn't been in touch with his brother, he said, but he believed her.

"I can pay for Lupita," he concluded, "but not for you." To get them to Mexico would cost $3,000 each, and she'd have to pay her share of that, then figure out some way to cross the border. A coyote would charge her at least $7,000 for the full trip, start to finish.

She wanted to make sure Lupita was safe, but sending her alone was out of the question. It could put her in even more danger, and even if she crossed safely, Maricela might never see her again. And who would take care of her up there—her absentee father? Her preoccupied uncles? The alternative, though, was to let her stay here with a revenge bounty on her head.

At home, locked in the dark quiet of the house, she saw Trump on TV. People were saying he wouldn't win, and her family wanted to believe that was true. This man, she understood, was one more obstacle to her escape plan.

"They want to kill me and Lupita," she wrote Ernesto and Raúl. "I have to leave."

WHEN the twins got Maricela's messages, they panicked and called Wilber. The three of them had a family conference.

If the gangs really were after Maricela and Lupita, she needed to get out of town fast. She couldn't hide out in the house forever, and if they wanted to kill her that bad, they could always break into the house. But the Flores brothers simply didn't have the money to pay for her trip, let alone to support her while she got on her feet here. They knew firsthand how bad the trip was for boys; for a young woman and a little kid, they could only imagine. Plus, their parents needed her at home.

"But if they really want to kill her?"

"They told Ricardo that if he joins, he has to kill Dad," Raúl said.

Wilber had seen pictures of Ricardo on Facebook looking bloated from drinking.

"If he does anything to Dad, I'll fly down there myself and kill him," Ernesto said, his face reddening.

How had it all come to this?

Maricela now entreated her brothers over Facebook daily. She said she needed to get there as fast as possible, "otherwise they will stop giving *permisos.*" There were no *permisos,* as her brothers and others had told her again and again. Best case, she would be in detention for a few weeks and then be allowed to await court in Oakland, likely with an ankle bracelet.

"No, they told me it's true." *They* being the coyotes—the people she would be paying to take her north. Maricela, simultaneously driven by fear and starry-eyed at the prospect of finally going north, could not be dissuaded. And she became obsessed with the deadline the coyotes had given her: November 2016.

The boys certainly couldn't put several thousand dollars together within a month. What was the urgency with November? they asked.

"Because then it will be the elections," she finally explained. "And if Trump wins, they will stop giving out *permisos.*" Never mind that there were no *permisos* in the first place, or that, even if Trump was elected, none of his policies would be enacted until the new year. The rumor stuck like truth: more walls, no *permisos,* no chance to start anew.

"It's very unlikely he will win," I told Raúl one day at school during lunchtime, as he slumped on the couch outside my office, ruminating over what to do.

"He's going to win," Raúl said. "I know it."

I told him he was always thinking the worst would happen.

"Maybe so, but I know he's going to win." He shook his head. "People love him. And then all the Latinos are going home."

Like Maricela, he couldn't be dissuaded. As much as this country had been good to him, he was—and always would be, he felt—an outsider.

"I swear to you—Trump will win."

IN mid-October, Ernesto was sleeping over at Sofía's house when she woke up in pain. "You okay?" he asked, and she bit into his shoulder, hard. Within a few minutes her water had broken and they loaded into her mother's car for the hospital. By the time they were situated in the hospital room, Sofía was red in the face and narrow-eyed with concentration. She labored for around ten hours, writhing and moaning with each contraction. Ernesto pressed into her back, as they had been taught at the parenting and birthing classes they'd attended after school last spring. But with each contraction, she seemed to lose a little strength.

"I can't," she said, sweating and shaking her head. "I can't do it."

"*Echale ganas,*" he encouraged. "Don't worry, just keep trying, you've got this."

"The baby's coming," he texted Raúl between contractions.

"My baby is on its way," he wrote Maricela, casting a virtual net across the city, the continent, to feel closer to his family.

Until his daughter was born, a part of Ernesto held to the possibility that his child might, in fact, be a boy. But with Sofía's final push, a little baby girl slipped out, tiny and messed with birth. Here was Isabella, alive and in the world.

As Ernesto held his daughter for the first time, he was overcome with the realness of her, the delicate little body that marked an unfathomable shift in who he was. He gingerly handed the baby back to Sofía and called Raúl to tell him the news.

Raúl took the bus to the hospital. Ernesto passed the baby cautiously, like a bowl filled with water, to his twin. Raúl took her in his arms comfortably. As he stared into his niece's eyes, his face softened into an old expression something like innocence or wonder—the one people had once used to tell him and his brother apart. Raúl rocked her gently. He was totally in love.

"She had the baby. It's a girl. She is happy and healthy and doing okay," he wrote Maricela.

Ernesto took a week off from work—a week without pay—to spend time with Sofía and Isabella. Sofía, according to tradition, was to spend forty days indoors recuperating. She plugged her ears with cotton balls to keep out any outside air and adhered to a strict diet. That first week the baby slept well enough and was easily soothed by breastfeeding. She developed a little birthmark over her eye that worried Ernesto, but when he found out it was normal and would likely fade, he began to love it. He liked playing with her tiny hands, finger by finger, those miniature copies of his own.

Each morning before work, he stopped in and sat on the couch, where Sofía passed him the baby. Some cartoon was often on the TV. It was sad when Isabella spent his whole visit sleeping—he got only so much time with her, after all. One morning Ernesto stared at his daughter and took her hand, shaking it slightly, rubbing the tip of his finger along her fuzzy cheek.

"Wake up," he whispered, "wake up." He wanted to see her eyes before he had to go to work.

He held his daughter awkwardly, as new dads often do. Raúl, though, was an instant natural. That morning he had come along and patiently waited for his turn with Isabella. She settled easily into his arms, and he walked around the room, then sat in a chair facing the corner, walling the two of them off from the world, rocking the warm, sleeping bundle.

"Let me have her," Ernesto said as a Spanish *Finding Nemo* blared from the screen in front of them. It was almost time to go. Raúl shrugged and gave her back. Across the room on the other couch, Sofía snuggled against Ernesto's shoulder, peeking at the baby. The three of them, along with Sofía's little brother and Raúl, turned their eyes to the TV. They watched raptly as Nemo, the lost little boy fish, made friends in the fish tank at the Sydney dentist's office and hatched an escape plan, and they laughed uproariously as the dentist's fish-crazed niece marched into the office, headgear and all.

When Nemo's father and his amnesiac friend, Dory, got swallowed by a whale, Ernesto checked his phone, careful not to rock his daughter. Time to go. He handed the baby to Sofía, kissed her on the forehead, and reluctantly walked out the door.

ERNESTO had started the school year taking classes in Alameda, but by Isabella's birth, he had quit. He'd go back later, he felt—now was the time for another job. Sofía had started taking classes at the school for teen moms before Isabella was born, and she'd return there in January.

Raúl enrolled in the twelfth grade at Oakland International with an amended schedule that meant he didn't have to come in until 10:10. But still he often didn't make it on time, or at all. He wanted to go to school, he needed to "for my future," he said, but sometimes he just couldn't pull himself out of bed. Staying in school kept him from getting another job, but he wasn't going often enough to actually earn the credits he needed to move toward his goal of graduating, let alone become fluent in English. (He was still very limited in his ability to speak, since he'd missed so much school over the years.) He'd take on the whole weight of the family debt, but he wanted to maintain some sliver of hope for a better future for himself. Being enrolled in school—even without really attending—served that purpose.

He sent $750 home to keep the lenders at bay.

"They're going to sell it," Maricela said.

"I'll send more," Raúl promised.

The lenders were making calls to find buyers for the land now. Raúl really was the only hope to stave them off.

"I'll suffer if it means saving them," he said. He was deadly serious. For two months he ate little, bought nothing, paid his rent, and sent money home. He knew well enough that his full-blown effort was late; he thought of all the money he'd wasted on clothes, on booze, the lost wallet, the bad choices. Still, he tried. He was taking the lead now, and he was both dignified and overwhelmed by this pitiless, solitary yoke. Every time he walked away from the bank with emptied pockets was a triumph.

But the money barely made a dent. And now it wasn't just the land; Maricela needed his help, too—her life, if the rumors were true, depended on it.

But it was no use. In time, the numbers, and his growling stomach, became a paralytic. The hole was just too deep. He called his mother in La Colonia one day, in broken sobs. "I can't, I can't do it alone," he whimpered. He explained his depression, his anxiety, and how, because of the baby, Ernesto couldn't help for now. Raúl wasn't sleeping, always had the jitters. "I'm afraid I'm going crazy," he told her.

"Don't worry," Esperanza said. "Take care of yourself." He mustn't let the stress kill him, she told him—she needed him safe and well. The debt was too much for all of them. They'd sell one parcel of their land to save the other and get out from under the creditors for good.

Raúl felt the mixed heat of shame and relief.

"Thank you," he said. "I'm sorry." He felt the urge to crawl into a quiet place and stay there for a while. But one can't just withdraw from the world, Raúl knew—he'd tried that before, until love and duty had beckoned him back. Independence didn't mean doing everything by himself; being his own man didn't mean being alone. He needed the rest of them. Even Ernesto. Him, most of all.

AFTER the phone call, Esperanza told Wilber Sr. and Maricela that it was over. There was no more debt, she said. It was driving Raúl crazy. They had to accept that the land was lost, the debt too high for them to ever climb their way out.

Wilber and Maricela protested, but Esperanza held her ground. She was determined. "Enough."

Wilber and Maricela sat down to do the math. If they sold one plot of land, valued now at around $40,000, they thought, they could pay off the debt, keep the other plot, and still have some money.

It pained Wilber to sell the land, which meant so much more than money. But it had to be done. "What's done is done," he told Maricela. But he didn't want to talk to his sons for a while. Esperanza didn't hold it against them.

"We're fine, everything's fine," Esperanza told Raúl. "We'll sell the land and have more money. We'll be okay!" Raúl knew she was lying, but all the same he felt somehow lighter. No more debt. Now, like Ernesto, he was free to start from scratch.

He broke the news to his brother gently: they were selling the land. No need to rub it in, to make him feel at fault. Ernesto sighed, then began to cry. He took it harder than Raúl had expected: he did care. As if through a series of sucker punches, they had kept uncovering more of the secret, beating heart of the world: its vastness, its cruelty, and now the interdependence of things.

When Raúl thought back to Guatemala now, or his enemies back home, he realized he no longer felt nauseated. The terror and the rage had faded. But this came at a price: he was also forgetting. The contours of his past were blurring, and even his mother's face now took time to focus against the screen of memory. The thing about growing up and moving on was that you also had to let some good things go.

He asked a friend to give him a tattoo: two black feathers on the inside of his forearm, alongside the word *Dream*. In El Salvador a tattoo would have been seen as the mark of a gangster. Here it could mean anything. The new tattoo covered up his scars.

The main parcel of the Flores family land, their *herencia,* went up for sale.

ONE month and a day after Isabella was born, it was Election Day.

As the news came in of Trump's potential upset victory, the guys who worked the kitchen in the sushi restaurant began shouting and swearing.

"Jesus Christ," one said.

"Pack your bags, boys—that's it," said another.

"Fucking racists."

Ernesto listened, head hung.

As they shut down the restaurant for the night, the owners, a Japanese family, seemed distraught. "There will be war," they said. "This man is going to cause many wars."

On November 9, 2016, the whole world seemed surprised by the election outcome, but not the Flores siblings. They always did prepare for the worst, even as they hoped for much, much more.

They talked to Wilber. The election had shaken him deeply. Trump was still promising to purge the country of illegals—to deport two million, probably three million, people. Starting, he said, with those who had a criminal record. Like him. That ridiculous parking lot DUI from so long ago wriggled at the edges of Wilber's mind like a parasitic worm. He had done his community service and paid the fines, but still it was all on his record, as he'd found out through the probate court investigation. After nearly a decade in the United States without papers, deportation seemed likelier than ever before and his future, in certain ways, all the more precarious. Who knew what tomorrow held for him?

He decided to make some changes.

Wilber called Raúl to let him know that he and Gabby had broken up for good. They had had too many fights, with too much stress. He had done everything for her, he said, and she didn't appreciate him. Raúl assumed they'd get back together as always, but the next day the news was the same, and the day after that.

Now Wilber had an idea. "I want to find an apartment for all three of us," he said. It bothered him that his brothers lived in a crappy room in a house where they couldn't use the kitchen or leave their shampoo in the shower or leave their door unlocked. Maybe, he thought, the three of them could make a real home together.

This way, too, Maricela would have a place to crash if she did come north.

Time, the election, and the troubles back home were a uniting force. They started looking for apartments together, the three Flores men. Maybe Maricela would join them, maybe not. The specter of violence down south, the specter of deportation up north, and the mess in between: their worlds were determined by it all.

At least Isabella was a citizen. They worried about her growing up in a place rife with racism, having fewer opportunities, being hated or scorned. But looking into her eyes, that seemed so improbable. Isabella, like all newborns, was a do-over, a clean slate—a chance for her family, and her world, to raise someone right. She'd inherit the earth, a full Salvadoran American. More than that, she'd make it better.

As to how the political landscape would settle, "all we can do is wait," said Raúl. Ernesto agreed.

All along, things had happened to them—the desert trip, the murder, the kidnapping, their country's unraveling, and now Ernesto's fatherhood—that were beyond reason. They knew they'd been dealt a terrible lot but had also had some unbelievable strokes of luck—beyond, they believed deep down, what they deserved. To be so very lucky and so terribly unlucky could disorient a person; you never knew where the next punch might come from, or if it would come at all.

Maricela sent them a message. Their cousin Juan was now the local MS-13 boss.

"We would have climbed over that wall, you know," Raúl said.

EARLY one morning in December in La Colonia, the Floreses heard shots from down the road. A farmer in his seventies, just a little older than Wilber Sr., had been executed by the side of the road. He died instantly, shot through the head and the chest. The police, they found out later, suspected Barrio 18. No one in the community would talk to the police or the press, except on condition of anonymity.

When Maricela heard the shots, she thought at first they were meant for her. The whole family stayed inside for a few days.

It rattled everyone—in La Colonia and in Oakland—that the shooting had happened so close to their home and in broad daylight. In fact, the number of homicides in El Salvador had declined: in November 2016, the police chief reported, there were nearly 20 percent fewer homicides country-wide than in the same period the year before. The first eleven months of 2016 registered 1,125 fewer homicides than in all of 2015, when over 6,600 people had been killed. But if the national homicide rate had fallen, it seemed to have got worse in La Colonia. They could picture right where the man had been gunned down.

The following week Maricela picked up the phone, curious about an unknown number that was calling.

"Listen, girl," the voice said. "You're going to pay us five hundred dollars, or we're going to kill you."

As with many threats in El Salvador, it was hard to know whether the call was coming from real gangsters. But it felt real to her, compounding the threats that already existed. Regardless of whether they were linked to Sebastian's brother, or whether the gangs really had her address, she wanted out of town.

She went and stayed with Cesar for a while and took the two girls with her, nervous on the bus lest someone see her, follow her, track her down. There, she stayed inside while Cesar went to work.

Along with a selfie of herself and Cesar, who wasn't her husband officially but might as well be, she posted online:

Me and my husband I love you Cesar.

Her trademark self-conscious smile complemented his reserved grin; his factory badge and blue uniform shirt were visible along the photo's edge.

She heard from her father that someone had agreed to buy the smaller parcel of land. "Thirty thousand dollars," he told her. Enough to pay off the debt—now around $24,000—and have some left over. They'd been hoping for more, but after so few bites, this was good news.

There was a catch.

"The man lives in the United States," Wilber Sr. explained. "He will pay off the land little by little." They'd still be relying on small monthly installments from the States, which they'd use to pay off their own debt over time. They took the deal. At least they still had their larger parcel of land. As long as they could farm it, they wouldn't starve.

Her second sister, Marina, the third-to-last Flores sibling, followed Lucia and joined the convent. It was the safest bet for both of them, to be protected and cared for. Maricela was the only sister left at home, living with Ricardo, the drunk who flirted with the gangs, and her two little brothers. No one to help her with the babies now, no one to talk to, her friends, her closest siblings, all gone.

If only they'd sent her to the North instead of, one after another, her brothers. For now Maricela wasn't leaving, but she hadn't given up her burning-ember hope. If she didn't go she knew she'd spend her whole life wondering what might have been, or what could still be. If she did go, leaving Cesar or her girls or her parents behind, she'd likely always wonder, as her brothers did, whether she'd made the right decision—whether, in fact, she'd had the option to stay.

For now, Cesar loved her and, more important, valued her. Men always had, and perhaps always would, determine her world. But she knew that she also had to find value for herself—especially in this world where women were still, so often, second class, and in this country where life was cheap. She was determined to forge a life distinct from the one she had inherited from convention and from her parents' circumstances (God bless them). What good, clean-hand choices were there for girls like her? They could go to the convent, they could go to the North, they could hunker down in their lives and live as quietly as possible, as if underground. She wanted Lupita and Leiny to find more than she had to give them, and to do that, she'd have to start them off better than where she'd begun. Here or there she would manage to better the hand she'd been dealt; she and her girls in her wake would—quietly, maybe, but unflinchingly—carry on. What other choice was there?

THE twins decided to take a bike ride up into the Oakland hills. They tore along a paved path that skirted the ridge from Inspiration Point, feeling their wheels catch air from time to time over the speed bumps. From up here they could see San Francisco and, beyond it, the ocean: the Pacific, the same ocean they'd visited as kids during the annual trip for good students in La Colonia. The dry and blistered hillsides reminded them of Texas. Ernesto took a photo and posted it with the caption:

Today in the desert.

Up here, above the lives they had built, and the country they had built them in, the look-alike brothers cruised over a cattle grate, past barbed-wire fences. Fences, walls, deserts, oceans. People got what they needed to survive or died trying. So far they'd made it.

"¡Animal!" Raúl shouted.

"Bitch, I'll kick your ass!"

It occurred to the Flores twins that there would likely never again be a time when their entire nuclear family, all eleven of them, were back together. Things had changed, forever. Half the family land was gone, too, a fact that would stay lodged in them like shrapnel, along with the other wounds. At the same time, there was a bright side: the debt was canceled. This moment offered the sense of a real beginning. Raúl would get to school on time, and next semester, Ernesto would re-enroll in the community college classes to get his certificate of completion. He wanted to set a good example for his daughter, after all. This month, they were sure, they could send some money home to help their family—pure help, not just a piddle toward an unbeatable debt. If they saved enough their father could buy another parcel of land he'd found for sale—a small one, but a fertile one, better, even, than the one they'd lost. They were getting another chance, and they'd do it right this time.

They dipped and soared in the parched folds of California, whooping and hollering like kids, until it was time to pack up the bikes and head back down to the flats, to work. Back at Inspiration Point, they looked out over the frenetic plane of Oakland, the shimmering bay, and across to the Golden Gate.

From up high, just the two of them, they could hold on to that notion of possibility. This, they supposed, was the irresistible tug of the American Dream. For a sunny instant, they were pulled in.

AFTERWORD

"Me tiraron," one of my students told me when I first started working at Oakland International. "They threw me." At that point my Spanish wasn't great, so I thought I'd misheard. He explained, "They put me in a bag, and when the guards weren't looking, they threw me over the fence." *Me tiraron.* His smugglers holding on to each end of the sack, they heave-ho'd my sixteen-year-old student over the twelve-foot wall and into the space between two immigration agents patrolling the other side. The boy undid himself from the sack and took off running. In spite of the fence and the agents within eyesight of him and each other, he wasn't caught. He would have done anything, he told me, to get to the United States.

My thirteen years of experience working with, interviewing, and reporting alongside thousands of refugees and migrants like the Flores twins have shown me that very few people actually want to leave their homes. People leave because something there has become untenable. Global poverty is a massive driver of migration to the United States and around the globe—and though poverty is not a legally recognized justification for crossing a border, who among us wouldn't move to a greener pasture in order to feed ourselves, to feed our children? "Economic" migrants worldwide are fleeing drought, famine, languishing economies, and the adverse impacts of globalization. But as the story of the Flores brothers reveals, along with the stories of others they and I met during the journey of living and reporting this book, today's unauthorized migration across our southern border is driven largely—though of course not entirely—by violence.

Since the change in administration and the initial publication of this book, MS-13 has become all but a household name in the United States. Trump has said that MS-13 members "have transformed peaceful parks and beautiful quiet neighborhoods into bloodstained killing fields." This he blames largely on the influx of Central Americans like the Flores twins, many of who are themselves fleeing MS-13 back home, but whom Attorney General Sessions has called "wolves in sheep's clothing." Trump claims unaccompanied minors are taking advantage of immigration loopholes and bringing in violent crime, thus criminalizing the profile of the new young immigrant, echoing the criminalization of new young immigrants of past centuries. Meanwhile, the administration's repeated invocation of MS-13 only helps bolster the gang's image as the biggest, baddest bunch around, and thus its power.

Another result of Donald Trump's anti-immigrant rhetoric is that undocumented immigrants like Wilber feel on shakier ground than ever before. And they are, because the Trump administration's policy shifts are not merely rhetorical. He has attempted and succeeded at real action, including a marked increase in arrests and deportations of those already living in the U.S. and a ban on new entrants from certain Muslim countries and he plans to expand detention facilities. Meanwhile, the current administration threatens to penalize so-called sanctuary cities, like Oakland, if local law enforcement refuses to cooperate with immigration authorities.

The resulting climate of fear and uncertainty also impacts immigrants living in the United States with official papers. In November, I got a text from a number I didn't recognize. "This is Raúl Flores one of the twins I have an important question," it read. I called him. "They say that they are taking away people's papers?" he said. I was confused at first—what was he talking about? And then I realized: he must have heard about the potential revocation of Temporary Protective Status for certain countries, which would impact nearly 200,000 Salvadorans. I insisted that wouldn't apply to him.

"You have a green card," I told him. "Unless you're convicted of a crime, you're safe. They can't just take your green card away from you."

"I hope not," he said, but with doubt in his voice. And then, "Are you sure, sure?"

Many things can be done here in the United States to improve our policies and systems for immigrants with paperwork, as well as the more than eleven million undocumented immigrants already living here, the tens of thousands in immigration detention at any given time, and the hundreds crossing the border every day. Though the United States is seen as a model for having created alternatives to detention programs for unaccompanied minors, and though the majority of youth maintain that they were well cared for in the long-term shelters, conditions in the short-term *hieleras* are often unconscionable, and allegations of abuse persist within ORR-contracted facilities like the one in which the Flores twins were housed.

Deplorable conditions in adult detention centers are also alleged to continue, particularly in those housing families—prolonged detention, malnourished children, scabies and lice outbreaks, limited access to health care, and cramped quarters (though according to the *New York Times,* ICE officials claim that these reports are exaggerated). Despite the Department of Justice's August 2016 decision to end the use of private contractors for incarceration in the criminal justice system, private corporations continue to profit off the adult immigration detention system and thus have an economic stake in immigration policy. They will continue to do so if the Trump administration's plans to expand immigration facilities continue.

The data clearly shows that access to counsel significantly determines the outcome of a child's ability to gain protection according to the law. Expecting children to represent themselves in a high-stakes situation that could significantly impact their well-being—and in some cases their very lives—is unethical.

In many ways, schools like Oakland International are on the front lines of immigration. Across the United States, English-language learners

are twice as likely to drop out of high school as those fluent in English—
and these statistics are even more dire for students newly arrived in
the country. As low-skilled jobs dwindle, far fewer careers are possible
without a high school diploma. The link between dropping out of school
and involvement in the justice system is evident: though nine out of
ten U.S. adults have a high school diploma or equivalent, 69 percent of
inmates in federal and local jails did not complete high school. A study
by the Alliance for Excellent Education claims it costs $12,643 to educate
a student for a year and costs more than twice as much—$28,323—to
house someone for a year in prison. The study also posits that reducing
U.S. dropout rates by just 5 percent would lead to $18.5 billion in an-
nual government crime savings and would increase national earnings by
$1.2 billion. Education, particularly for newly arrived immigrants, who
lack many or any connections to the larger community, can, when done
right, provide a sense of community, belonging, and purpose. We have
seen all over the world, and throughout history, that when young people
feel excluded from society they seek belonging in its fringes, among its
shadows. This could very easily have happened to the twins.

RELATED policy shifts would be important steps in ensuring the justice
and humanity of the U.S. immigration system. But even more critical
problems affecting immigration must be addressed outside our borders.

When a patient has a hemorrhage, the surgeon doesn't just sew up
the body to stop the bleeding; they look for the breach, the root of the
problem. Concerning immigration, the questions we should be asking
are: Why is Central America hemorrhaging people? And what can be
done to stop it at the source?

Many politicians, including President Trump, have made border
protection the central issue, the notion being that securing the border
would make the problem of "illegal" immigration go away. Though immigration enforcement walls are now being built all over the world, from
Hungary to Norway to Thailand, the fact is that walls do not secure
borders; they simply make them more complicated to cross. Hundreds
of thousands of undocumented migrants cross U.S. borders every year,

undeterred by the threat of death in desert hinterlands or the crime-riddled territories they pass through. Nor are they deterred by the 650 miles of wall that already exist.

Rhetorical bombast and sweeping policy change may, however, serve as a deterrent—at least at first. The number of unauthorized crossers into the U.S. dropped sharply after Trump's inauguration, including the number of unaccompanied minors. Yet not a single new mile of wall had been built. Were people too scared to try their luck now that Trump was in office? In May and June, the number of apprehensions at the border began rising once again; the problems south of our border, after all, had not gone away. This suggests that the real wall is exclusionist rhetoric and policy—such as keeping immigrants out by nationality and increasing arrests.

But exclusionist policy ignores the legacy of U.S. responsibility for the Central American catastrophe. A war is raging to our south, though we seem to refuse to call it one, and American policy fueled the wars that preceded it. We supplied guns to and trained mercenaries and death squads who ended up perpetrating scorched-earth massacres like the one in El Mozote, where bodies, as I chronicle in this book, are still being exhumed and identified today, over two decades later. We created free-trade deals that not only adversely impacted Americans but also gutted the prospects of small-scale farmers south of the Mexican border. Transnational corporations like Chiquita, Dole, and Del Monte bought up land and cornered the export markets for local medium- and small-scale businesses, making it more difficult for rural families to earn a living.

The 2016 U.S. presidential election revealed on a massive scale that long-ignored economic despair and societal sidelining have spurred political unrest. Such economic despair has been going on in El Salvador for decades. The same kinds of investment that could assuage the "forgotten" U.S. working class could also help create alternatives to the Northern Triangle's gang economy: investment in infrastructure to create jobs in local markets, in products made "here at home." The United States cannot at once be isolationist—build a wall, kill the trade deals—

and global, selectively reaping the benefits of an international economy, like lower-cost imports, cut-rate outsourced workforce, and cheap labor in our fields here at home. We have played a major part in creating the problem of what has become of Central America, and we must play a major part in solving it.

This argument is more than moral: it is also pragmatic. It's easy enough to dismiss the Central American crisis as not our problem. But we know that when young men lose agency in determining the outcomes of their lives and their prospects are narrowed, they tend to radicalize. If every kid could go to school and get a job in Central America, they would have slim incentive either to join a gang or to leave home. But this scenario cannot become a reality without deep international investment—not just in projects but in whole systems: education, health, economic infrastructure, community policing. Recent successes in peaceably ending internal unrest—in northern Uganda, South Africa, Rwanda, and even the Central American civil wars—can provide guidance on conflict demobilization and societal reconciliation. Disbanding the gangs would require providing a real, systemic alternative, and the United States must play a part.

People migrate now for the same reason they always have: for survival. The United States can build a wall, dig a two-thousand-mile trench, patrol with drones and military-grade vehicles and machine guns, and put thousands more guards at the border. Desperate migrants will still find another way. They'll take to the sea, they'll stuff themselves into bags, they'll dig tunnels (see El Chapo), they'll push into rougher and rougher territory. They'll send their children alone. Plenty of work must be done here in the United States to achieve responsible immigration reform—but to focus only on our side of the border is to miss the urgent and persistent realities at the very heart of undocumented immigration. It is also to understand far too narrowly the lives and motivations of the millions who have made this country their home. Immigrants to the United States were and still are determined by the places from which they came, and we in turn are determined by them. Whether by choice, by necessity, or both, they are also Americans. Just ask the Flores twins.

NOTES

METHODOLOGY

To write this book, I spent two years traveling on and off throughout the United States, Mexico, Guatemala, and El Salvador to get a glimpse of the perilous migration trail north, as well as the scope of violence in Central America. I spent countless hours with the Flores twins and their extended family in Oakland and in El Salvador, interviewing and getting to know them so I could render their very personal stories and very challenging circumstances.

I relied heavily on my professional experience working with immigrant families at Oakland International High School and at other organizations, and on my past reporting on unaccompanied minors and El Salvador for *VICE, Pacific Standard, VQR,* and *The New Republic.* All this figured into my narrative both explicitly (some scenes in this book are edited versions of stories that appeared in those magazines) and as background.

This book was written through a combination of firsthand reporting and reconstructed scenes. The vignettes between each main chapter are all products of my reporting in El Salvador, Mexico, Texas, and California. I was present for many of the Oakland-based scenes in this book, though I also reconstruct many scenes during which I was not present or that occurred before I met the twins. For them, I relied on repeated interviews with the people who had been present, as many of them as possible, to ensure that I had the facts straight; that a given memory was as strong as the memory could be; and that there were no discrepancies among their accounts. Where there were discrepancies, I have noted them in the text and offered whatever sense I could make of the variance. Wherever possible, I fact-checked the twins' accounts using available research and data. (I also employed the help of a professional fact checker.) Though I am fluent in Spanish, I often used interpreters and translators to ensure that I wasn't missing any nuances of a story. The Flores family endured question after question from me, and often repeated questioning, so I could be sure I fully understood their accounts.

I could not interview several key people because there was no way to find them or because the interview would endanger the Flores family. For these same security reasons, I have changed the names of the "Flores" family members, the name of their town, and some of their identifying features. I have changed the names of some of the other characters as well. I have used the testimony of as many sources as possible without putting the subjects of this book in harm's way.

In my career as a journalist, vulnerable and marginalized people have let me into their lives based on my promise—one they really had no reason to believe—that I would tell their stories justly, respectfully, and carefully, if not necessarily to their liking. While reporting on migrant farmworkers in California, unaccompanied teenagers in Texas, girl gangsters in El Salvador, war prison survivors in Slovenia, Ethiopian climate migrants in Kenya, destitute farmers in Guatemala, and others, I've pledged to tell the stories as fairly as I can without objectifying or endangering my subjects.

This book, however, posed a particular ethical question: I knew the Flores twins (and some of the other people in the book) from my capacity as a school administrator, not as a reporter. The twins were interested to learn that I had written magazine stories about young people in circumstances similar to theirs, that I'd been to Texas, where they'd been apprehended and detained, that I'd spent time in El Salvador, and that I was thinking about writing a book. They encouraged me to write a book about "kids like us" because, they felt, people needed to understand how hard things were in Central America, on the journey north, and even in Oakland. When it occurred to me that the best book I could write would be about them, I asked the twins (by then legally adults) what they thought about my telling their story—with their names and some identifying details changed. They took some time to think about it and finally agreed.

I agonized over the ethical question, discussing it with fellow writers, colleagues, editors, my bosses and co-workers at the school, the twins, and the twins' family. I finally came to the conclusion that if I could trust myself to tell their story respectfully and carefully, and if the twins accepted and encouraged the idea, it was appropriate for me to write this book. Ultimately, as nineteen-year-olds, they made the choice that yes, they wanted their story told.

AUTHOR'S NOTE

xv **their historical annual average:** Office of Refugee Resettlement, "Year in Review, 2013," https://www.acf.hhs.gov/orr/resource/office-of-refuge e-resettlement-year-in-review-fy2013.

THE MISSING

6 **the 1981 massacre of El Mozote:** "El Salvador Judge Reopens Case of 1981 Massacre at El Mozote," *Guardian,* October 1, 2016. For an excellent and groundbreaking investigation of the El Mozote massacre and the death squads of the civil war, see Mark Danner, *The Massacre at El Mozote* (Vintage Books, 1993), which was adapted somewhat from Danner's "The Truth of El Mozote," *New Yorker,* December 6, 1993.

7 **around 95 percent of crimes in the Northern Triangle go uncharged:** Cristina Eguizábal et al., "Crime and Violence in Central America's Northern Triangle: How U.S. Policy Responses Are Helping, Hurting, and Can Be Improved," Woodrow Wilson Center Reports on the Americas no. 34 (2015).

CHAPTER 1

9 **MS-13, or Mara Salvatrucha:** Originally formed in Los Angeles in the 1980s then brought back to El Salvador among deportees, MS-13 is now an international, though relatively decentralized, crime organization, operating in countries around the globe, including the United States. Since taking office, the Trump administration has focused much attention on the increasing (and increasingly visible) activities of MS-13 in the United

States, particularly in Long Island. "They have transformed peaceful parks and beautiful quiet neighborhoods into bloodstained killing fields. They're animals," Trump said in a speech to Long Island law enforcement officers in July of 2017. Trump and Sessions have publicly blamed MS-13 activities on the influx of immigrants from Central America.

12 **85 percent of the atrocities:** Commission on the Truth for El Salvador, "From Madness to Hope: The 12-year War in El Salvador," U.S. Institute for Peace, January 26, 2001, http://www.usip.org/sites/default/files/file /ElSalvador-Report.pdf.

18 **along with them came the gang culture:** Christine J. Wade, *Captured Peace: Elites and Peacebuilding in El Salvador* (Ohio University Press, 2016).

19 **"by an army of flies":** Óscar Martinez, Efren Lemus, Carlos Martinez, and Deborah Sontag, "Killers on a Shoestring: Inside the Gangs of El Salvador," *New York Times,* November 20, 2016.

20 **over 350,000 people:** Aaron Terrazas,"Salvadoran Immigrants in the United States," Migration Policy Institute, January 5, 2010.

22 **nearly 2 million Salvadorans resided:** Gustavo López, "Hispanics of Salvadoran Origin in the United States, 2013," Pew Research Center, September 15, 2015.

22 **a higher percentage than even Mexico's:** Lauren Markham, "The Prince of Peace," *VQR,* Fall 2016, republished as "Can a Millennial Mayor Save One of the World's Most Violent Cities?" *Guardian,* October 18, 2016.

22 **approximately $4 billion:** World Integrated Trade Solutions, "El Salvador at a Glance," 2015, http://wits.worldbank.org/CountrySnapshot/en /SLV/textview; and Pew Research Center, "Remittances Flows Worldwide in 2015," August 31, 2016.

22 **"El Salvador's biggest export is people":** Nayib Bukele (mayor of San Salvador), interview by author, January 2016. See also Lauren Markham, "The Prince of Peace," *VQR,* Fall 2016, republished as "Can a Millennial Mayor Save One of the World's Most Violent Cities?" *Guardian,* October 18, 2016.

25 **Shaggy, the Little Devil of Hollywood:** Óscar Martínez, Efren Lemus, Carlos Martínez, and Deborah Sontag, "Killers on a Shoestring: Inside the Gangs of El Salvador," *New York Times,* November 20, 2016.

25 **the Boxer:** Steven Dudley, "Barrio 18 in El Salvador: A View from Inside," *Insight Crime,* March 25, 2015, http://www.insightcrime.org/news -analysis/barrio-18-el-salvador-view-from-inside.

THE FLOOD

28 **4,354 people will be murdered by the end of the year:** Overseas Advisory Council, "El Salvador 2012 Crime and Safety Report," U.S. Department of State, April 7, 2012, https://www.osac.gov/pages/contentreportdetails .aspx?cid=12336.

29   **Temporary Protective Status:** As of November 2017, according to the
      Pew Research Center, 195,000 Salvadorans living in the United States
      were recipients of Temporary Protective Status, more than any other coun-
      try by far. (Hondurans, the next highest population of TPS recipients,
      numbered 57,000.) The Trump administration has already ended TPS for
      Nicaraguans, and, citing that Temporary Protective Status was meant to
      be a temporary, and not long-term, immigration relief, has suggested that
      it will consider ending TPS for other nationalities as well.

30   **The next year it will climb to 57,496:** Office of Refugee Resettlement,
      "Facts and Data," U.S. Department of Health and Human Services, n.d.,
      http://www.acf.hhs.gov/programs/orr/about/ucs/facts-and-data.

CHAPTER 2

34   **"The dead and pieces of the dead":** Joan Didion, *Salvador* (Vintage
      Books, 1983), p. 19.

35   **an average of twelve people murdered a day:** Overseas Advisory Coun-
      cil, "El Salvador 2012 Crime and Safety Report," U.S. Department of
      State, April 7, 2012, https://www.osac.gov/pages/contentreportdetails
      .aspx?cid=12336; Overseas Advisory Council, "El Salvador 2013 Crime and
      Safety Report," U.S. Department of State, April 11, 2013, https://www
      .osac.gov/pages/contentreportdetails.aspx?cid=13875.

35   **than people:** Christopher Ingraham, "There Are Now More Guns Than
      People in the United States," *Washington Post,* October 5, 2015.

37   **a well-known Catholic faith leader:** The 2012 gang truce is mired in
      controversy, and its exact terms, as well as who was driving the effort,
      remain unclear. Then-president Mauricio Funes publicly embraced the
      truce in 2012, but after it fell apart, he posited that it was carried out by
      civil society actors without his knowledge or permission.

THE CHURN

47   **When the Zeta and Gulf cartels splintered in 2010:** Paul Imison,
      "Mexico's End-of-Year Crime Stats Paint a Mixed Picture," *Latin Corre-
      spondent,* December 30, 2015.

47   **major spike in homicides and other crime:** Christopher Wilson and
      Eugenio Weigend, "Plan Tamaulipas: A New Security Strategy for
      a Troubled State," Woodrow Wilson Center, Mexico Institute, Octo-
      ber 9, 2014, p. 7, https://www.wilsoncenter.org/sites/default/files/New_
      Security_Strategy_Tamaulipas_0.pdf.

47   **an unconventional war zone:** Ibid., p. 8.

48   **a few chime in or shake a maraca:** Much of this section in the migrant
      shelter is reprinted from my article "The Prince of Peace," *VQR,* Fall
      2016.

THE WALLS

69 **the Rio Grande:** Much of this section is reprinted and reworked from my article "First the Fence, Then the System," *VQR,* Summer 2013.

70 **tens of billions of dollars:** Glenn Kessler, "Trump's Dubious Claim That His Border Wall Would Cost $8 billion," *Washington Post,* February 11, 2016.

71 **the remains of hundreds of migrants:** U.S. Border Patrol, "Sector Profile: Fiscal Year 2015," U.S. Customs and Border Protection, January 12, 2016, https://www.cbp.gov/sites/default/files/documents/USBP %20Stats%20FY2015%20sector%20profile.pdf.

71 **found in Brooks County, near Falfurrias:** Adam Isacson and Maureen Meyer, "Border Security and Migration: A Report from South Texas," Washington Office on Latin America, January 23, 2013, https://www .wola.org/analysis/border-security-and-migration-a-report-from-south -texas/.

72 **tossed into a common pit:** Maya Srikrishnan and Molly Hennessy-Fiske, "Mass Graves of Unidentified Migrants Found in South Texas," *Los Angeles Times,* June 21, 2014.

CHAPTER 4

80 **24,668 minors:** Office of Refugee Resettlement, "Facts and Data," U.S. Department of Health and Human Services, n.d., http://www.acf.hhs .gov/programs/orr/about/ucs/facts-and-data. Not all children apprehended by immigration authorities are transferred into ORR custody. Minors from countries with contiguous borders to the United States— Mexico and Canada—can be directly returned across the border if they do not assert that they have a fear of returning home.

82 **release to an official detention center:** Guillermo Cantor, "Detained Beyond the Limit: Prolonged Confinement by US Customs and Border Protection along the Southwest Border," American Immigration Council, August 18, 2016, https://www.americanimmigrationcouncil.org/research /prolonged-detention-us-customs-border-protection.

82 **an average of four days:** Ibid.

82 **within seventy-two hours:** Global Detention Project, "United States Immigration Detention Profile," May 2016, https://www.globaldetention project.org/countries/americas/united-states.

82 **In June 2014 a consortium of human rights:** "Systemic Abuse of Unaccompanied Immigrant Children by U.S. Customs and Border Protection," a June 11, 2014, complaint issued to the U.S. Department of Homeland Security by the National Immigrant Justice Center, Americans for Immigrant Justice, the ACLU Border Litigation Project, the Florence Immigrant Rights and Refugee Project, and Esperanza Immigrant Rights Project.

82 **temporary custody in the *hieleras*:** Ibid.

83   *hieleras* **were leaked to the press:** The first leaked images of detention
      conditions for minors appeared in Brandon Darby, "Leaked Images Re-
      veal Children Warehoused in Crowded U.S. Cells, Border Patrol Over-
      whelmed," *Breitbart News,* June 5, 2014. The following week additional
      photos provided by Congressman Henry Cuellar (D-TX) appeared in
      Susan Carroll and David McCumber, "Photos Show Logjam of Immi-
      grants Detained at Government Facility," *Houston Chronicle,* June 11, 2014.

85   **short-term housing and care of unaccompanied minors:** Administra-
      tion for Children and Families, "Justification of Estimates for Appro-
      priation Committees, Fiscal Year 2017," U.S. Department of Health and
      Human Services, p. 240, https://www.acf.hhs.gov/sites/default/files
      /olab/final_cj_2017_print.pdf.

85   **Flores Settlement:** "Flores Settlement Agreement and DHS Custody,"
      Lutheran Immigration and Refugee Services, Women's Refugee Commis-
      sion, and Kids in Need of Defense, n.d., http://docplayer.net/20957066
      -Flores-settlement-agreement-dhs-custody.html.

85   **transferred the responsibliity:** Office of Refugee Resettlement, "Unac-
      companied Children's Services," U.S. Department of Health and Human
      Services, n.d., https://www.acf.hhs.gov/orr/programs/ucs.

85   **DHHS budgeted $175 million:** Administration for Children and Fami-
      lies, "Justification of Estimates for Appropriation Committees, Fiscal Year
      2017," U.S. Department of Health and Human Services, p. 240, https://
      www.acf.hhs.gov/sites/default/files/olab/final_cj_2017_print.pdf.

86   **$373 million from 2016:** Administration of Children and Families, "Jus-
      tification of Estimates for Appropriations Committees," FY 2017, U.S. De-
      partment of Health and Human Services, p. 16, https://www.acf.hhs.gov
      /sites/default/files/olab/final_cj_2017_print.pdf.

86   **allegations of sexual abuse:** Hernán Rozemberg, "Immigrant Youth
      Shelter Ordered Closed," *San Antonio Express News,* April 14, 2007.

86   **2014 *Houston Chronicle* exposé:** Susan Carroll, "Crossing Alone: Chil-
      dren Fleeing to U.S. Land in Shadowy System," *Houston Chronicle,* May
      24, 2014.

86   **thirty-four days:** Administration for Children and Families, "Justifica-
      tion of Estimates for Appropriation Committees, Fiscal Year 2017," U.S.
      Department of Health and Human Services, pp. 268–69, https://www
      .acf.hhs.gov/sites/default/files/olab/final_cj_2017_print.pdf.

87   **between $200 and $500 per night:** Eighty percent of the budget was al-
      located to shelter costs. Eighty percent of the budget, divided by the total
      number of unaccompanied minors, divided by the average length of stay
      (thirty-four days) for that year, amounts to $200 to $500 per night.

87 **including bonuses and incentives:** According to the 1099 forms from Southwest Key.

90 **courthouse is packed:** Much of this section is reprinted and reworked from my article "First the Fence, Then the System," *VQR,* Summer 2013.

96 **According to the 1982:** U.S. Supreme Court, *Plyler v. Doe,* June 15, 1982, https://www.law.cornell.edu/supremecourt/text/457/202#writing-USSC_CR_0457_0202_ZO.

97 **rose steadily from around 3.5 million in 1990:** "Unauthorized Immigrant Population Trends for States, Birth Countries and Regions," Pew Research Center, November 3, 2016.

97 **2.3 million lived in California:** "U.S. Unauthorized Immigration Population Estimates," Pew Research Center, November 3, 2016.

97 **that number spiked to 1.7 million:** Ibid.

97 **individual tax identification number:** "The Facts About the Individual Tax Identification Number," American Immigration Council, April 5, 2016.

98 **the undocumented paid $11.8 billion:** Ibid.

99 **he thought he might get papers:** If an undocumented immigrant marries a U.S. citizen, he or she is indeed able to acquire citizenship but is required to leave the country for a minimum of ten years before that occurs.

100 **eligible to enroll in school:** California Education Code, Compulsory Education Law, 48200, http://leginfo.legislature.ca.gov/faces/codes_display Section.xhtml?lawCode=EDC&sectionNum=48200.

107 **entire U.S. public school population:** National Center for Education Statistics, "Fast Facts," https://nces.ed.gov/fastfacts/display.asp?id=96.

107 **the state's public school population:** Laura Hill, "California's English Learner Students," Public Policy Institute of California, September 2012, http://www.ppic.org/main/publication_quick.asp?i=1031.

107 **English-language learners:** Oakland Unified School District, http://www.ousd.org/Page/12187.

111 **a cut rate of $94.95 per immigrant:** From the service agreement (contract) between the U.S. Department of Homeland Security, Immigration and Customs Enforcement, and the Geo Group, provided to Human Rights Watch on April 29, 2015, following a Freedom of Information Act request.

111   **raking in $140 million per year since 2012:** "Immigration and Deten-
        tion Map and Statistics," End Isolation, n.d., http://www.endisolation
        .org/resources/immigration-detention/.

111   **once Donald Trump was elected president:** Caitlin Huston, "Gun
        Stocks Fall and Prison Stocks Jump after Trump Win," *MarketWatch,* No-
        vember 9, 2016, http://www.marketwatch.com/story/gun-stocks-fall-and
        -prison-stocks-jump-after-trump-win-2016-11-09.

111   **initiating new contracts:** Madison Pauly, "The Private Prison Industry
        Is Licking Its Chops Over Trump's Deportation Plans," *Mother Jones,* Feb-
        ruary 21, 2017.

112   **deported over 450,000 people:** Immigration and Customs Enforce-
        ment, "FY 2015 ICE Immigration Removals," U.S. Department of
        Homeland Security, https://www.ice.gov/removal-statistics/2015#wcm
        -survey-target-id; Office of Immigration Statistics, "DHS Immigration
        Enforcement 2016," *Annual Flow Report,*" U.S. Department of Homeland
        Security, https://www.dhs.gov/sites/default/files/publications/DHS%
        20Immigration%20Enforcement%202016.pdf.

112   **9 percent of total removals:** Immigration and Customs Enforcement,
        "FY 2015 ICE Immigration Removals," U.S. Department of Home-
        land Security, https://www.ice.gov/removal-statistics/2015#wcm-survey
        -target-id.

112   **more than any administration to date:** Human Rights Watch, "United
        States: Events of 2016," 2016. https://www.hrw.org/world-report/2017
        /country-chapters/united-states.

112   **prosecution for facilitating smuggling:** DHS Memo, "Implementing the
        President's Border Security and Immigration Enforcement Improvement
        Practices," February 20, 2017.

CHAPTER 6

114   **as of 2007:** Oakland City Council Resolution 80584, May 15, 2007, http://
        observatoriocolef.org/_admin/documentos/Resolution%2080584%20
        Oakland%20Ca.pdf.

114   **"sanctuary city":** Matthew Green and Jessica Tarlton, "What Are Sanc-
        tuary Cities and How Are They Bracing for Trump's Immigration Crack-
        down?" KQED, February 7, 2017.

115   *notarios,* **who promised help:** Attorney General's Office, "Attorney Gen-
        eral Submits Bill to Fight Notario Fraud, Government of the District of
        Columbia," DC.gov, April 29, 2016, https://oag.dc.gov/release/attorney
        -general-submits-bill-fight-notario-fraud.

115   **47 percent of those who secured legal representation:** "New Data on
        Unaccompanied Children in Immigration Court," Syracuse University,
        July 2014, http://trac.syr.edu/immigration/reports/359/.

115   **a child without a lawyer:** "Advocacy Factsheet," Kids in Need of Defense,

November 3, 2016, https://supportkind.org/wp-content/uploads/2016/11/Advocacy-KIND-Fact-Sheet-Nov-2016.pdf.

115 **children were over three times more likely to show:** "A Humanitarian Call to Action: Unaccompanied Children in Removal Proceedings," American Bar Association Commission on Immigration, May 2016, http://www.americanbar.org/content/dam/aba/administrative/immigration/uacstatement.authcheckdam.pdf.

116 **Legal Services for Children (LSC):** At the time, LSC was the only agency specifically dedicated to supporting unaccompanied minors in the Bay Area, and very few other agencies were taking these cases. But before the end of the year, this would change. In response to the 2014 immigration crisis and media attention, the City of Oakland, along with several local philanthropic organizations, stepped up funding to provide free legal services to these young people. By the fall of 2014, Centro Legal de la Raza and East Bay Sanctuary had hired new attorneys and prioritized these cases, taking on the lion's share (along with several other smaller organizations and LSC) of unaccompanied minors living in Oakland.

118 **"young persons who are perceived to be affiliated":** Executive Office of Immigration Review, "Matter of E-A-G Decision," U.S. Department of Justice, July 30, 2008, https://www.justice.gov/sites/default/files/eoir/legacy/2014/07/25/3618.pdf.

118 **two other gang-related asylum cases:** Executive Office of Immigration Review, "Matter of M-E-V-G Decision," U.S. Department of Justice, February 7, 2014, https://www.justice.gov/sites/default/files/eoir/legacy/2014/07/25/3795.pdf; and Executive Office of Immigration Review, "Matter of W-G-R Decision," U.S. Department of Justice February 7, 2014, https://www.justice.gov/sites/default/files/eoir/legacy/2014/07/25/3794.pdf.

126 **whom LSC highly recommended:** "Amy Allen" is a pseudonym.

133 **if we missed their eighteenth birthday:** At the federal level, Special Immigrant Juvenile Status (SIJS) can be granted up until the age of twenty-one, but in California, until October 2015, the finding had to be done before one's eighteenth birthday. On October 9, 2015, California governor Jerry Brown signed into law AB-900, which allowed California courts to recommend SIJS for youth between eighteen and twenty-one: "Given the recent influx of unaccompanied immigrant children arriving to the United States, many of whom have been released to family members and other adults in California and have experienced parental abuse, neglect, or abandonment, it is necessary to provide an avenue for these unaccompanied children to petition the probate courts to have a guardian of the person appointed beyond reaching 18 years of age." California

Assembly, Bill 900, Chapter 694, approved October 9, 2015, https://leginfo
.legislature.ca.gov/faces/billNavClient.xhtml?bill_id=201520160AB900.

THE ARREST

135   **The block outside San Salvador's Policía Nacional Civil:** For a previ-
ous version of this section, see Lauren Markham, "The Prince of Peace,"
VQR, Fall 2016; republished as "Can a Millennial Mayor Save One of the
World's Most Violent Cities?," *Guardian,* October 18, 2016.

136   **about 3 percent of the country's GDP:** "The Gangs That Cost 16% of
GDP," *Economist,* May 21, 2016.

136   ***agrupación ilícita,* or illicit congregation:** Decreto #459, Asamblea Leg-
islativa, Republica de El Salvador.

136   **third incarnation . . . since 2003:** Christine Wade, "El Salvador's 'Iron
Fist': Inside Its Unending War on Gangs," *World Politics Review,* June 6,
2016, http://www.worldpoliticsreview.com/articles/18982/el-salvador-s
-iron-fist-inside-its-unending-war-on-gangs.

136   **the sheer number of gang members:** "The Gangs That Cost 16% of
GDP," *Economist,* May 21, 2016.

137   **even years awaiting trial:** Institute for Criminal Policy Research, "World
Prison Brief: El Salvador," http://prisonstudies.org/country/el-salvador.

CHAPTER 7

139   **get their green cards:** "Chapter 4: Special Immigrant Juvenile Status
(SIJS)," Kids in Need of Defense (KIND), n.d., https://supportkind.org
/wp-content/uploads/2015/04/Chapter-4-Special-Immigrant-Juvenile
-Status-SIJS.pdf.

147   **busy Martin Luther King Jr. Way:** Because the twins were going to Alameda County probate court, the courthouse was in Berkeley rather than
Oakland.

155   **"for victims of certain crimes":** Citizenship and Immigration Services,
"Victims of Criminal Activity: U Nonimmigrant Status," U.S. Department of Homeland Security, n.d., https://www.uscis.gov/humanitarian/
victims-human-trafficking-other-crimes/victims-criminal-activity-u-
nonimmigrant-status/victims-criminal-activity-u-nonimmigrant-status.

THE GIRLS

156   **Dr. Fortín Magaña:** Dr. Magaña left his post at the Instituto de Medicina
Legal in December 2015.

156   **smiling against a backdrop of greenery:** Much of this section is reprinted and reworked from my summer 2017 article from *Pacific Standard.*

156   **in the world:** Julio Jacobo Waiselfisz, "Mapa da Violencia 2015: Homici-
dio de Mulheres No Brasil," FLASCO Brasil, 2015, http://www.mapada
violencia.org.br/pdf2015/MapaViolencia_2015_mulheres.pdf.

157   **right before the gang truce:** ORMUSA, "Indicatores de Violencia," http://observatoriodeviolencia.ormusa.org/index.php.

158   **a 2015 study by the United Nations Population Fund:** "Mapa de Embarazos en ninas y adolescentes en El Salvador 2015," United Nations Population Fund (UNFPA) El Salvador, July 2016, http://www .inclusionsocial.gob.sv/wp-content/uploads/2016/09/El-Salvador-Mapa -de-Embarazos-2015.pdf.

158   **jailed for miscarriage:** UNICEF, "At a Glance: El Salvador, Statistics," n.d., https://www.unicef.org/infobycountry/elsalvador_statistics.html. For more details on women being jailed for miscarriage, see Rachel Nolan, "Innocents: Where Pregnant Women Have More to Fear than Zika," *Harper's,* October 2016.

158   **a 2016 USAID report:** "El Salvador: Education," USAID, updated November 7, 2016, https://www.usaid.gov/el-salvador/education.

158   **in 2016 it was 33 percent:** Office of Refugee Resettlement, "Facts and Data," U.S. Department of Health and Human Services, n.d., http:// www.acf.hhs.gov/programs/orr/about/ucs/facts-and-data.

159   **more than 32,000 cases of parents traveling:** This number reflects the number of families, not of individuals. See Jens Manuel Krogstad, "U.S. Border Apprehensions of Families and Unaccompanied Children Jump Dramatically," Pew Research Center, May 4, 2016, http://www.pew research.org/fact-tank/2016/05/04/u-s-border-apprehensions-of-families -and-unaccompanied-children-jump-dramatically/.

159   **six out of ten:** "Invisible Victims: Migrants on the Move in Mexico," Amnesty International, April 28, 2010, https://www.amnesty.org/en /documents/AMR41/014/2010/en/.

159   **even higher:** Erin Siegal McIntyre and Deborah Bonello, "Is Rape the Price to Pay for Chasing the American Dream?" Fusion.net, September 10, 2014.

CHAPTER 8

169   **In May 2014 alone authorities caught over 9,000:** Customs and Border Protection, "Southwest Border Unaccompanied Alien Children FY 2014," U.S. Department of Homeland Security, updated November 24, 2015, http://www.cbp.gov/newsroom/stats/southwest-border-unaccompanied -children/fy-2014.

169   **That made 47,000 since ... October:** Customs and Border Protection, "An Open Letter to Parents of Children Crossing Our Southwest Border," U.S. Department of Homeland Security, June 23, 2014, https://www. dhs.gov/news/2014/06/23/open-letter-parents-children-crossing-our- southwest-border.

170   **356 percent increase over the year before:** Customs and Border Protection, "CBP Border Security Report, Fiscal Year 2014," U.S.

Department of Homeland Security, December 19, 2014, https://www
.cbp.gov/document/report/cbp-border-security-report-fiscal-year-2014.

170 **the Women's Refugee Commission:** Sonia Nazario, "The Children of
the Drug Wars: A Refugee Crisis, Not an Immigration Crisis," *New York
Times,* July 11, 2014.

171 **"within 50 miles of major city":** Much of the reporting and writing in
this section comes from Lauren Markham, "FEMA Wants to House Migrant Children in Empty Big Box Stores," *New Republic,* July 20, 2014.

171 **over $156 million in government grants:** This information comes from
the Southwest Key forms 1099.

171 **"It is dangerous to send a child":** Customs and Border Protection, "An
Open Letter to Parents of Children Crossing Our Southwest Border," U.S.
Department of Homeland Security, June 23, 2014, https://www.dhs.gov
/news/2014/06/23/open-letter-parents-children-crossing-our-southwest
-border.

172 **often confused with a *permiso*:** Julia Preston, "Migrants Flow in South
Texas, as Do Rumors," *New York Times,* June 16, 2014.

THE FAILED

183 **3,000 from Mexico:** From an August 2015 interview with Ana Solorzano, Chief of the Office Concerning Migrants, of the government of El
Salvador.

183 **from 57,496 in 2014 to 33,726:** Adam Isacson, Maureen Meyer, and
Hannah Smith, "Increased Enforcement at Mexico's Southern Border,"
Washington Office on Latin America, November 2015, p. 3, http://www
.wola.org/files/WOLA_Increased_Enforcement_at_Mexico's_Southern_
Border_Nov2015.pdf.

CHAPTER 9

186 **Though increasingly safe, in 2013 Oakland was home:** Sam Brock and
Kinsey Kiriakos, "Reality Check: Is Oakland Really the Most Crime Rid-
den City in California?" *NBC Bay Area,* November 18, 2014.

186 **In 2014 aggravated assault:** "City of Oakland Weekly Crime Report,"
http://www2.oaklandnet.com/oakca1/groups/police/documents/web
content/oak050910.pdf.

THE HALT

202 **a forced bus strike:** "El Salvador Bus Drivers Strike as Gang Violence
Surges," Reuters, July 27, 2015.

203 ***El Diario de Hoy* reported:** Pedro Carlos Mancia, Patricia Garcia, and Ev-

elyn Chacon, "Comercios pierden $60 millones por boicot al transporte," *El Diario de Hoy,* July 30, 2015.

203   **"The criminals want to hold talks"**: "Sánchez Cerén ofrece militarizar las unidades de transporte," *La Página,* August 9, 2015, http://www.la pagina.com.sv/nacionales/109213/2015/08/09/Sanchez-Ceren-garantiza -seguridad-en-transporte-ante-rumores-de-nuevo-paro.

CHAPTER 10

207   **In just June and July, over $100 million**: "Drought Causes $100 Million in Crop Losses in El Salvador," Phys.org, August 10, 2015, http://phys .org/news/2015-08-drought-million-crop-losses-el.html.

210   **harsher prison sentences**: Arron Daugherty, "El Salvador Supreme Court Labels Street Gangs Terrorist Groups," *Insight Crime,* August 26, 2015, http://www.insightcrime.org/news-briefs/el-salvador-supreme-court -labels-street-gangs-as-terrorist-groups.

217   **created a special . . . Task Force**: Immigration and Customs Enforcement, "Identity and Benefit Fraud," U.S. Department of Homeland Security, n.d., https://www.ice.gov/identity-benefit-fraud#wcm-survey -target-id.

217   **an aggressive ad campaign**: Immigration and Customs Enforcement, "ICE Leading Nationwide Campaign to Stop Marriage Fraud," U.S. Department of Homeland Security, April 2, 2014, https://www.ice .gov/news/releases/top-story-ice-leading-nationwide-campaign-stop -marriage-fraud.

217   **"If you walk down this aisle"**: Immigration and Customs Enforcement, "Marriage Fraud Is a Federal Crime," U.S. Department of Homeland Security, June 2016, https://www.ice.gov/sites/default/files/documents /Document/2016/marriageFraudBrochure.pdf.

THE LONG WALK

228   **around the front lawn**: Some passages in this section appeared in my article for #VQRTrueStory segment, "Northbound," *VQR,* December 14, 2015.

230   **Los Angeles, 4,025**: The distances displayed on the map in the shelter were not totally accurate down to the kilometer.

THE LAND

249   **a national water shortage emergency**: "El Salvador Declares Drought Emergency for First Time Ever," Reuters, April 14, 2016, http://www .reuters.com/article/us-el-salvador-drought-idUSKCN0XB2YM.

249   **Some 3.5 million people in Central America:** "Central America Drought: 2014-16," *Relief Web,* http://reliefweb.int/disaster/dr-2014-000132-hnd.

CHAPTER 12

262   **the same period the year before:** "Homicides in El Salvador Fall 18.5 Percent Through November 2016," Reuters, December 7, 2016.

262   **than in all of 2015:** Ibid.

262   **over 6,600 people had been killed:** Nina Lakhani, "Violent Deaths in El Salvador Spiked 70% in 2015, Figures Reveal," *Guardian,* January 4, 2016.

AFTERWORD

268   **Deplorable conditions in adult detention centers:** Wil S. Hylton, "The Shame of America's Family Detention Camps," *New York Times Magazine,* February 4, 2015.

268   **incarceration in the criminal justice system:** United States Department of Justice, "Phasing Out Our Use of Private Prisons," *Justice Blogs,* August 18, 2016, https://www.justice.gov/opa/blog/phasing-out-our-use -private-prisons.

269   **as those fluent in English:** Lesli A. Maxwell, "Stemming the Tide of English-Learner Dropouts," *Education Week,* March 14, 2013, http:// blogs.edweek.org/edweek/learning-the-language/2013/03/stemming_the _tide_of_english-l.html?cmp=ENL-EU-NEWS2.

269   **without a high school diploma:** "National Unemployment Rate Steady, but Those Without a High School Diploma Still Struggle," Employment Policy Institute, April 2010, https://www.epionline.org/release/national -unemployment-rate-steady-but-those-without-a-high-school-diploma -still-struggle/.

269   **high school diploma or equivalent:** "Educational Attainment in the United States: 2015," United States Census Bureau, March 2016, https:// www.census.gov/content/dam/Census/library/publications/2016 /demo/p20-578.pdf.

269   **increase national earnings by 1.2 billion:** "Saving Future, Saving Dollars: The Impact of Education on Crime Reduction and Earnings," The Alliance for Excellence in Education, September 2013, http://all4ed.org /wp-content/uploads/2013/09/SavingFutures.pdf.

ACKNOWLEDGMENTS

I owe thanks to many people who supported me during the process of dreaming about, researching, and writing this book.

Many books offered me insight and revelation, including Joan Didion's *Salvador*, Luis Alberto Urrea's *The Devil's Highway*, Ted Conover's *Coyotes*, Sonia Nazario's *Enrique's Journey*, Óscar Martínez's *The Beast* and *A History of Violence*, Mark Danner's *The Massacre at El Mozote*, Carlos Henríquez Consalvi's *Broadcasting the Civil War in El Salvador*, and Marc Zimmerman's *El Salvador at War: A Collage Epic*. *Insight Crime* and the dogged, masterful reporting of *El Faro* offered invaluable information and perspective; I owe much gratitude to their work.

I found my brilliant and loving agent, Sylvie Greenberg, at exactly the right time, when the seeds of this book had just begun to germinate. I couldn't have found a better champion or friend in this pursuit. My unparalleled editor, Meghan Houser, provided constant guidance, cheerleading, insight, and patience, and I am forever grateful to her for taking a chance on this project and for breathing life into it. My fact-checker, Sharon Riley, is a research wizard who took great pains to ensure that I'd gotten things right. Thanks, too, to the whole team at Crown for the invisible work behind bookmaking.

I have been blessed with the best and most supportive of teachers.

Early on, there was Andy Johnston, Randy Barnett, David Loeb, Ed Mc-Catty, and Trevor Peard. Thank you to Robert Cohen and David Bain at Middlebury College for pushing me further while cheering me on. My professors at Vermont College of Fine Arts helped me fuse craft, language, and the arc of story. Thank you Jess Row, David Jauss, and most of all Abby Frucht; thank you also to Mary Ruefle, Larry Sutin, and Ralph Angel for invaluable mentorship and inspiration postgraduation ("Your job is to write the best sentences possible," Ralph reminds me, "no matter what you're writing about"). Deep gratitude to the folks from the Middlebury Fellowship, Bill McKibben, Janisse Ray, Rebecca Solnit, Chris Shaw, and Sue Kavanagh, who model the art of righteous writing and living, and who believed in my first feature story, which set me on the path to becoming a journalist. Likewise, Malia Wollan, Jack Hitt, Alan Burdick, and Michael Pollan at the UC Berkeley 11th Hour Food and Farming Fellowship provided me the generous support, community, and guidance I needed to continue to report on unaccompanied minors. Thank you.

Paul Reyes at *VQR* urged me to pitch him my very nebulous, notional story about kids who came to this country alone. That encouragement launched this book. Wes Enzinna took a chance on my second unaccompanied minors story. Each time Paul and Wes have edited my work over the years they have taught me how to be a better journalist and a better writer.

Funding from the French American Foundation and the Pulitzer Center for Crisis Reporting supported the research of key sections of this book. The Rotary Foundation provided me the time and perspective that allowed me to conceive of this project, and the Mesa Refuge offered quiet and space on the edge of California where I could hunker down and write, and also dream. Clarity for the original idea I owe to the Southern California Vipassana Center, and the desert.

Tom Verner and the North Branch School were the reason I ended up in El Salvador in the first place, years ago. Friends in El Salvador have helped me immeasurably since then: Melisa Oliva, Lucy Guzman, Vilma Ortiz, Emilia Estrada, Luis Mario, Billy, and Irma. And to the woman who dragged me up the stairs into her shop and cared for me after I passed out in the middle of Santa Tecla with a case of dehydration: thank you.

Langan Courtney, Nate Dunstan, Ariana Flores, Sylvia Townsend, and Igor Radulovich have imparted much wisdom over the years as colleagues and as friends. Jean Yamasaki and Eleni Wolf Roubiatis are incredible human beings and tireless advocates who have taught me and heartened me along the way. Katie Annand did the same, and more—thank you for being open to this project.

I knew the day I met Carmelita Reyes that I would find a home at Oakland International—even though the school didn't exist yet. Carmelita, Sailaja Suresh, Thi Bui, Liza Richheimer, and all the founding teachers, thank you for your brilliance and incarnating that world and letting me be a part of it. Thank you to the later staff, too, especially Salem Peterson, Mallory Moser, Brooke Toczylowski, Cormac Kilgallen, Raquel Franker, Michelle Rostampour, and Shahrzad Makaremi (these last three held down the fort any time I was away writing or researching this book, and I am forever grateful). The people of OIHS are the most dedicated and inspirational people I know; I love them all like brothers and sisters, and like siblings, they have enriched my life and my perspective on the world. The students have done this perhaps most of all. And Mr. David Hansen: this book might not exist if it weren't for you. Thank you for your uplifting work, for introducing me to the twins, and for always pushing my thinking forward.

Thank you to the wide circle of beloved friends who endured my anxiety and chatter as the book took shape. My porch people, my friend family: thank you for patience and intelligence and joy. Luke Carson, Eric Skaar, and Liz and John Frankel helped me understand the issues. Thank you to the Middlebury Fellows and the UC Berkeley Food Fellows, and most especially to Heather Gilligan and Bridget Huber for helping me turn so many ideas into stories. Carrie Nazzaro, Theresa Kenney, Dani Fisher, Evan Bissell, Kendra Ing, Niko McConnie-Saad, Melissa Chou, and Anna Goldstein, as well as journalist pals Diane Jeantet, Ian Gordon, and Holly Haworth, offered love, wisdom, smarts, adventure, and fun. Thank you to Liara Tamani for unbridled positivity and inspiration; Robin MacArthur for her courage and singing prose and cross-continental good vibes; and Sierra Crane Murdoch for her grace and commitment to truth telling. (I read everything these three women write with pride and a small pang of loving envy—you should, too.)

Lindsay Whalen provided me with laughter, moral support, expert guidance, edits, and suggestions the whole way through—how I am so lucky to have a best friend who is also an editor and a brilliant writer, I'll never quite know. I can, and do, talk to Hannah Epstein from takeoff to landing on any flight, literal or metaphoric. Her love and encouragement have carried me through so many triumphs and heartaches on the page and in my life. I cannot imagine earth without these two. (Thanks, too, to the Epstein and Whalen families, and the extended Gucciardis, who have taken me in as their own.)

I am lucky to come from a loving and supportive family who, regardless of political beliefs, have loyally bolstered my pursuits while training me in the art of storytelling. Thank you to the extended Markham/Read clan, and most especially to Uncle Read for reading this book with an open heart. Thank you to my father, John Markham, for being my unwavering champion, someone committed to the notion of a vocation, and the best raconteur I know; to my mother, Liz Read, who is as selfless and supportive as they come and will accompany me on any journey near and far; and to my brother, Chris, who always pushes me to see the other side of things and can make me laugh and think.

Ben Gucciardi is the anchor of all anchors, righteous and brilliant, a man who walks to the thump of the world's heartbeat. Thank you for keeping me healthy, happy, rooted, full of wonder, and for helping me clear the path for this book.

Thank you to the entire "Flores" family for letting me into your worlds so as to be able to tell this story. And thank you, gentle readers, for making it to the end.

INDEX